WISDOM'S WORK

"J. Daryl Charles is a scholar who works at the intersection of faith, culture, and public life. His interests range widely, but they are all concerned with 'the Augustinian burden'—how to live, responsibly and with wisdom, as citizens both of this world and of the one to come. Written with insight and grace, these essays will encourage thoughtful Christians everywhere."

— Timothy George
Founding Dean of Beeson Divinity School;
General Editor, *Reformation Commentary on Scripture*

"Daryl Charles is unique. He is one of the most ebullient, courageous, and penetrating Christian moral thinkers on the scene today, a man whose irresistibly joyful personality bubbles over with the love of Christ, but whose careful and lucid prose in support of a recovery of natural law serves to illuminate the common ground that joins us all, whether we know it or not. He has a rare talent for connecting theology with everyday life, especially in his treatment of the enduring importance of vocation and labor in human existence. This collection is not to be missed."

— Wilfred M. McClay
G. T. and Libby Blankenship Chair
in the History of Liberty,
University of Oklahoma

"Daryl Charles is a Christian public intellectual with deep roots in the Evangelical, Reformed, and Catholic traditions. Both deeply learned and utterly challenging, this set of essays exhibits the wide-ranging nature of his thought on, for example, cultural discipleship, the natural law as the foundation for moral dialogue in contemporary culture, Christian anthropology, and the Christian's vocation in education and work. Charles's essays display theological, philosophical, and cultural insights, modeling the normative interplay of the dynamics of faith and reason in the intellectual life. This book should not be missed."

— Eduardo Echeverria
Professor of Philosophy and Systematic Theology,
Sacred Heart Major Seminary

"Western society is more confused than ever about the nature of reality, and the church is unsure about whether and how it should address this confusion. J. Daryl Charles is one of our best Protestant guides in today's fog of ideological war."

— GERALD R. MCDERMOTT
Beeson Divinity School;
Author of *Everyday Glory:
The Revelation of God in All of Reality*

"With an eye toward the deep disagreements of our post-consensus culture, Daryl Charles wants to demonstrate the merits of natural law thinking coupled with a caring, winsome attitude toward all our neighbors for defending the truth and working toward a moral consensus that can strengthen the common good. His work is cut out for him because many reasonable people, including many Christians, disagree even about the meaning of natural law and what constitutes the common good. Yet readers will find in this volume many insights into our cultural predicaments and into the importance of taking our vocations seriously in service to God and neighbors."

— JAMES W. SKILLEN
President (retired),
Center for Public Justice, Washington, D.C.

WISDOM'S WORK

ESSAYS ON ETHICS, VOCATION, AND CULTURE

J. Daryl Charles

ACTONINSTITUTE

Wisdom's Work: Essays on Ethics, Vocation, and Culture

© 2019 by J. Daryl Charles

All rights reserved. No part of this publication may be reproduced, stored in a retrieval system, or transmitted in any form or by any means, including electronic, mechanical, photocopying, recording, or otherwise without the prior permission of the publisher.

Scripture quotations marked (NIV) are taken from The Holy Bible, New International Version®, NIV® Copyright © 1973, 1978, 1984, 2011 by Biblica, Inc.® Used by permission. All rights reserved worldwide.

Scripture quotations marked (RSV) are taken from the Revised Standard Version of the Bible, copyright © 1946, 1952, and 1971 by the Division of Christian Education of the National Council of the Churches of Christ in the United States of America. Used by permission. All rights reserved.

Scripture quotations marked (NASB) are taken from the New American Standard Bible®, Copyright © 1960, 1962, 1963, 1968, 1971, 1972, 1973, 1975, 1977, 1995 by The Lockman Foundation. Used by permission.

Scripture quotations marked (KJV) are taken from the King James Version. Public domain.

Scripture quotations not otherwise noted are the author's translation.

ISBN 978-1-880595-03-9 (paperback)
ISBN 978-1-880595-05-3 (ebook)

Cover image: David Commissions Solomon to Build the Temple (1 Chronicles 28), iStock illustration 827715474

ACTON INSTITUTE
for the Study of Religion & Liberty

98 E. Fulton
Grand Rapids, Michigan 49503
616.454.3080
www.acton.org

Interior composition: Judy Schafer
Cover: Scaturro Design

Contents

Preface	vii
1. Post-Consensus Culture, Natural Law, and Moral Persuasion: Translating Moral Conviction in a Disbelieving Age	1
2. The Human Person and the Common Good	27
3. Ethical Integrity and the Ethics of Humanitarian Intervention	53
4. Natural Law and Protestant Reform: Lessons from a Forgotten Reformer	61
5. The Kuyperian Option: Cultural Engagement and Natural-Law Ecumenism	89
6. Why Do Economic Issues Merit Moral Reflection?	107
7. Take This Job and Shove It: Theological Reflections on Vocation, Calling, and Work	121
8. Education as Vocation	141
9. Wisdom and Work: Perspectives on Human Labor from Ecclesiastes	155
Bibliography	177
Subject and Author Index	187
Scripture Index	199

Preface

The collection of essays before you, interdisciplinary and multi-faceted in its nature, is an accurate—and current—representation of my deeply held convictions about the intersection of faith and culture, of theology and public life. Its intention springs from motivations that are simultaneously academic and pastoral, for the interaction of these two domains has been my personal life's calling, as best as I understand the notion of *vocatio*. It furthermore springs from an Augustinian burden that Christians take seriously their dual citizenship in this world, that they think long and hard about the nexus of religious faith and meaningful cultural involvement. There is a pressing need to relate our deepest convictions about all of life—convictions anchored in the doctrines of creation, providence, redemption, incarnation, and consummation—to the public sphere in all its variety. But this task incurs particular challenges and obstacles. Several of these are in-house in nature.

One challenge confronting Christian social witness is what we might call the sectarian Tertullian temptation. I refer here to the church father's answer, in his treatise *Prescription against Heretics*,[1] to his own rhetorical question, What does Jerusalem have to do with

---

1. This treatise is reproduced in volume 3 of *The Ante-Nicene Fathers*, ed. A. Roberts and J. Donaldson (New York: Charles Scribner's Sons, 1903), and can be accessed electronically at http://www.newadvent.org/fathers/0311.htm.

Athens? For Tertullian, the latter represented intellectual culture and the life of the mind, while the former represented our spiritual heritage through Christ. The divide, he argued, was clear. After all, he reasoned, we will not be judged in the last day on the basis of how much worldly wisdom and cultural refinement we have assimilated. At bottom, then, Tertullian was asking about the relative worth of those things comprising the present life. Does not, therefore, intellectual pursuit, cultivation of the life of the mind, and the realization that ideas have consequences in the end constitute an unnecessary luxury? Or, in the words of one commentator, by cultivating the life of the mind and taking temporal life seriously, are we not simply "fiddling while Rome is burning"?[2]

The difficulty with the Tertullian mind-set—at least the later, sectarian Tertullian—is that it is fundamentally escapist in character. Its focus is eschatological to the extent that it severs, at least in meaningful ways, any allegiances to the temporal order in the interest of remaining faithful to the heavenly. But our dual citizenship, even when our *ultimate* allegiance is to the city of God, nevertheless requires that we take our responsibilities to the city of man in earnest. A proper eschatological perspective holds the temporal and the eternal in a proper tension, and it does not release that tension.[3] This posture, in turn, allows the Christian community neither to succumb to the entrapments of its cultural surroundings nor to flee the world and eschew responsible participation. Anchored in an awareness of divine providence and common grace and recognizing that the sovereign Lord Almighty places us in particular cultural contexts for a purpose, we take our stewardship of that calling seriously.

A related challenge to orthodox Christian believers in the twenty-first century needs identifying. It is one that is located in the pulpits of our own churches and parishes, as well as in those institutions entrusted with the training of our pastors and priests—namely, our seminaries and divinity schools. Particularly among more evangeli-

---

2. John F. Crosby, "Education and the Mind Redeemed," *First Things*, no. 18 (December 1991): 23–28.

3. Hence the title of the important volume by Paul Marshall with Lela Gilbert, *Heaven Is Not My Home: Living in the Now of God's Creation* (Nashville: Word, 1998).

cally minded Protestants (and wider evangelical Protestantism happens to be my own particular location within the body of Christ), the focus of standard teaching and preaching is a distinctly private—as opposed to public—faith. That is, we emphasize the work of God within the believer—namely, the requisite need for cleansing from sin and forensic imputation of God's holiness through Christ by faith. Well and good. The emphasis, again, is personal faith. At the same time, it needs stating (and restating) that mere personal fellowship with the living God, important as that is, does not answer the larger question, Why are we here on earth to serve the Lord? This is simply to ask why (on earth!) we as Christian believers were not raptured away from earthly responsibilities immediately following our conversion (if, that is, we can identify any sort of conversion experience[4]). For if personal communion with God is the sole—or even chief—reason for our earthly existence, then we should ultimately disdain our earthly existence, wishing only to be in the presence of the Lord, even to the point of justifying suicide in order to leave this present life.[5]

The problem here, lest I be viewed as some sort of heretic, is not with a "personal relationship with Christ." Far be it from this author to contest a matter so basic. What *is* problematic, however, is the broader inability of our churches to teach and preach a *public* faith. Thereby Christian leadership, in general, has been AWOL in asking and addressing the question of faith's application in the public sphere. Mainline Protestants, of course, often have completely reversed the process, perverting the historic Christian faith by negating its confessional "fundamentals"—that is, those things that

---

4. For example, my own three children doubtless would be hard-pressed to identify a specific time and place of "conversion." They simply grew up in an environment that assumed the lordship of Christ over all things. Hence, even when they went through particular seasons of confusion, challenge, or questioning, they probably could not identify a time or season in which they were not Christian.

5. It is well known that in the patristic era the church battled with Manichean and Gnostic tendencies that are addressed forcefully already by Paul in his first letter to the Corinthians. Those tendencies seem still to be with us. Much of contemporary Christianity, for varying reasons, denies the fundamental goodness of material creation.

we all confess on bended knee at the altar—while at the same time prostituting themselves at the altar of social relevance.[6] The same would apply to "cafeteria Catholics" as well. Protestant or Catholic, the perversion nevertheless is unacceptable.[7] A further obstacle, if we may set aside chiefly ecclesial concerns for the moment, is the tendency, particularly among Protestant believers, to neglect the rich resources of the church's theological heritage—resources that are indispensable to its public witness. I refer here inter alia to the symbiotic relationship of faith and reason, and natural-law reasoning.

---

6. Here I am reminded of the rather remarkable decision by Princeton Theological Seminary (PTS) in April 2017 to rescind the Abraham Kuyper Prize for Excellence in Reformed Theology and Public Life, which was to have been awarded to the Rev. Timothy Keller of Manhattan's Redeemer Presbyterian Church at the annual Abraham Kuyper and Public Theology conference that April at PTS. The award is typically given to someone who has demonstrated "innovation and excellence" in the sphere of public theology. Past recipients of the award include Congressman John R. Lewis (2015); Nicholas Wolterstorff, Noah Porter Professor of Philosophical Theology emeritus, Yale University (2014); Marilynne Robinson, writer and Pulitzer Prize winner (2011); Lord Jonathan Sacks, chief rabbi of the United Hebrew Congregations of the Commonwealth (2010); Alvin Plantinga, professor of philosophy emeritus, University of Notre Dame (2009); Richard Mouw, former president of Fuller Theological Seminary (2007); and Jan Peter Balkenende, former prime minister of the Netherlands (2004). The seminary's president, in announcing the reversal only two weeks before the April event, claimed to be responding to protests from students and Presbyterian Church (USA) pastors who denounced Keller's and his denomination's (the Presbyterian Church in America) views on the ordination of women and on same-sex causes. (The seminary's official statement can be found at http://www.dailyprincetonian.com/article/2017/04/theological-seminary-rescinds-award.) The sheer irony of the decision is that Kuyper himself desired a lively and pluralistic public arena in which Christians were free to contend. Clearly, the seminary cannot tolerate such pluralism. And although it claims to tolerate—even encourage—"diverse viewpoints," it obviously cannot tolerate disagreement on matters of gender and sexuality. In truth, it is saying that such disagreement dare not be tolerated. And therewith it is declaring that historic Christian orthodoxy is unacceptable.

7. Lest the reader conclude that I lack sufficient ecumenical vision to include the Orthodox Church, the verdict is still out regarding that church's public witness in Western nations, Rod Dreher's "Benedict Option" notwithstanding.

Regarding the relationship between faith and reason, no one can improve on John Paul II's final encyclical, *Fides et Ratio* (1998). Therein the former pontiff not only offers an extraordinarily robust cultural critique but also explicates—in both theological and philosophical terms—the very nature of this relationship that resides in our being created in the *imago Dei*. Not infrequently a strong emphasis on piety—and this species of Christian faith is unquestionably more often Protestant than Catholic in character—has the tendency to look down on or distrust the rational side of our faith, as if a fundamental tension exists between reason and piety based on creation. When this sort of mind-set enters the public sphere (or attempts to do so), it has immense difficulties relating the nature and content of Christian faith to unbelievers. Why? Because of its deep suspicion toward reason—namely, the very thing that is needed to build bridges to the unbeliever's life and mode of thinking. In a similar vein, this deficient approach to faith is likely to view Paul's work in Athens (Acts 17) as a failure rather than as faithfulness to and empathy with his audience and the host culture.[8] This leads us to the importance of natural-law reasoning, about which much could be said and, in fact, much is said in the essays that follow. Here, alas, we stumble across one of the greatest—and most unfortunate—present-day distinctions between Catholic and Protestant faith. While a minor renewal of natural-law thinking among orthodox Protestants over the last two decades can be detected,[9] Protestants

---

8. I read and interpret Acts 17:16–34 in light of Paul's autobiographical confession found in 1 Corinthians 9:19–23: Christian faith will seek to clothe itself in meaningful ways, given the social and cultural location to which God calls us as individuals. It should be noted that even though Luke mentions nothing more about Dionysius, the convert from Paul's Areopagus address (Acts 17:34), and the New Testament never mentions his name again, this one convert ended up becoming a bishop of the church in Athens and a martyr for Christ. We learn of this from Eusebius in his *Church History*. Thus, my interpretation of Paul's work in Athens is that the apostle to the Gentiles was immensely successful.

9. See, for example, Stephen J. Grabill, *Rediscovering the Natural Law in Reformed Theological Ethics* (Grand Rapids, MI: Eerdmans, 2006); J. Daryl Charles, *Retrieving the Natural Law: A Return to Moral First Things* (Grand Rapids, MI: Eerdmans, 2008); idem, *Natural Law and Religious Freedom: The Role of Moral First Things in Grounding and Protecting the First Freedom* (New

generally remain suspicious of natural-law thinking. Their reasons for this suspicion are for the most part theological and hence need to be taken seriously. But this suspicion (or outright rejection) of natural-law thinking, it needs emphasizing, is more recent and cannot be ascribed to the Magisterial Reformers of the sixteenth century, all of whom affirmed the natural law as a moral bedrock and who, despite their theological and ecclesiological differences with the Catholic Church, maintained continuity on ethical matters with their Catholic counterparts.

For theologically orthodox Protestants, the resistance to natural-law thinking retains strong overtones of the sixteenth-century conflict between Protestants and Catholics, even when, as I note above, their opposition to natural law actually mirrors *later* Protestant commitments. For example, such overtones are detected in the assumption that natural law is a medieval construct that imposes an unwarranted opposition between nature and grace, a supposed rejection by Jesus and the New Testament of Old Testament law, a correlative negative orientation toward law in general, and a concern that law or legalism might trump the Christocentrism of our faith. In ways that I hope the following essays illuminate, natural law in fact resides at the very heart of the church's apologetic mission.[10] That is to argue, the church bears witness in the public sphere on the basis of certain moral truths that are inviolable, woven into the very fabric of the universe. What is morally true for twenty-first-century human

---

York: Routledge, 2018); David VanDrunen, *Natural Law and the Two Kingdoms: A Study in the Development of Reformed Social Thought* (Grand Rapids, MI: Eerdmans, 2010); idem, *Divine Covenants and Moral Order: A Biblical Theology of Natural Law* (Grand Rapids, MI: Eerdmans, 2014); and Owen Anderson, *The Natural Moral Law: The Good after Modernity* (New York: Cambridge University Press, 2012). See, as well, Jesse Covington, Bryan McGraw, and Micah Watson, eds., *Natural Law and Evangelical Political Thought* (Lanham, MD: Lexington, 2013).

10. We can understand why some Protestants have these concerns about natural-law thinking and why they are still fighting as the Reformers did five hundred years ago. In the twenty-first century, however, the problem lies at the other end of the theological spectrum: law is equated with legalism; consequently, it is insufficiently appreciated—when not outright rejected—as a mirror of God's character.

beings, regardless of their worldview or faith orientation, was true for those living in imperial Rome in Paul's day; as it was for those of ancient Greek, Persian, and Babylonian cultures; as it was for those of ancient Israel; as it was for those from Adam to Israel. In classical Reformed Protestant terms, one might speak of this abiding moral reality as part of common grace. As distinct from special grace or special revelation, common grace is that representation of God's providence, based on creation, that guides and preserves all of human existence and without which human beings and human culture would be nonexistent.

One final obstacle to our thinking needs identification at the outset of this volume. As with natural-law thinking, this obstacle, too, is the fruit of gross misperception within the wider Christian community. I refer here to the much misunderstood—and supremely neglected—notion of vocation. While it is true that our hypersecularized culture has stripped vocation of its inherent religious meaning, the greater tragedy is that vocation has been ignored or misconstrued *in our own* Christian circles. Both Catholics and Protestants have succumbed—wittingly or unwittingly—to a bifurcated view of divine calling that for much of the church's history has resulted in a distorted "sacred-versus-secular" view of human endeavor and human labor. Since very few of us, in any typical parish or congregational setting, are called to the pastorate or the priesthood as a life work, that leaves approximately 99.9 percent of the Christian community "consigned" or "resigned" to the marketplace. Such, tragically, is the thinking of far too many believers. The numbers (99.9 percent) are correct, but the perception—and the unfortunate language expressing that perception—is distorted and wholly incorrect. As several of the essays in this collection argue, if God has created us to work, having fashioned us in his own image, then we are stewards of all creation—coregents, as it were, and hence stewards over all arenas of life, *including the marketplace*. Now, if this is the case, where, then, are the teaching and preaching that will equip businesspeople, lawyers, psychologists, plumbers, medical professionals and health-care providers, social workers, teachers, electricians, computer programmers, politicians, and farmers to flourish in that environment to which they—the 99.9 percent of the Christian community—are called? Are our pulpits and our training institutions (i.e., our seminaries and divinity schools) capable of such vision? Based on the evidence, major reform in the church is needed. My concerns here should be understood by the reader as an observation, not a condemnation.

The Acton Institute has invited me to produce a volume that might address these and related issues. And to this invitation I have gratefully responded.[11] Since coming into association with Acton as one of its affiliate scholars, I have had the high honor and privilege of meeting men and women—Catholic and Protestant and, on occasion, Orthodox and Jewish—who are committed to the overarching Acton goal of "a free and virtuous society." In the essays that follow—several of which have their origin in particular addresses at various institutions—the baseline assumptions governing my own way of thinking about faith and culture are laid bare. At the most basic level, there is no free society without virtuous people. That is, without moral formation, without the ability to engage in moral reasoning publicly, and without the freedom to make moral judgments publicly, there is, quite simply, *no such thing* as a free people. John Paul II sounded this warning repeatedly in the teaching of his encyclicals: no trust in what we understand as liberal democracy can create—or preserve—a truly free society. For unless that society, that democracy, is renewed from within, unless the people inhabiting that democratic regime *themselves* undergo moral renewal, in time that regime will become totalitarian. What remains to be determined is whether that corrupted society takes on a "softer" or a "harder" totalitarian cast.

At this point, perhaps the reader is put off by my "moralizing" or my sense of cultural earnestness. Permit me simply to say that I am not, nor have I ever been, an alarmist or apocalypticist. While I am reasonably certain that the forty-eighth installment of the Left Behind series is floating around out there and soon to appear in Christian bookstores everywhere, and while in the last century (and indeed my lifetime) all too many Christians have adopted the outlook that culture is "going to hell in a handbasket, so why rearrange chairs on a sinking ship?," I resolutely reject that outlook as systematic error and as wholly unbiblical in terms of its theology.

---

11. In this regard, special thanks are due to Jordan Ballor and Drew McGinnis of the Acton Institute—both of whom I consider to be kindred spirits—for extending this kind invitation.

To escape the world—or to wish to escape—is a repudiation of the doctrines of creation, redemption, and incarnation. At the same time, in our day the pendulum would seem to have swung in the opposite direction. The great challenge in our era may be that Christians have become absorbed into the culture as a result of their lack of critical discernment so that they are scarcely identifiable from the surrounding culture. Let us be clear: both isolation and capitulation are marks of unfaithfulness; both are a negation of the biblical witness. In theological terms, I vigorously adopt the vision that animates the Acton Institute. That is, as stewards of all of creation and God's good gifts, we utilize *everything* within our means and at our disposal—creatively, winsomely, and soberly—with a view to honor the Creator.

Such is an *ethical* mandate. It is also a *vocational* mandate. And, undeniably, it is our *cultural* mandate.

One

Post-Consensus Culture, Natural Law, and Moral Persuasion: Translating Moral Conviction in a Disbelieving Age*

The Situation: Our Post-Consensus Culture and Metaphysical Realities

Post-Consensus Culture and the Tyranny of the Majority

In Western history, periods of social and political upheaval have often given rise to a renewed interest in moral law. For example, the important universal human rights declarations that we take for granted today and that were forged immediately following World War II and the Holocaust are owing to natural-law assumptions. How can there be universal human rights apart from fixed moral law in the universe? Presently in the West we may be at one of those defining junctures of cultural upheaval.

Much has been said and written in recent years about ours being a post-Christian era. Our time has been variously called post-traditional, post-modern, post-literary, post-historic, post-collectivist, post-bourgeois, post-capitalist, post-industrial, post-Protestant,

---

* A version of this essay was presented under the same title in June 2018 at the Acton Institute's annual conference, Acton University, in Grand Rapids, Michigan.

post-civilized, and, of course, post-Christian.¹ Cultural critique from another corner has been telling us in recent years of the need for a new St. Benedict—the so-called Benedict Option—with the implication that we need quasi-monastic communities in order to survive the current collapse of culture as we know it.² The suggestion is that we are "moral cave-dwellers," entering a new "dark age" of sorts in which the social and cultural conditions that make character possible are no longer present.³

I often wonder what sort of critique a certain Frenchman who visited our young nation in the 1830s would offer us today. Cataloguing his insights in what may be the most important book ever written about both democracy and America, Alexis de Tocqueville in *Democracy in America*[4] distinguished between two types of tyranny—a

---

1. Lest one think that this sort of "post-everything" language is a more recent phenomenon, already in the 1970s it was appearing in some versions of cultural commentary; so, for example, Richard John Neuhaus, *Time toward Home: The American Experiment as Revelation* (New York: Seabury, 1975), 1.

2. Rod Dreher, *The Benedict Option: A Strategy for Christians in a Post-Christian Nation* (New York: Sentinel, 2017).

3. This is the basic argument set forth almost two decades ago by James Davison Hunter, *The Death of Character: Moral Education in an Age of Good and Evil* (New York: Basic Books, 2000). Though cited less often than Alasdair MacIntyre's *After Virtue*, from whose final paragraph Dreher draws his fundamental thesis, Hunter is far more accessible. Hunter, nevertheless, would surely agree with MacIntyre's conclusion:

> What matters at this stage is the construction of local forms of community within which civility and the intellectual and moral life can be sustained through the new dark ages which are already upon us. And if the tradition of the virtues was able to survive the horrors of the last dark ages, we are not entirely without grounds for hope. This time however the barbarians are not waiting beyond the frontiers; they have already been governing us for quite some time. And it is our lack of consciousness of this that constitutes part of our predicament. We are waiting not for a Godot, but for another—doubtless very different—St. Benedict.

After Virtue: A Study in Moral Theology, 3rd. ed. (Notre Dame: University of Notre Dame Press, 2007), 245.

4. Alexis de Tocqueville, *Democracy in America*, ed. Harvey Mansfield and Delba Winthrop (Chicago and London: University of Chicago Press, 2000).

tyranny of the minority (typical of the European experience) and a tyranny of the majority. The latter type, he worried, would be the challenge for the young American nation. An important question emerging from Tocqueville's reflections is this: *Can a tyranny of the masses be enshrined in law?* Tocqueville believed that it could. Laws are typically a reflection of their people, and laws can be unjust and immoral. When morality is separated from law, totalitarianism ensues, and this tyranny can be either "soft" or "hard" in character. When law, politics, and government lack people who are committed to operating on moral principle, we prepare the soil for a soft totalitarianism. Thus, Tocqueville's worries were legitimate.

On Making Moral Judgments: The Sin of Judgmentalism

What gives rise to a majoritarian tyranny? One of the defining features of our present cultural condition is that we are loath to make moral judgments. We dare not offend others by publicly advocating categories of right and wrong, good and evil, virtue and vice. To do so is to commit the cardinal cultural sin of judgmentalism and to be decried as hate-filled, bigoted, and intolerant. To insist on making moral judgments, then, is profoundly out of step with the times and deemed, well, intolerable.

Given the contemporary hegemony of tolerance turned on its head, Americans are accustomed to adopting any number of creative strategies in order to avoid naming right and wrong, good and evil. Creativity and ingenuity, after all, are hallmarks of American life. We Americans are truly awash in victimhood, exoneration, exculpating, plea-bargaining, and general immunity from wrongdoing. In the end, no one—at least no one *alive!*—in our culture can be found guilty. One common method of exculpation, of course, is to deny that evil exists. This strategy, let us be clear, is not merely the province of Eastern pantheistic religion; it also inhabits the lives of metaphysical materialists, agnostics, and nihilists. Alas, free will, depraved intention, egregious human rights violations, and evil as a concept are conveniently explained away. In this context, one thinks, for example, of Albert Camus's intriguing novel *The Plague*, an allegorical tale depicting the psychology of emergent tyranny, wherein evil as a concept is not allowed to inhabit the minds of human beings.

Notwithstanding the fact that rats are overrunning the city of Oran, its citizens have convinced themselves that these vermin do not exist. Why? Because they *may not* exist.

At the intellectual level, of course, a scientific justification for the view that evil does not exist lies in the "new biology" and Darwinian assumptions about life. The moral sense that is unique to the human species is explained through our genetic nature, which prepares us as humans, through endless adaptation, to live civilly, morally, and empathetically. Why some people are less civil, moral, and empathetic than others is not so readily explained, even when "default" reasoning is tethered to brain structure and genetic predilection. But this seems like a theory in search of a justification as opposed to a legitimate explanation that fits the evidence. To argue that moral ideas reflect biological processes at work in the natural world is to concede a certain inevitability about human nature and human behavior. If this is true, then *there is no need to convince a person to pursue moral judgment or be ethical*, since that person has been programmed genetically anyway. In fact, the very assumption that a political system can work is rendered absurd since nature has already programmed people differently (namely, some *not* to cooperate).

Writing seventy years ago, C. S. Lewis foresaw the tendency in Western societies to utilize science in an attempt to avoid moral self-responsibility. Lewis fully expected that someday punishment per se would be abolished while religious belief would be viewed as neurotic, with both crime and religious conviction being treated as a mental disorder.[5] Precisely at the time that Lewis was predicting the eclipse of rationality and moral agency, very much in line with what has been called "the triumph of the therapeutic," B. F. Skinner was trumpeting, "If man is free, then a technology of behavior is impossible," and "I deny that freedom exists at all. I must deny it—or my program would be absurd."[6]

Another strategy, short of denying the existence of evil, is to regulate it—that is, to reduce it to manageable proportions. While this

---

5. C. S. Lewis, "The Humanitarian Theory of Punishment" (1949), in *God in the Dock: Essays on Theology and Ethics*, ed. Walter Hooper (1970; repr., Grand Rapids, MI: Eerdmans, 2002), 287–94.

6. B. F. Skinner, *Walden Two* (New York: Macmillan, 1948), 213, 242, 257.

is standard fare today for how we deal with crime and incivility, its critique was offered already a generation ago by the late senator from New York Daniel Patrick Moynihan.[7] In identifying a moral calculus that he called "defining deviancy down," Moynihan observed that social evil and aberrant behavior dare not be found to reach outlandish proportions that would cause a cultural stigma. What to do? Redefine what constitutes normal and abnormal, acceptable and unacceptable. Thus, for example, rather than suffer the embarrassment of acknowledging staggering levels of criminal deviance and having to hold people accountable for their behavior, as a society we simply redefine—through psychosocial, economic analyses—what we deem aberrant. In this way we conveniently—and painlessly—make society "safer" and criminal behavior less frequent.[8]

In the post-consensus cultural climate of ours, however, the stratagem of choice seems to have become branding others with the sin of judgmentalism. This is an extremely effective means of silencing the public expression of religious or moral conviction. Though far more subtle than overtly totalitarian tactics, accusing people of judgmentalism is a powerful psychological tool insofar as it plays on people's self-perception, in the end paralyzing them in the face of genuine moral evil and injustice. While religious and nonreligious people find recourse to this method, a particularly effective tool for both groups is citing Jesus's words from Matthew 7:1: "Do not judge, or you too will be judged" (NIV).

To be accused of judgmentalism in American culture these days is worse than to be branded a murderer. After all, suspected manslayers at least can find exculpation in a tragic childhood, high blood-sugar levels, or the cruel biological joke of a "violent gene." But let us pause for a moment to reflect. Is judging indeed *not* to be tolerated? Is judging inherently unjust? Is moral judgment impermissible? Or is it perhaps possible—heaven forbid—that human beings are

---

7. Daniel Patrick Moynihan, "Defining Deviancy Down," *American Scholar* 62, no. 1 (Winter 1993): 17–30.

8. Of course, a related way of reducing evil and criminality to "manageable" proportions is to limit them to a few cases from history—e.g., Mao, Stalin, Hitler, Idi Amin, Pol Pot, Jeffrey Dahmer—which allows us to remove the scourge of human depravity lodged in the human heart and apply it to only a few select, outrageous instances.

actually capable of doing so in a correct and just manner? Or are we consigned always and eternally to be open-minded, careful never to offend others as we live out our lives?

An important though rudimentary distinction needs to be made, and it is the distinction between prejudice and judgment. Judgment, rightly construed, is "to call things by their real names."[9]

Thus, moral judgment is predicated on our ability to discern between good and evil, just and unjust, hypocritical and authentic, and as a result to call them each accordingly. In the end, open-mindedness—a healthy attitude when qualified but a scourge when used to refuse moral self-responsibility—is not enough. Self-esteem and victimhood negate a society's ability to do good and to work for the common good. Jesus's anger, lest we miss the lesson of the aforementioned biblical text, is aimed at hypocritical religion, vindictiveness, and Pharisaism; the Son of Man is not calling for the elimination of moral judgment, even when Psychological Man does.[10]

Tolerance Old and New

Along with its siblings diversity and sensitivity, tolerance has achieved remarkable status in our culture's hierarchy of values.[11] *Tolerance* is one of those "thought-killer" words that has come to constitute our cultural lexicon, requiring uncritical acceptance for all reasons in all seasons. In fact, the commandment "Thou shalt not judge" seems to have superseded all revealed commandments. But how far—and how much—*should* we tolerate? What are toleration's limits, and how is toleration best understood?

---

9. Jean Bethke Elshtain, "Judge Not?," in *The Moral Life: An Introductory Reader in Ethics and Literature*, ed. Louis J. Pojman (New York: Oxford University Press, 2004), 195.

10. Sociologist Philip Rieff used the descriptors "moral man" and "psychological man" to describe American culture before and since "the triumph of the therapeutic." See *The Triumph of the Therapeutic: Uses of Faith after Freud* (New York: Harper & Row, 1966).

11. Elsewhere I have argued in similar fashion as in this section of the essay. See J. Daryl Charles, *Retrieving the Natural Law: A Return to Moral First Things* (Grand Rapids, MI: Eerdmans, 2008), 248–51.

In the English language, *toleration* in the sense of "bearing" or "indulging" (from the Latin *tolerare*) came into prominence in the late seventeenth century. It denoted a policy of forbearance in the face of something disliked or unpopular. It was a foremost political virtue, demonstrated by a government's readiness to permit a variety of religious beliefs and illustrated in John Locke's *Letter concerning Toleration* (1689) and *Two Treatises of Government* (1690). In its conception, then, tolerance took on the cast of a virtue because of its concern for the common good and its respect for people as persons. We endure particular customs or habits—sometimes even unpleasant ones—in the interest of preserving a greater unity. Recall that in the Lockean context, tolerance was advocated for religious nonconformists. Never was it construed, however, to imply—much less to sanction—morally questionable behavior, as it often is today. The culture of tolerance in which we presently find ourselves is a culture in which people believe nothing, possess no clear concept of right and wrong, and are remarkably indifferent to this precarious state of affairs. As a result of this transmutation, tolerance becomes indistinguishable from an intractably intolerant relativism. The challenge, then, is learning how to purify tolerance so that it remains a virtue without succumbing to the centripetal forces of relativism.

Thus, in order to avoid the relativist tendency, it is crucial that we distinguish between pluralism as a sociocultural fact of life and pluralism as an ideology.[12] And precisely because people use the term *tolerance* indiscriminately without noting the difference, preserving this distinction is critically important. At stake in the former are negotiable issues such as language, customs, ethnic habits, and group preferences. Social, cultural, and ethnic pluralism is to be welcomed and praised, for it is part of the created order. At stake in the latter, however, are issues of moral reality; hence, discernment is needed. Ideological pluralists demand that we tolerate alternative explanations of reality, while at the same time pressuring us

---

12. On this see Lesslie Newbigin, *The Gospel in a Pluralist Society* (Grand Rapids, MI: Eerdmans, 1989); idem, *Truth to Tell: The Gospel and Public Truth* (Grand Rapids, MI: Eerdmans, 1991); as well as Alister E. McGrath, *A Passion for Truth* (Downers Grove, IL: InterVarsity, 1996), esp. chap. 5 ("Evangelicalism and Religious Pluralism").

to negotiate—and abdicate—claims to ultimate truth. If tolerance is allowed to devolve into an indifference to what is true, then the result is a baneful permissiveness toward all manner of evil and a collapse of the common good and civil society.

The tone of the ideological pluralist or inclusivist, of course, sounds so epistemologically modest and so eminently reasonable. By contrast, exclusivists strike us as rather arrogant, even oppressive. Yet precisely the opposite is the case.[13] This is why martyrdom is an abiding Christian reality, even when it is not the norm in Western societies at the moment. Ideological pluralists, after all, do not offer up their lives in the name of being radically inclusive.

Holding Culture Accountable:
Thoughts on "Legislating Morality" and the Common Good

Despite the prevailing mood of perverted tolerance and of nonjudgmentalism, however, we discover, alas, that we all do make judgments that are moral in nature.[14] That is, all people make moral discriminations as to what they will tolerate and what they will not. All people—at all times and in all places—make moral judgments. They simply draw the line between acceptable and unacceptable at different places and use different criteria. But, wonder of wonders, all people—everywhere—find themselves using the language of "should" and "should not." Isn't that instructive! Where does that discrimination originate?

In practical terms, however, where exactly do we draw the line? How do we as a society determine what behavior is acceptable and what is unacceptable? Our answer is this: we must draw the line *where private preferences that undermine the common good make claims in the public sphere.* Therefore, whatever the cost and inconvenience (and in the days ahead the cost will get much higher), Christians are not only free to contend in the public arena but they are required to do so, and that for the purposes of preserving the common good and the moral order. This response, of course, will lead to charges ad infinitum that we are "imposing our morality" on those

---

13. Peter J. Leithart has very succinctly made this point in "Pluralism's Pride," *Touchstone* 18, no. 7 (September 2005): 15–17.

14. See Charles, *Retrieving the Natural Law*, 251–57.

around us. Christians are reminded ad nauseam by secularists that because we live in a pluralistic democracy, we are forbidden from such imposition. But are we?

If morality were indeed a private affair, as some contend, then critics of Christianity would be justified in excluding the Christian voice from the public arena. But since the square is public (and recall Richard Neuhaus's classic argument that the public square is not "naked"[15]), this means that all people may contend. In this vein, we will need to counter the received wisdom that the public sphere—and the state—must remain neutral. We must ask, Is there such a thing as moral neutrality?

If there are particular goods identified by a society that need protecting, then society cannot be neutral about those goods. Rather, it has a vested interest in maintaining and preserving them. Tolerance is an authentic virtue if it is rooted in a commitment to what is true and good for society; correlatively, it is a vice if it is indifferent to these realities. Thus, tolerance is not—indeed, it cannot be—neutral toward what affects society.

But we must proceed one step further. By contending that there is no such thing as moral neutrality, we are also declaring that *someone's morality will be imposed*. It is a well-worn axiom that you cannot legislate morality. But this is nonsense. In the end, someone's morality will be legislated. The public nature of the marketplace, the public nature of social institutions, and the very public nature of requisite Christian witness together confront us with a hard truth:

> A society cannot function well, cannot survive ... without a large measure of intolerance. Yes, intolerance—of theft, burglary, cruelty, classroom hooliganism, disrespect for parental authority, and violent crime of all sorts; [intolerance] of substance abuse, infidelity, illegitimacy, perversion, pornography, rape, and child molestation; [intolerance] of fraud, envy, covetousness, and knavery; [intolerance] of sloth, mediocrity, incompetence, maleducation, improvidence, irresponsibility, and fecklessness. A society tolerant of those things would soon find itself in seri-

---

15. Richard John Neuhaus, *The Naked Public Square: Religion and Democracy in America*, 2nd ed. (Grand Rapids, MI: Eerdmans, 1988).

ous trouble, even facing dissolution, and many people in that society would be in peril of their lives.[16]

For those of us who tend to shy away from confrontation and wish for greater toleration on the part of Christians, we do well to remember that Christian social presence and witness compel us to work for the common good using any and all permissible means. Everyone has claims on the public square—most notably, Christians, whose cultural mandate rests on a firm commitment to the redemption of all things. While it is not a given that everyone's claims in public will be tolerated, tolerance properly understood mirrors a strong and principled commitment to promote moral truth and to work for the common good. Christian conviction and cultural presence will necessarily be anchored in two fundamental orientations. We must insist that the religious viewpoint—even those characterized by a close adherence to traditional religious confessions—be allowed within the public arena, thereby refusing to succumb to the temptation to privatize faith. Christian confession, after all, has a leavening effect on humanity and culture. At the same time we must be cognizant of the limits of political and legal action within pluralistic society, and we must refuse to view activism as salvific.

Perhaps it is high time in Western culture—and specifically the American context—that we return a good word that has been hijacked—*tolerance*—and reinstate its proper meaning.

The Ethical Imperative: Translating Moral Conviction in a Post-Consensus Culture

Alternative Responses to the Culture by the Christian Community

How, then, might we respond to the present social climate that tolerates the intolerable but will not tolerate moral principle? I see three possibilities. One alternative is to be resigned to the impossibility of the task and to withdraw, or at least to develop a theological or philosophical rationale for withdrawing. This can be done in multiple

---

16. John Attarian, "In Dispraise of Tolerance, Sensitivity and Compassion," *The Social Critic* 3, no. 2 (Spring 1998): 22.

ways. One is to fatalistically think, "Well, why rearrange the chairs on a sinking ship anyway?" Another rationale would be that of the Anabaptists, who were part of a minority movement in sixteenth-century Protestantism that confessed a separation from the world (and from any vocations that reminded them of the world). To this day, many adherents of this tradition are separatistic. Regardless of the various justifications for this alternative, we may call it isolation.

A second response to the cultural situation is the opposite of isolation—that is, being insufficiently critical and discerning of the social and philosophical assumptions that drive the culture so that we end up capitulating and being absorbed into the culture. This is typical of the Protestant mainline, but it also mirrors what John Paul II called "cafeteria Catholicism." In any case, if the first tendency is isolation, the second represents capitulation.

A third response, it seems to me, is the proper way, and it is the willingness to count the cost and to be engaged citizens. It is neither retreating nor withdrawing, nor being spiritually dull and undiscerning, but being committed stewards of the culture, using our gifts and callings to build up the common good—whether we are butchers or bakers or candlestick makers, whether we are nurses or artists or drivers of hearses. We may describe this third alternative as faithful stewardship. Being a steward entails what we might view as bridge building—that is, looking for creative, resourceful, and strategic ways in which we can penetrate the culture and find points of commonality for the purpose of translating our moral convictions.

This challenge, of course, is not easy; it is full of complexity and at times ambiguity, and, frankly, it is hard work. But it is nevertheless our calling, if I may here use a theological term. Thus, we utilize everything within our means, we utilize a full array of unlimited gifts and abilities, and we utilize any and all open doors that present themselves. In the end, however, translating our convictions in responsible and compelling ways is not about success as Americans typically understand it. The steward's motivation is faithfulness, not success so-called.

On the Content and Manner of Our Witness

In terms of Christians' social presence and witness, there is an unfortunate tendency to separate truth and charity, as if they are distinct and at times conflicting entities. This is the product of split thinking and is devastating in terms of its ethical consequences. We must keep truth and charity wedded together since they are unified in the character of God (even when they manifest themselves in different ways). I submit that the results are disastrous when truth and charity are divorced, for at that point our ethic becomes diluted and our social presence lacks a backbone.

In his important 2009 encyclical *Caritas in Veritate*, Benedict XVI writes: "Charity in truth, to which Jesus Christ bore witness by his earthly life and especially by his death and resurrection, is *the principal driving force behind the authentic development of every person and of all humanity*."[17] In this final encyclical of the pontificate of Benedict XVI, we find the extension of a theme that was recurring not only in his work but in that of his predecessor, John Paul II. *"Only in the truth does charity* shine forth, *only in the truth* can charity be authentically lived. Truth is the light that gives meaning and value to charity."[18] Benedict does not deny love's importance, but given that love is often presumed to have priority in terms of Christian social witness, he does argue that love—at least as it is understood today—needs strong qualification.

The problem, as Benedict is aware, is that "charity has been and continues to be misconstrued and emptied of meaning, with the consequent risk of being misinterpreted, detached from ethical living and, in any event, undervalued." But this emptying also occurs "in the social, juridical, cultural, political and economic fields"—that is, contexts which are "most exposed to this danger" and where moral

---

17. Benedict XVI, Encyclical Letter on Integral Human Development, *Caritas in Veritate* (June 29, 2009), no. 1 (emphasis added), http://w2.vatican.va/content/benedict-xvi/en/encyclicals/documents/hf_ben-xvi_enc_20090629_caritas-in-veritate.html.

18. John Paul II, Encyclical Letter on Certain Fundamental Questions of the Church's Moral Teaching, *Veritatis Splendor* (August 6, 1993), no. 3 (emphasis added), http://w2.vatican.va/content/john-paul-ii/en/encyclicals/documents/hf_jp-ii_enc_06081993_veritatis-splendor.html.

responsibility is urgently needed.[19] Hence the need to link charity with truth not only in the sequence given by Paul, *veritas in caritate* (Eph. 4:15), but also in the inverse and complementary sequence of *caritas in veritate*.

Not only does truth need to be "sought, found and expressed within the 'economy' of charity," but "charity in its turn needs to be understood, confirmed and practised in the light of truth."[20] The reason for this mutual and reciprocal relationship is significant and should give pause to anyone who takes the moral life seriously. In a cultural context that downplays truth at best and despises it at worst, Benedict worries that *love*—perhaps properly understood in generations past—now is devoid of meaning. He elaborates:

> Without truth, charity degenerates into sentimentality. Love becomes an empty shell, to be filled in an arbitrary way. In a culture without truth, this is the fatal risk facing love. It falls prey to contingent subjective emotions and opinions, the word "love" is abused and distorted, to the point where it comes to mean the opposite. Truth frees charity from the constraints of an emotionalism that deprives it of relational and social content, and of a fideism that deprives it of human and universal breathing-space. In the truth, charity reflects the personal yet public dimension of faith in the God of the Bible, who is both Agápe and Lógos: Charity and Truth, Love and Word.[21]

The implications of the organic linkage between charity and truth become apparent. Because of this linkage, charity can be "understood," "shared," and "communicated," even cross-culturally, transcending the normal cultural barriers that limit communication and communion.[22] Truth, thus seen, has the capacity to open minds and unite people in their experience. In the present social and cultural climate wherein the tendency is to relativize truth, Benedict wishes to admonish us that "practising charity in truth helps people to understand that adhering to the values of Christianity is not merely

---

19. Benedict XVI, *Caritas in Veritate*, no. 2.
20. Benedict XVI, *Caritas in Veritate*, no. 2.
21. Benedict XVI, *Caritas in Veritate*, no. 3.
22. Benedict XVI, *Caritas in Veritate*, no. 4.

useful but essential for building a good society and for true integral human development."[23]

And what would a Christianity consisting of charity without truth breed, if tolerated? In Benedict's assessment, it would be "more or less interchangeable with a pool of good sentiments, helpful for social cohesion, but of little relevance."[24] But more specifically, "there would no longer be any real place for God in the world. Without truth, charity is confined to a narrow field devoid of relations. It is excluded from the plans and processes of promoting human development of universal range, in dialogue between knowledge and praxis."[25]

For this reason, Benedict reminds his readers, the church's social teaching is *caritas in veritate in re sociali*; it is "the proclamation of the truth of Christ's love in society" and "the principle around which the Church's social doctrine turns."[26] Therefore, while social ethics is a service of charity, "its locus is truth," which will have a "preserving" and "liberating" power in the face of "ever-changing events of history."[27] Correlatively, without truth, "without trust and love for what is true, there is *no social conscience and responsibility*."[28] Thereby "social action" ends up serving private or misguided interests, gutting the very source and goal of moral action.

Moreover, without truth, in addition to love collapsing into subjectivism and sentimentalism, "it is easy to fall into an empiricist and sceptical view of life, incapable of rising to the level of praxis because of a lack of interest in grasping the values—sometimes even the meanings—with which to judge and direct it."[29] To be faithful to human nature, for Benedict, is to be faithful to the truth, which alone is the guarantee of freedom (cf. John 8:32) and human development.

But let us pause for the moment and consider, in very practical terms, what the divorce of love and truth might mean for that part of civil society we call criminal justice. Out of fear of driving crimi-

---

23. Benedict XVI, *Caritas in Veritate*, no. 4.
24. Benedict XVI, *Caritas in Veritate*, no. 4.
25. Benedict XVI, *Caritas in Veritate*, no. 4.
26. Benedict XVI, *Caritas in Veritate*, nos. 5, 6.
27. Benedict XVI, *Caritas in Veritate*, no. 6.
28. Benedict XVI, *Caritas in Veritate*, nos. 5, 6 (emphasis added).
29. Benedict XVI, *Caritas in Veritate*, no. 9.

nals even further away and of being rigid or intolerant, we decide not to punish or prosecute. Or out of a distorted view of forgiveness, we decide not to punish according to the degree of the crime. So we "forgive" them, letting them off the hook. The end result? We make society unsafe for everyone, and injustice reigns. In ethical terms, we need to be reminded of moral truths that are fixed and not subject to alteration. One such principle is that love will never sacrifice what is true and real in order simply to show compassion or "save the relationship." The other side of that ethical coin is that truth will always look for ways to clothe itself that dignify the human being. Charity can be tough and demanding; truth can be dignifying, even when it is just or seemingly harsh. Love is not sloppy sentimentalism, and truth does not lose sight of human dignity. In the words of C. S. Lewis, we hold people accountable for their actions *precisely because* they are made in the image of God and are responsible moral agents.[30]

Just as our ethic must keep truth and charity wed, so too the manner of our moral persuasion must be creative and winsome. The public square is a place for all citizens, with none excluded; this we call a principled pluralism. At the same time, our method does matter; in fact, it matters enormously. Our countenance—that is, the tone and bearing with which we engage others—is important. The truth will offend others, yet we must be careful that it is the *substance* and not the *style* of our engagement which does the offending.

As we presently wrestle with translating our convictions in the public sphere, we should bear in mind and learn from intergenerational wisdom. Here I refer to continuity of the message, on the one hand (after all, we are part of the historic Christian *tradition*), yet discontinuity of method or strategy, on the other hand. Methods that may have worked in previous generations might not be effective today. Thus, it is incumbent on us to adapt creatively to our audience without sacrificing the message. Creativity is wonderful and has a divine precedent: in theological terms we call it the incarnation. The Logos (or reason) of God the Creator took on flesh (cf. John 1:1–5, 14). God communicates through human language. God "translates."

---

30. Lewis, "The Humanitarian Theory of Punishment," in *God in the Dock*, 287–300.

The challenge before us, then, is building bridges to our fellow citizens in ways that are relevant and faithful. In the fourth section below, I will set before us two individuals who serve as good models, useful exemplars, of bridge building through natural-law thinking. But before we consider the merits of those two models, however, in the next section I would like to reaffirm the necessary resources for moral persuasion, which are theological in nature.

The Ethical Foundation: Affirming Our Requisite Resources

The Moral Function of Doctrine

A vibrant, morally guided social ethic does not descend out of thin air. It issues out of particular doctrinal commitments that we share at the altar as we confess the historic creeds together and for which we would lay down our lives. Novelist Dorothy Sayers was a contemporary of C. S. Lewis and was known to many as the creator of Lord Peter Wimsey, the aristocratic amateur detective. Perhaps less well known are her forays into the realm of theology, which turn out to be exceedingly rich. In her theological writing, Sayers was rather impatient with those who viewed doctrine to be "hopelessly irrelevant" to the life of the ordinary Christian.[31]

Creed or Chaos? constitutes Sayers's witty, imaginative, and at times acerbic call to take dogma seriously. Sayers writes, "The word *dogma* is unpopular, and that is why I have used it. It is our own distrust of dogma that is handicapping us."[32] In truth, "the dogma *is* the drama," she insists.[33] But sadly, in her view, our failure to appreciate fully the role of theology has rendered Christian cultural witness impotent, cutting us off at the knees, as it were. Thereby, she laments, we have "very effectively pared the claws of the Lion of Judah" and "certified him [to be] meek and mild."[34]

---

31. Dorothy Sayers, *Creed or Chaos?* (repr., Manchester: Sophia Institute, 1974), 50.
32. Sayers, *Creed or Chaos?*, 40.
33. Sayers, *Creed or Chaos?*, 5.
34. Sayers, *Creed or Chaos?*, 9.

For Sayers, doctrine possesses two inviolable functions in the life of the Christian. First, it defines what is distinctive about our world- and life-view. To lose sight of the importance of doctrine is to lose the backbone of the faith we profess and to invite spurious alternatives. Second, doctrine alone furnishes the basis for a uniquely Christian social ethic. Christian theology, after all, is an attempt to describe the nature of reality, which includes human nature and our place in the cosmos. Relatedly, without a theological foundation the church is utterly incapable of explaining, let alone embodying, the contours of a Christian social ethic. Theology alone allows us to contend for a baseline morality in the public square, which depends on our awareness of an objective moral order as displayed through creation and the cosmos.

Creation, Redemption, and Incarnation: The Theological Bedrock of Our Ethical Witness

Historically, Christian theology has been based on a creation-fall-redemption-consummation scheme of biblical theology. Previous generations of Protestant evangelicalism—and here I am referring to much of the twentieth century—have often been more concerned about consummation, which is to say eschatology or end-times matters, than they have been to affirm a full-orbed theology of creation and redemption. This preoccupation with end-times scenarios inter alia has had a debilitating effect on the church's cultural witness. Consider the fruit of that sort of outlook: religious believers, as a result, will tend to withdraw from meaningful and strategic participation in social life. Thus, a proper understanding of creation and redemption—and the resultant cultural mandate that confronts God's people—is imperative.

Not only were all things created by God "in the beginning" but all things are being sustained, preserved, and guided by the sovereign Creator in the present created order. Thus, to *create* and to *rule* belong together; they are inseparable.[35] Not for one moment should we lose sight of the Creator's sovereign activity both in creating

---

35. This is the essence of Albert Wolters's argument set forth in *Creation Regained: Biblical Basics for a Reformational Worldview*, 2nd ed. (Grand Rapids, MI: Eerdmans, 2005).

and in upholding and guiding all things in the created order. And because of this creation order, law—both physical and moral—has significance. It is through law that the sovereign Lord mediates his rule over creation. In this sense we can understand both science and morals: the Creator mediates his rule of the universe through physical laws (laws of nature) just as he governs human affairs through moral law (the natural law).

Moreover, all creation is declared in biblical revelation to be "good." This is critically important in light of the effects of sin. On several occasions in Genesis 1, God pronounces his work of creation to be "good." The implication is that we dishonor the Creator by taking a negative or deficient view of any aspect of creation. This was the chief error of the Gnostic heresy in the early centuries. Gnosticism understood salvation as flight from this evil world, a prison from which people needed to be rescued.

The ramifications of the goodness of creation are far-reaching. In contrast to, for example, Anabaptists, for whom withdrawal or separatism is a governing motive, a proper view of creation liberates the Christian to serve in multitudes of ways *within* the culture. Being stewards of the culture offers a sense of reward and fulfillment as we apply our gifts and callings accordingly and broadly.

But the pious Christian will surely object by insisting, *What about the fall?* What about the effects of sin, which are thoroughgoing and universal in scope and character? The biblical response is that not even the fall and human depravity undo the essential goodness of creation. Does sin affect it? By all means; sin distorts everything in creation. But does it undo the goodness of the created order? By no means.

Moreover, a proper understanding of the doctrine of creation has crucial ramifications for the doctrine of redemption. Redemption, as taught in the New Testament, encompasses all things and is not narrowly restricted to the so-called spiritual realm. Paul's letters to the Ephesian and Colossian Christians press this point: redemption achieved by Jesus Christ is cosmic in scope in the sense that it restores the whole of creation. As underscored in Colossians 1, Paul is emphatic that *all things*—everything seen and unseen, material and nonmaterial—were created *by* and *for* Christ (cf. also John 1:3 and Heb. 1:2). And not only is Jesus both the agent and the goal of everything in creation, he is also redeemer thereof. That is, all things are restored through and to Christ. This has bearing not only on our understanding of human nature and human behavior but it also adjusts our vision for vocation and service in the world. Christ being both creator and redeemer restores the meaning and purpose to our work in every part of life. This means that nothing vocationally is off-limits; there is no sacred-versus-secular distinction, and we are to be stewards of all areas of life and culture.[36] Redemption, then, is as wide as the universe.

But the doctrines of creation and redemption are magnified by the doctrine of incarnation. If we truly believe that based on the image of God through creation we are coregents with God over all of creation—to develop, expand, shape, and mold it for his glory—and if we believe that God incarnated himself in Christ, the Word made flesh; and Christ incarnates his life among and through his people, then there ought to be no such thing as withdrawal or isolation from the created order. The doctrine of the incarnation entails God manifesting his life in and through the created order. During the present age it is the people of God, because of Christ, who incarnate the life of God in everything around them. That is, they carry on the redemptive scope of God's plan. For what needs redemption is not merely the soul per se but human nature and human life in its composite unity. Part of this task is to reverence the work of the Creator, the One who is creator not merely of nonmaterial reality but material reality as well. From the standpoint of an "incarnational humanism," there is value in all that is natural, human, and earthly. That is to say, the heavens and the earth, which mirror the created order, "are not destined for an eternal ash-heap, but for a transformation."[37]

---

36. This was one of the critically important aspects of the Protestant—and especially Lutheran—breakthrough in the sixteenth century. Previously, *vocatio* was understood as a "calling" to the monastery or the priesthood. Based on his reading of Scripture, Luther, in reacting to this long-standing bifurcation of sacred versus secular, insisted that *all* were priests and that *everyone* is called to a particular station in life. There is no sacred as opposed to secular division of life before God, he contended. Every work is *holy* in the sight of God when properly motivated.

37. Thus, John Courtney Murray, *We Hold These Truths: Catholic Reflections on the American Proposition* (New York: Sheed and Ward, 1960), 190. Murray

Indeed, all of creation will be "new," but at the same time we will still recognize it as part of God's good creation.

Natural Law and Common Moral Ground

At the outset of this essay, I noted that natural-law thinking contributed to the emphasis on universal human rights immediately following World War II. In theological terms, natural law is part of what is called general revelation, as distinct from special revelation. General revelation is that knowledge of the Creator, of the self, and of moral reality that is accessible to all people. What are the sources of general revelation? They are chiefly two: creation and conscience, which is to say external evidence and internal evidence, with the two realms working together. Paul identifies these two in the beginning of his letter to the Romans. What is his argument? It is that all people everywhere, Jew or Gentile, have a minimum natural knowledge of the Creator, of the self, and of moral reality. That minimum knowledge is enough to hold a person accountable so that, according to the apostle, all people everywhere, based on this minimum, are "without excuse" (Rom. 1:20).

The moral impulse is unique to the human species and is part of the image of God in each person. Every human being, by virtue of creation, mirrors this divine image. And because of this commonality, we may speak of a common humanity, the common good, and common moral ground shared by all. Because of the *imago Dei*, we have a "nature," a *common nature*, which not even sin and evil can eliminate. This is why we can appeal to people on the basis of our commonalities and natural law.[38]

---

pressed this point by contrasting what he called an "incarnational humanism" with an "eschatological humanism."

38. John Calvin expresses it well: despite human depravity, flickers of the divine light still shine. See *Institutes of the Christian Religion*, ed. John T. McNeill, trans. Ford Lewis Battles (Louisville: Westminster John Knox, 1960), 1.15.4, 2.2.2, and 2.2.12.

The Model: Two Examples of Natural-Law Reasoning and Bridge Building

Paul, the Apostle to the Gentiles

In 1 Corinthians 9 we find Paul describing his own "philosophy" of engaging others. He illustrates this approach to engagement with these fascinating words:

> Even though I am free before all people, I've made myself a servant to all, in order to persuade some. To the Jews I became as a Jew, in order to persuade Jews.... And to those who are outside the law ..., I become the same, in order to persuade those outside the law.... I have become all things to all men, in order that by all means I might save some. (vv. 19–22)

"I have become all things to all men." What is Paul saying here? He seems to be saying that he is infinitely ready and willing to adapt to his surroundings in order to be persuasive. Those of us who have lived for an extended period in a foreign culture know precisely why accommodation is so important. As "strangers in a strange land," we must find meaningful touch points with the host culture. The first step, of course, is learning the language. No one will be effective or successful in any endeavor abroad if he or she does not learn to speak the language. This demonstrates to people that we value the culture, inasmuch as human culture is the vehicle through which truth is expressed.

Although in much of the book of Acts we see Paul in action, it is in the university city of Athens, the cultural capital of the ancient world and home to several ancient schools of philosophy, where we find Paul adapting himself in ways that might initially strike us as strange (or unorthodox). Luke's narrative found in Acts 17:16–34, which is tantalizingly brief, nevertheless contains some intriguing details. Initially the apostle is out in the agora, the marketplace, where social and philosophical disputes and discussions typically occurred in Athens. There he is able to mix it up, as it were, with both Jews and Gentiles. This takes dexterity, and not everyone can do it with the facility of Paul. Peter surely could not have held his own as did the apostle to the Gentiles.

Following his work in the agora, he is invited to address an elite audience, the council of the Areopagus (or "Mars Hill" in some translations). The council in the first century was an elite presidium of honored cultural leaders—thirty in number and Stoic and Epicurean in their worldview. By Paul's day the council, in its revived state, had been in existence for roughly four centuries already.[39] In Paul's address to the Areopagus council, as Luke recounts and summarizes it (Acts 17:22–34), we find two principal parts. The first part is preparatory or apologetic—that is, establishing a rapport with his audience through evidence, utilizing cultural artifacts with long-standing meaning from the city, and citing two poet-philosophers who had long-standing ties to Athens. One other element in this bridge-building strategy needs to be noted. Paul utilizes general revelation and natural-law assumptions about the cosmos, the creation of humans, and humans' relationship to the divine. And with this he then transitions into the second part of his address: fuller revelation of the Divine.

My focus here is not as much the content of Paul's message as it is his particular method. What do we observe? His introduction is clearly bridge building; he is establishing common ground. To have cited the Hebrew Scriptures in this context, given the framework of reality of Paul's audience, would have been meaningless. Rather, Paul's intention is to draw from evidence of reality that is both external to them (the cosmos) and internal (the human conscience) in order to present a fuller understanding of the divine purpose. This type of strategy we might call accommodation or adaptation.

C. S. Lewis

While C. S. Lewis does not use the phrase "natural law" in his writings, he does speak of the "law of nature" while employing the term "the Tao," and he uses related imagery in his fantasies (for example, in the Narnia chronicles), such as the "deeper wisdom"

---

39. In fact, mention of the Areopagus continues up to the fourth century AD, suggesting that its influence even during the Roman period was considerable. On distinctions between the earlier period of the Areopagus (pre-fourth century BC) and the later period (from the fourth century BC onward), see Gertrude Smith, "The Jurisdiction of the Areopagus," *Classical Philology* 22, no. 1 (1927): 61–79.

that has existed before time. When he speaks of the "law of nature," Lewis is not using the language of the biologist or the naturalist. He is referring to the natural law. We gain insight into this interpretation when he uses the expression "the Tao" throughout *The Abolition of Man* to describe the moral law, the law written on the heart (cf. Rom. 2:14–15), which "scientism" or the misguided application of science, he worries, empties or eviscerates. When moral emasculation occurs, people become "men without chests."

What surely is Lewis's most important commentary on the natural law, however, is found in the initial chapter of *Mere Christianity*. Under the title "Right and Wrong as a Clue to the Meaning of the Universe," Lewis, in a brilliantly subversive way, seeks to smuggle in the question of universal morality—that is, the natural law—but without arguing for God formally. As much of his philosophical writing, this chapter is written for the modern skeptic—well educated but agnostic or atheistic. How this initial chapter functions is significant. Lewis does not assume Christian faith on the part of his audience; as Paul did in Athens, he builds a bridge to his skeptical audience and utilizes natural-law reasoning. Assuming that his audience is not theistic, Lewis poses a rhetorical question in the essay: *Why does everyone—every single person—react the same way when he or she is slighted? Why do people—all people—instinctively react with resentment or outrage when they are treated unjustly?*[40]

Indeed, this type of question is useful in getting people, whether of a previous generation or today, to think seriously about the nature of the human moral impulse. And it is a question that thoughtful Christians need to be asking. *Why this predictable moral impulse on being wronged, and where does this originate?* The material realm, for Lewis, is incapable of offering a plausible explanation not only for the human moral impulse in general but for the supremely consistent moral impulse in all people—occurring 100 percent of the time—when they are mistreated. Based on the empirical evidence, Lewis concludes, it would seem as though there is a moral law at work in the universe. And if there *is* a moral law (the "law" of react-

---

40. The text of "Right and Wrong" on which I am relying is found in C. S. Lewis, *Mere Christianity*, rev. ed. (New York: HarperCollins, 2001), 3–32.

ing to injustice), then the evidence is compelling that behind this law stands a lawgiver.

Both Lewis and Paul, I would suggest, each in his own way, serve as helpful models as we struggle in our post-everything cultural climate to connect meaningfully with those around us. Here we are wise to bear in mind the role that general revelation plays. While it does not save, God's revelation of a general nature gives evidence of a Creator, and it is for this evidence that all people will be held accountable, as Paul in early Romans makes abundantly clear. It is precisely for this reason that the natural law is so important.

Conclusion

Persuasion and the Public Square: Concluding Thoughts on Our Mode of Engagement

Not only must Christians know what they believe but they must also know how to articulate those convictions. This, alas, is hard work. Because the public sphere is *public*, as we have insisted, we must wrestle with creative and winsomely expressed strategies as we seek to persuade those around us and the wider culture. And until our own society becomes totalitarian and unfree, we are responsible for marshaling and articulating public arguments. While not all are called to be public apologists, we all must represent our convictions in the public sphere in some form.

Persuasion has always been at the heart of the Christian message. In theological parlance, Christians are responsible for setting forth an "apology," or "defense" (a legal term), of their views before the world. Persuasion is inherent in our cultural stewardship. After all, as we have attempted to argue, the Word, which was God, took on flesh, came among us, and we beheld his glory (John 1:1, 14). Inspired by the Logos, we are *called* to communicate to the culture.

Requisite, then, for both individual Christians and the Christian community corporately is the need to learn how to translate our convictions in a compelling manner. We have taken note of two exemplars—each an "apostle to the Gentiles" in his particular era. In conjunction with this we have considered the openness of Paul's attitude: "all things to all people" and "by any and all means." Paul appears to be saying that there are an infinite number of strategies that can be utilized to persuade others, and that these can be employed without moral compromise. He is willing to adapt to his social and cultural surroundings in order to find open doors. Effective translation, then, seems to require a measure of creativity. At bottom, nothing that is good is off-limits, including work in social and public policy.

Correlatively, an important tool of translation is an appeal to natural law, given the *imago Dei* and the law written on the heart (cf. Rom. 2:15). Hence, we appeal to what is common to all. While Protestants may not be as comfortable with the grammar and moral reasoning that inhere in natural law as Catholics are, they need to be reminded that the Magisterial Reformers of the sixteenth century were unabashed in their affirming of the natural law as part of general revelation. While the Reformers protested vehemently on matters of theology and ecclesiology, as to the bedrock of their ethical thinking, they were one with their Roman Catholic counterparts.

We have also noted the importance of tone and bearing as we wrestle with how to translate our convictions in the public sphere—particularly today, in a period of cultural turmoil, social unrest, and aggressive or abrasive speech. For the Christian, this means that our message can be discredited by the manner in which we attempt to translate our convictions. To be sure, this does not mean that we will not on occasion need to employ "rhetorical tough-mindedness."[41] There are situations in which confrontation is necessary because issues of truth and falsehood are at stake. But to be tough-minded or unyielding does not mean that we must be abrasive or abusive in our mode. Tough-mindedness and moral fiber need not negate magnanimity and generosity of spirit.

The Church's Responsibility for the World: Serving the Common Good

I conclude with a question: What responsibility does the church have for the world? Recall our earlier premise, anchored in Paul's letter to the Colossians, John 1, and Hebrews 1:2: all things were created through and for Christ. What is the goal of creation? It is to

---

41. Michael Gerson and Peter Wehner, *City of Man: Religion and Politics in a New Era* (Chicago: Moody, 2010), 122.

be reconciled, in its totality, to God in Christ. And recall a further premise: redemption is not merely a rescue operation before impending disaster or after a disaster. The church, hence, is responsible for the world in every way, including morally, since the earth is the Lord's and everything in it (cf. Ps. 24:1). The Christian church of every generation needs the reminder of Augustine's two cities metaphor: we have two citizenships, one in the city of God and the other in the city of man, both of which we take seriously, even when the first commands our ultimate allegiance. Because all things were created for and unto Christ, we are therefore stewards of all aspects of culture (the city of man).

Finally, we need to be reminded that stewardship is a matter of faithfulness, not success as Americans tend to understand it. What if Western culture were to go through a spiritually dark period of, say, multiple generations? How would Christians respond? We must live, work, and serve with the long term in view. And we must do this in such a way that we do not isolate ourselves, retreat, or withdraw from public life, as is the temptation in any age when the cost for Christian faith is considerable. Every Christian believer has been given various talents and giftings with which to serve God and the common good. Here we do well to recall the parable of the talents (Matt. 25:14–30) in Jesus's teaching: some are given ten, some five, some two, and some one. We bring great honor and joy to the Master by investing those gifts he has given to us. Conversely, we dishonor him by taking lightly or not using what he himself has given us to invest in this life. The moral is that we *use* whatever we have been given, as stewards of the King of creation. Let us do that—creatively, winsomely, and faithfully.

Two

THE HUMAN PERSON AND THE COMMON GOOD*

The Human Person and the Creator

Anatomy of a Christian Worldview

Who am I? Why am I here? What is a human being? What is the meaning of suffering? What purpose does my life serve? In what relation does my life stand to others? Human beings have a deep-seated need to be able to explain—to ourselves if not to others—our own existence and our place in the cosmos. Giving answers to these basic questions depends on one's world- and life-view—that is, a scheme for interpreting reality that transcends mere opinions and feelings and that entails certain baseline assumptions about reality. All people make certain baseline assumptions about ultimate reality, even when they cannot readily explain or articulate these in a coherent fashion. An inability to make sense of reality with some coherence can lead, literally, to self-destruction. And if this statement seems exaggerated, we need only think how many people—and how

---

*A version of this essay was presented at the Acton Institute's symposium "The Church and the Common Good" in Seattle, Washington, in October 2017.

often people—wrestle with suicidal thoughts (perhaps many who are reading this very text).

Humans instinctively avoid or react against a fragmented life that does not offer some sort of meaningful explanation or interpretation of reality. World- and life-views are very much like climates insofar as they affect us regardless of whether we are aware of them. One simply cannot escape their influence. And every person, past or present, has an interpretive framework for ultimate reality. This was true of Aristotle, Caesar Augustus, the apostle Paul, Attila the Hun, Henry VIII, Martin Luther, Friedrich Nietzsche, Adolf Hitler, and Mother Teresa. It is true of every person born "under the sun," everyone who experiences life in this cosmos.

Our contemporaries not infrequently wonder why it is that the knottiest social issues and most contentious disagreements between people typically arise over issues of politics and religion. Whether in personal relations or public policy, the reason lies in the clash of world- and life-views—that is, in competing views of ultimate reality, human nature, and humans' place in the world. What is not immediately apparent in these disagreements is the level of presuppositions or unspoken assumptions at play—assumptions about God (theology), human nature (anthropology and psychology), human behavior (ethics), human knowledge (epistemology), human relations (sociology), and the universe (cosmology). But thinking in terms of world- or life-views and about ultimate assumptions is not something simply reserved for philosophers or theologians; it is the responsibility of every Christian.

I can distinctly recall my deep anxiety and nervousness in September 1992 when I arrived at the building lot in a suburban community outside of Baltimore to inspect the foundation of the first house we built; that foundation had been poured the morning before. My nervousness had been magnified by the fact that forty-five truckloads of dirt were needed to help raise the building site, which was said to be the lowest in the neighborhood (and what seemed like the lowest on the East Coast!). Holding my breath, I went walking around the perimeter of the freshly poured concrete and steel on which the house was supposed to rest. What was I doing, and why was I so nervous? The cause of my anxiety was that I was looking for flaws. Instinctively, though I know nothing about home building and cannot fix anything, I knew that *everything* in the house would ultimately be dependent on the quality of that slab. Any blemish or crack would affect the total structure and render the house permanently flawed—that is, until the house was reduced to rubble and a new foundation laid. That reality was unsettling: the foundation *is* the house.

Our frameworks by which we interpret ultimate reality, our world- and life-views, are like houses; at the foundational level they are informed and propped up by unseen governing assumptions about reality. Usually, assumptions are taken for granted since they remain largely hidden. Even when most people may not consciously work through these very foundations, their lives are nevertheless expressions of those particular deeply held, underlying convictions. Whether conscious or unconscious, a person's precommitment to a set of presuppositions leads to inevitable and ineluctable results. This has profound implications for ethics, since moral convictions are formed out of one's convictions about ultimate reality.

Creation, the Imago Dei, and Inherent Human Worth

In recent years it has become increasingly evident that most—if not all—of our culture's pressing ethical and bioethical issues hinge in some way on the question of human personhood.[1] At the center of these issues is lodged the matter of human nature. Post-everything culture has difficulty acknowledging an abiding consensus about what constitutes the human person. What distinguishes human life from other forms of life as utterly unique? Such, of course, is to ask, *What is the nature of the human person?* Our answer to this question will have notable bearing on the social policies of our day.

A useful starting point to begin answering this question might be Aristotle's example of the oak and the acorn.[2] Resident within

---

1. I explore human personhood and human dignity in greater detail in chapter 6 ("Contending for Moral First Things in Ethical and Bioethical Debates: Critical Categories—Part 1") of *Retrieving the Natural Law: A Return to Moral First Things* (Grand Rapids, MI: Eerdmans, 2008), esp. 198–204.

2. Aristotle, *Metaphysics* 9.8 (1049b14–28). Aristotle's wider discussion of potentiality and teleology based on genus is found in *Metaphysics* 1.3, 9.8, and *Physics* 2.3, 2.7.

the acorn is all the potential that distinguishes the genus oak. This potential furnishes a sufficient explanation of both the sameness and the diversity existing within the genus, and it offers an adequate description of the nature of the oak, at any stage in the oak's development. It needs emphasizing that this description of the oak's nature has nothing to do with the oak's strength and characteristics, how the oak might be used, how large it might grow, or how well it might weather the various elements throughout its growth process. Nor does this understanding of the nature of an oak vary among Asians, Africans, Europeans, or North and South Americans. Rather, there is a sameness in all forms of the genus oak, despite its great diversity. This sameness corresponds to its essence, which is intrinsic.

We might, therefore, make certain conclusions regarding the interrelation of the oak and the acorn:

- Without the oak tree the acorn would not exist, and without the acorn the oak could not exist.
- The acorn and the oak tree are dependent on each other for their continued existence.
- The acorn may or may not grow sufficiently, but this possibility does not bear on its essential nature.
- The oak tree may or may not grow to the size of other oaks, but that does not bear on its essential nature.

Notice what remains true of both the oak and its earliest form, the acorn. Whether and to what degree either develops does not alter the fact that, from their inception, both belong to the genus oak. Using a different analogy allows us to make the same point: consider the nature of a computer. While a central processing unit, random-access memory, various drives, computer chips, and electromagnetic circuitry are all elements that contribute to what a computer *does* and how it *functions*, without the software the computer is not operational. The computer software may be said, albeit crudely, to have "intrinsic" value.

These analogies, which admittedly are unpolished, nevertheless help illustrate what is unique and essential to human nature. Here I speak of the human being's intrinsic worth or dignity, which distinguishes humans from the rest of the created order. Not for nothing has someone observed that when animals run out of biological opportunities and activities—such as seeking food and shelter, mating and reproducing, playing, avoiding pain and predators—they fall asleep. When human beings, by contrast, run out of biological functions they tend to ask questions.[3] The nature of this questioning always and again returns to *what it means to be human*. Who am I? Why am I here? Where am I headed? Is truth knowable? Is there an ultimate good? Are there consequences for my actions? To what or whom am I morally accountable?

The specific character of this "dignity" needs qualification. Humans' dignity exists by virtue of their being human, and no other criterion.[4] Were this not the case, then their value, their worth, would rise and fall according to the development or deterioration of their functions. Such valuation, based on utility and functionality, is extremely subjective and fluctuates according to the interests, whims, and circumstances influencing the person doing the valuing. Human sanctity and human rights are therefore meaningless apart from the notion of inherent dignity.[5] Human dignity, then, corresponds with who we *are*, not what we *do*. Dignity is neither to be confused with human autonomy and the fact of our choices,[6] nor is it to be confused with status, performance, or enhancement.

---

3. Bernard Lonergan, *Insight: A Study of Human Understanding*, ed. F. E. Crowe and R. M. Doran (Toronto: University of Toronto Press, 1992), 34.

4. For a comprehensive treatment of the matter of human dignity in the context of contemporary bioethical developments, see *Human Dignity and Bioethics: Essays Commissioned by the President's Council on Bioethics* (Washington, DC: The President's Council on Bioethics, 2008).

5. Therefore, to claim that the concept of human dignity is "useless," as the influential medical ethicist Ruth Macklin famously did in 2003, is cavalier at best and inhumane at worst. See her "Dignity Is a Useless Concept," *British Medical Journal* 327 (2003): 1419–20. In a similar vein, see Steven Pinker, "The Stupidity of Dignity," *The New Republic*, May 28, 2008, https://newrepublic.com/article/64674/the-stupidity-dignity. Pinker, however, is less concerned to probe the importance of dignity in moral terms than to lament the presence of theological conservatives who were serving at the time on the President's Council on Bioethics. It seems wise and proper to ask whether *anything good* can possibly come from *denying* human dignity. One only need look to tyrants, despots, and totalitarian schemes to answer that question.

6. Contrary to conventional thinking about bioethics.

But an increasingly regular question regarding personhood is being posed in the public sphere, and not infrequently in the context of social and policy issues. What if a person has not reached full potential? What if the person's existence seems to lack demonstrable social utility? What if the person's brain structure seems to inhibit or work against moral agency? Recall the implications of the oak and the acorn. The acorn may or may not reach its full potential; it may never become a towering oak. And yet as such, undeveloped and "fetal" though it may be, it contains the genetic code for the oak. It is reasonable to apply this way of thinking to human beings. Shall a handicapped neonate, whatever the handicap, be called human? Shall a preemie born several months prematurely (and often remarkably so) not be considered human, even though wanted and loved by the parents? Shall the elderly, the demented, or the infirm, because of decreased functionality and social utility, be rendered nonhuman?

For those who believe that personhood is determined by external qualities, capacities, functions, and social utility, all of which can decrease or even disappear, such beings are not *true* persons. And it follows, then, that having been denied personhood, such beings will need someone—obviously, someone possessing true personhood—to determine at what point personhood was achieved and at what point it disappeared. Complicating that decision-making process is the fact that every less-than-perfectly-functioning human being—from the womb to the grave—differs only by a matter of degree. Alas, in the end, establishing or denying personhood becomes a wholly subjective endeavor, since there is no consensus, only a personal choice as to what version of human life is desirable or undesirable at a particular stage of life growth.

In historic Christian theology, the significance of the doctrine of the *imago Dei* is that every human creature points toward a Creator. The image is a reflection of its origin and hence the reason for our intrinsic dignity. It follows, then, that our full imaging of the Creator expresses itself through our fundamental nature and not merely our functions, social utility, or qualitative development. Significantly, Scripture does not equate dignity with attributes, traits, or abilities; rather, dignity is expressed in terms of likeness to God.[7] What is intrinsically valuable does not derive its value from mere utility, functionality, or perceived quality. As knowing, reasoning, and serving beings, we always mirror the Creator in our humanness, from conception until death. Because the image of God is an endowment, personhood is neither developmental nor incremental; nor is it the product of performance.[8] Thus, the image of God in us is *never removed* from the human creature. This fact has critically important ramifications for our social witness, for it allows us to engage fellow human beings around us on moral matters, on the basis of the natural law, regardless of culture, time, and location. This moral-spiritual component to the human person, what we call the "soulish dimension," is part of a body-soul composite, with the soulish dimension continuing to exist in spite of physical or external obstacles and after physical death. This material-nonmaterial duality leads one theologian to describe the image of God in terms of the incarnation: God cannot incarnate himself in a pig, a cow, a dog, or an ape because those creatures are incapable of reflecting the divine image.[9] God has, however, incarnated himself in the form of a human, mysteriously choosing to send the eternal, uncreated Logos to become one of us.

---

7. While attributes such as rationality, dominion, and sociality are often thought to express the divine image, it is more accurate to identify them as symptoms, effects, or evidence of that dignity, not the *cause* or reason for it. (One need not, however, deny that capacities such as reason, dominion, righteousness, and sociality are related to our being made in the image of God, contra John F. Kilner, *Dignity and Destiny: Humanity in the Image of God* [Grand Rapids, MI: Eerdmans, 2015], 177–230. Here we wish only to distinguish between cause and consequence.) Again, the danger of identifying abilities, functionality, and social utility as the measurement of dignity is that we thereby undermine the personhood of those human beings who seem to be lacking or deficient in these capacities, as the parents of a child with disabilities will confirm. This erroneous thinking about dignity is a grave threat today both in totalitarian and liberal democratic regimes.

8. This is not to deny that an infant progresses through developmental stages, only that the infant has the natural capacity to do so because of human nature and the image of God within.

9. William E. May, "The Sanctity of Human Life," in *In Search of a National Morality: A Manifesto for Evangelicals and Catholics*, ed. William Bentley Ball (Grand Rapids, MI: Baker; San Francisco: Ignatius, 1992), 105.

An important implication of the fact that humans are divine image-bearers is that human moral activity will transcend mere impulse and desire. Reason by its very nature, based on the *imago Dei*, is oriented to truth. Because of the image of God, humans by nature seek what is true, what is good, and what is in harmony with their intrinsic nature. Operating in harmony with this nature permits human beings to flourish and allows them to distinguish between ultimate and less-than-ultimate ends. When humans use their moral freedom in ways that correspond with their created nature, they discover a "law" deep within their interior life—the natural law, the law written on the heart (cf. Rom. 2:14–15)—which they themselves did not create but nevertheless feel obliged to obey. The Ten Commandments and the so-called Golden Rule simply mirror the general contours of this moral law, serving as moral guidelines for all people, not just for those who are religiously inclined. While it is true that moral guidelines such as the Ten Commandments and the Golden Rule are universal in their scope, applying to all of humankind, apart from a theistic framework, the concept of dignity is groundless. Apart from theism, dignity and meaning are shifting entities. One simply cannot extract moral obligation (what ought to be) from what simply evolves randomly (what is). World War II and the Holocaust surely taught us that. Hence the postwar declarations on human dignity and universal human rights.[10] Atheistic materialism, therefore, would seem to be parasitic in nature. Universal human rights assumptions do not flow from a materialist metaphysics.

In the human person, observes John Paul II, "there shines forth a reflection of God himself," and "the sacredness of life gives rise to its inviolability, written from the beginning in man's heart, the conscience."[11] It is in this light that we may understand the divine warning after the flood and recorded in Genesis 9. Because of the image of God in each human being, absolute boundaries may never

---

10. It is significant that the language of human dignity does not really figure into declarations and constitutions of European nations until after the Second World War.

11. John Paul II, Encyclical Letter on the Value and Inviolability of Human Life, *Evangelium Vitae* (March 25, 1995), nos. 34, 40, http://w2.vatican.va/content/john-paul-ii/en/encyclicals/documents/hf_jp-ii_enc_25031995_evangelium-vitae.html.

be breached with regard to innocent human life. These boundaries are summarized and reiterated later in the command "Thou shalt not kill" (Exod. 20:13 KJV).[12] Because of the sacred dignity that issues from our creation in the *imago Dei*, violating innocent human life results in sanctions that have universal applicability: "And from each human being, too, I will demand an accounting for the life of another human being" (Gen. 9:5 NIV). While "Thou shalt not" expresses the command in negative terms, the implicit meaning of the declaration is positive insofar as it safeguards and protects human life. One cannot "over-respect" human life;[13] rather, the continual tendency throughout human history is to undervalue it. And this continues to be the crisis of our time.

The Imago Dei *and the Problem of Sin*

In our discussion thus far of the *imago Dei*, we have observed that the image cannot be eliminated from human beings. This is particularly important to grasp in the light of the reality of human fallenness. Someone has said that human beings simultaneously represent "the crown jewel of creation and the scum of the earth." And so it is. We dare not forget either pole of the human condition—dignity *and* depravity; moral realism depends on it. To emphasize the one without the other is not only to have a faulty view of the human being at the theoretical level but to end up sanctioning misguided social policy at the practical level. How corrupt is the human heart? Thoroughly, we rightly respond. Is there any realm of human existence that has gone untouched by sin? Emphatically, no. But to acknowledge the pervasiveness of sin and human depravity is not to

---

12. Or, more accurately, "Thou shalt not murder." The Old Testament depicts a very clear distinction between the shedding of innocent blood and the killing that takes place lawfully through war or criminal justice.

13. I prefer to speak of human "dignity" rather than "respect" in referring to that which is intrinsic to created human nature based on the *imago Dei*. Frequently in our day, "respect" has to do with the acknowledgment of—or acquiescence to—an individual's so-called rights to privacy and self-determination, to the unfettered choice of the autonomous individual. Significantly, not *dignity* but "respect" joins "autonomy" and "justice" as the three cardinal virtues that are thought to guide contemporary bioethics.

obliterate the rudimentary moral sense in each person. John Calvin describes it in this way:

> When men have an awareness of divine judgment adjoined to them as a witness which does not let them hide their sins but arraigns them as guilty before the judgment seat—this awareness is called "conscience." It is a certain mean between God and man, for it does not allow man to suppress within himself what he knows, but pursues him to the point of making him acknowledge his guilt.[14]

Despite Calvin's well-known reputation for stressing human depravity, he cannot be interpreted as saying that humans are incapable of basic moral reasoning. Quite the contrary. Rather, he sides with Paul: "Natural law is that apprehension of the conscience which distinguishes sufficiently between just and unjust, and which deprives men of the excuse of ignorance, while it proves them guilty by their own testimony."[15] The Reformer is adamant: despite human beings' "perverted and degenerate" tendencies, the image of God is "not totally annihilated and destroyed"; rather, "some [divine] sparks still gleam" in human nature.[16] Sin does not annihilate or remove the image of God.

But we err if we conclude that this point about the preservation of the image of God despite our fallen nature only amounts to some academic form of philosophical gnat-straining. It does not. We need only consider the heated debate between Karl Barth and Emil Brunner during the 1930s and 1940s that centered on natural law—a debate that continues to be instructive. Barth was adamant that sin has obliterated any possibility of the unbeliever intuiting natural moral knowledge. No secondary or natural knowledge, he insisted, could exist in the aftermath of the fall, so depraved are human powers. Reason simply cannot regain its original powers that it had before humans sinned. By contrast, Brunner represented the position that nature can in fact teach us, based on the fact of our fundamental

---

14. John Calvin, *Institutes of the Christian Religion*, ed. John T. McNeill, trans. Ford Lewis Battles (Louisville: Westminster John Knox, 1960), 4.10.3.

15. Calvin, *Institutes*, 2.2.22.

16. Calvin, *Institutes*, 1.15.4, 2.2.12.

awareness of God embedded in creation and conscience. As Brunner saw it, the reality of sin does not eradicate reason and conscience, based on the *imago Dei*. Rather, by nature humans are inclined toward truth and have the capacity to recognize it, even when those capacities have been darkened by sin. And because of some awareness of the natural law, people can work for justice.[17] The difference between Barth and Brunner is instructive, for it sheds important light on the utility of the natural law and how we engage culture around us. The critical question is this: Is human apprehension of basic moral truth universal, present, and operative within fallen human beings *by nature*, and hence, *can human beings be held accountable for their actions*? That is the baseline question. The historic Christian tradition answers in the affirmative. And on this matter, Paul could hardly be clearer, insisting that all people are "without excuse" (Rom. 1:20).

Constrained and Unconstrained Visions of the Human Person

At this point in our discussion of the human person, a word about competing social visions is in order. Social visions differ, at the most basic level, in their conceptions of human nature. How societies view human nature—regardless of whether those societies are Marxist or democratic, utopian or religious, totalitarian or free—will have important ramifications for political theory, economic theory, legal theory, and more. Social theorist Thomas Sowell has contrasted two visions, two ways of understanding human nature and social theory, labeling them the "constrained" and "unconstrained" visions.[18]

The unconstrained view of human nature is characterized by a human optimism. Rejecting the fundamental notion of people being fallen and hence depraved in nature, the unconstrained vision understands sin and self-interest as not constitutive of human nature, but only as occasional digressions from its essence. Rather, humans have great untapped moral potential, and over time they develop a

---

17. See in this regard Emil Brunner and Karl Barth, *Natural Theology*, trans. Peter Fraenkel (repr., Eugene, OR: Wipf & Stock, 2002).

18. Thomas Sowell, *A Conflict of Visions: Ideological Origins of Political Struggles* (New York: Basic Books, 2002).

higher sense of morality and social duty. Over the long term, human behavior, according to this view, becomes perfectible, based on moral and social progress. And while the word *perfectibility* has faded in our time, the concept has survived. Much of nineteenth-century socialism and twentieth-century liberalism has been built on this ideological premise. Given the unconstrained potential of human beings, it is thought that the great evils of society—such as war, poverty, and crime—can be alleviated by human solutions. C. S. Lewis, in *The Abolition of Man*, saw strains of this sort of thinking in his day, evidenced by society's unconstrained attempt through science to manipulate and perfect human nature. In the end, he warned, this view of human nature ends up destroying what it means to be human.

By contrast, the constrained vision presupposes the moral limitations and fallibility of human beings. Given this pessimistic rather than optimistic bottom line, responsible social and political agendas consequently will attempt to make the best of this reality rather than dissipate energies and programs in an attempt to perfect or realize humans' full or unlimited potential. Moral sentiment and activity thus are directed toward guarding the common good and protecting members of society, through law, from the effects of human self-interest and depravity rather than attempting to achieve, over the long haul, a utopian version of society.

The two great revolutions of the eighteenth century—in France and in America—serve to illustrate the practical applications of these competing visions. The underlying premises of the French Revolution reflected the unconstrained vision of human nature that prevailed among its proponents. By contrast, the founding fathers and framers of the American experiment in ordered liberty reckoned with the flaws in human nature. The elaborate system of checks and balances in the Constitution attest to the underlying and guiding premise that no one and no part of the state could be *wholly* entrusted with power since, as the saying goes, "power tends to corrupt and absolute power corrupts absolutely."[19] The writers of the *Federalist Papers* were keenly aware of the truth of the constrained view of human nature, writing that it is "a reflection on human nature that such devices

---

19. Lord Acton to Mandell Creighton, April 5, 1887, in *Selected Writings of Lord Acton*, ed. J. Rufus Fears (Indianapolis: Liberty Fund, 1985–1988), 2:383–84.

[i.e., checks and balances] should be necessary to control the abuses of government."[20] To the founders, evil was inherent in the human condition; therefore, social and political institutions were imperfect but necessary means by which to cope with this reality. The authors of the *Federalist Papers* ask, "Why has government been instituted at all?" Their answer is, "Because the passions of men will not conform to the dictates of reason and justice without constraint."[21] The truth of this anthropological reality needs reaffirming in every successive generation.

The constrained vision, then, is one that is undergirded by a moral realism rather than an idealist or utopian vision. It understands human nature as essentially unchanged across the ages and around the globe. How the human condition is conceived, in the end, informs society's approach to morality, politics, law, power, war, and freedom—its *entire* social vision. The two general visions—constrained and unconstrained—do not merely differ; rather, they stand in diametric opposition.

The Capacity for Suffering in the Human Person

Before we turn our attention to the person and society, it is appropriate to consider one further aspect of the human condition that tends to be avoided not only in wider culture but in the pulpits of our land. I refer to the question of suffering. In recent decades animal rights apologists (the most celebrated perhaps being Peter Singer) have advanced the argument that animals can experience suffering or enjoyment, and thus have moral status. We are justified in responding, however, that it is not suffering per se that conveys moral status—since all animals can and do suffer—but rather the capacity to reflect on that suffering. Pigs and cows and apes do not reflect on the meaning of suffering; reflection is a uniquely human trait—and a vexing one at that. Why do I suffer? is a peculiar mark of the human person, not the great apes.

While the confines of the present essay prevent a wider discussion of the problem of evil and suffering, we may take some comfort

---

20. Alexander Hamilton et al., *The Federalist Papers* (New York: New American Library, 1961), 322.

21. Hamilton et al., *The Federalist Papers*, 110.

in the fact that humans—since the beginning—have wrestled with this mystery. And only in the Christian scheme of reality do we find any assurances that there exists a redemptive side to the problem of suffering. Few attempts to reflect on the meaning of suffering have been more pastorally sensitive than John Paul II's 1984 pastoral letter titled *Salvifici Doloris*.[22] Here John Paul adds to the traditional Christian theodicies, or answers to the question of why we suffer—for example, (1) that suffering is a necessary consequence of God's permitting free will to exist; (2) that it is the consequence of a natural law (i.e., that we reap what we sow, or that what goes up must come down); (3) that it is caused by spiritual warfare; or (4) that it builds character and virtue (and, hence, aims at the greater good). All of these answers contain a measure of truth. Some suffering is caused by free will; some evil is a result of reaping what we have sown; some is a result of spiritual warfare; and some is for character development. But none of these answers is complete, offering justification for all suffering. One need only consider Job, for example, who suffered due to no fault of his own (hence, the error of his friends' attempts at theodicy) and whose vexing "why" question, in the end, is never answered. But for John Paul there is yet another perspective—a perspective that seeks to discern the redemptive side of suffering and which he calls "suffering love."[23] The basis for his argument is that meaning can be found in suffering only when we consider Christ's substitutionary suffering on the cross and the subsequent redemption of humankind. Christ's suffering drew us near to God and was redemptive in its trajectory. Christians' ability to "draw close" to those who suffer, therefore, can have a "redemptive" effect as we engage fellow human beings with a heart of compassion.[24] Because suffering is a "universal theme" that accompanies all humans, John Paul describes it as being "essential

---

22. John Paul II, Apostolic Letter on the Christian Meaning of Human Suffering, *Salvifici Doloris* (February 11, 1984), https://w2.vatican.va/content/john-paul-ii/en/apost_letters/1984/documents/hf_jp-ii_apl_11021984_salvifici-doloris.html.

23. As John Paul presents it, we "bear witness to love in [our] suffering." *Salvifici Doloris*, no. 29.

24. John Paul II, *Salvifici Doloris*, nos. 4, 15, 16, 17, 19, 20, 24, 27, and 30.

to the nature of man."²⁵ Consequently, he argues, pain and suffering have an "apologetic" function, whereby the church potentially builds bridges to the surrounding culture. While all evil produces suffering, John Paul reminds us that not all suffering is evil. Rather, it may take the form of "something good," before which, he writes, "the Church bows down in reverence with all the depth of her faith in the Redemption."²⁶ Finally, and importantly for John Paul, the question of suffering for the Christian is inextricably linked to the parable of the good Samaritan (Luke 10:25–37), for it is precisely the Samaritan who shows himself to be the real "neighbor" to the sufferer—unlike Job's so-called friends. The Samaritan is good because he is sensitive to the suffering of others. In this concrete expression of love, John Paul is convinced, the redemptive meaning of suffering reaches its definitive dimension and achieves its apologetic goal.²⁷ Here, as well, we see the dignity of the human person being expressed. Redemptive suffering suggests human dignity.

A Christian view of the human person keeps two poles in tension. We bear the divine image even while we bear the marks of sin and fallenness. The latter, it needs reiterating, does not cancel out the former. Both are constitutive of a Christian anthropology. A vision of human nature that fails to account for both poles will have disastrous effects for social-public policy and the maintenance of civil society as we know it. And it will determine the extent to which Christians participate meaningfully—and redemptively—in society.

The Human Person and Society

Participation in Social Life:
Taking Seriously Our Two Citizenships

Moral principle will find its application to society's moral quandaries not in philosophical abstraction but in humans working with other humans. After all, the human person is a "social animal" in constitution. But how, precisely, do we as people of faith proceed?

---

25. John Paul II, *Salvifici Doloris*, no. 2.
26. John Paul II, *Salvifici Doloris*, 24.
27. John Paul II, *Salvifici Doloris*, nos. 28–30.

What does the Christian propose for society? Assuming that we do have a stake in how society operates—that is, in contrast to certain religious fundamentalists and ideological pacifists—and at the same time rejecting the idea of a Christian society, we may ask, *How might we leaven culture* without succumbing to the distortions of theocracy, isolation, or capitulation that so frequently accompany Christian attempts at public witness?

Augustine's two cities metaphor from *The City of God* is useful here not because it offers a specific blueprint for Christian activity in the culture but because, at the general level, it prevents us from mistakenly adopting misguided approaches toward participation in society. While our ultimate allegiance is to the city of God, Augustine reminds us that we have two citizenships, which means that we take seriously our citizenship in the city of man. This prevents us—or at least *should* prevent us—from abandoning the culture, withdrawing for whatever reason—a constant temptation for every generation. It also prevents us from attempting to construct a Christian society—the theocratic temptation—since there exists a "sphere sovereignty" among various parts of society (for example, the church, the state, education, and intermediate structures). And it also should prevent the church from caving in and morally compromising with the world. Thus, we avoid those three perennial errors—theocratization, isolation, and capitulation—that are by no means purely Western or American in character.[28]

A society by definition is bound together by certain nonmaterial commitments. Every society, it needs emphasizing, has a hierarchy of values, whether explicit or implicit. These values require that its members subordinate physical, material, and instinctual impulses to the rational, interior dimension of life, a realm governed by moral and spiritual values. This assumes, at least in comparatively free societies, that citizens are relatively free to voice these commitments in public and not merely in private, with a view to advance the common good.[29]

---

28. For a most helpful—and accessible—discussion of alternative approaches to Christian interaction with surrounding culture, see Robert Benne, *Good and Bad Ways to Think about Religion and Politics* (Grand Rapids, MI: Eerdmans, 2010).

29. The alternative is either a "hard" or "soft" form of totalitarianism.

The guiding principle of Christian social morality and of public participation is the great commandment of neighbor-love, which in obedience to Christ joins our ultimate allegiance (the city of God) with our penultimate allegiances (the city of man). In addition to obedience, this view possesses a high view of the human person and society. In the Catholic context, this has produced teaching on the principle of subsidiarity; among Reformed Protestants, we find the principle of sphere sovereignty. Both notions mirror an awareness that God has willed not to reserve to himself all exercise of authority in the universe; rather, he entrusts it, in relative terms, to human creatures via government, representatives of which Paul calls "servants" and "ministers" of divine providence (Rom. 13:4, 6). Both notions also acknowledge that higher as well as lower communities of structure and order have their own relative autonomy, with a view to the common good so that these various spheres do not interfere with one another.[30] Without these limitations, statism and totalitarianism ensue.

Christians, therefore, whatever their individual callings, should be opposed both to the extreme forms of individualism so prevalent in our day, since they violate the social nature of human beings, and collectivism (such as communist socialism), since, based on a divinely instituted sphere sovereignty of various realms within human culture, the state is not permitted to dissolve the responsibility of either individuals or intermediate communities.

Our participation in the city of man, then, requires that we work for the common good. The common good may be defined properly as the sum total of social conditions that allows people, whether as groups or individuals, to reach their fulfillment as human beings within society.[31] So understood, it is concerned to protect all people. In its treatment of "Participation in Social Life," the *Catechism of the Catholic Church* identifies three components to the common good. First, it presupposes respect for the person and human dignity, from

---

30. For a useful examination of these two concepts side by side, see Kent A. Van Til, "Subsidiarity and Sphere Sovereignty: A Match Made in...?" *Theological Studies* 69, no. 3 (2008): 610–36.

31. So John Finnis, *Natural Law and Natural Rights* (Oxford: Clarendon, 1980), 155.

which flow inalienable rights and basic freedoms that are indispensable for human living, such as freedom of conscience, privacy, and freedom of religion. Second, it presupposes an environment in which the human person can develop and flourish. Legitimate authority will arbitrate, in the name of the common good, between various particular interests, whether group or individual in nature. Third, the common good requires a justly ordered peace, which creates the environment of security and stability for society's members.[32] Inasmuch as human society cannot function harmoniously without legitimate authority to safeguard its institutions, it is the responsibility of the state to promote and guard the common good, an order that is "founded on truth, built up in justice, and animated by love."[33]

How Society Functions: Justice, Law, and the State

The term *justice* is perhaps one of the most prostituted words of the English language in the twenty-first century. At least in North America, every conceivable political interest group locates its interests and grievances in the nebulous yet all-encompassing authority of "social justice." The definition of *justice*, therefore, is subject to the whims of whoever invokes it. But if justice is truly justice, it is not—nor *can* it be—a fluid entity. Justice as developed philosophically both in the Judeo-Christian moral tradition and in pre-Christian philosophy—Plato's *Republic*, for example, is dedicated to the theme—is a cardinal virtue. Historically, justice has been described as that which is due each person—a definition affirmed from Aristotle to Cicero to Aquinas.[34] The language of justice fills the entire Bible, giving the clear impression that it is a hallmark of biblical ethics. And correctly so, since justice defines human relationships and how a society should function.

For this reason, justice is the moral tissue that binds together society, regulating human relations at every level. It regulates human relations, first, among individuals; second, in our relations with a

---

32. *Catechism of the Catholic Church* (Washington, DC: United States Catholic Conference, 1994), nos. 1907–9.

33. *Catechism of the Catholic Church*, no. 1912.

34. Aristotle, *Nichomachean Ethics* 5.1–11 (1129a–1138b); Cicero, *On Duties* 1.5.15; Thomas Aquinas, *Summa Theologica* II-II Q. 58.

community; and third, in nations' relations with other nations.[35] The Christian moral tradition, following Thomas Aquinas, has generally maintained that justice can manifest itself in differing ways: it can be punitive or vindictive; it can be distributive; and it can be restorative, compensatory, or reconstructive.

Because justice is nonfluid in character, it is thus universally the same, establishing *the* criterion by which human behavior is established and judged. Where justice *is* fluid and changing, in Western culture we tend to call this sort of phenomenon a "travesty" or "miscarriage" of justice. Why? Because justice cannot be different for different people. At the most basic level, justice is impossible without a commitment to the transcendent dignity of the human person. Thus, it is the church's role to remind society of human dignity and attendant human rights, neither of which finds its origin in human law or the state per se. Rather, civil law and the state merely *recognize* human dignity and human rights, both of which transcend law and the state. Justice, we might argue, is an implication of the *imago Dei*, insofar as equal dignity and equality as persons are the substance of justice rightly understood. The equality of which we speak, it needs emphasizing, is an equality of personhood, of human dignity, and of inalienable rights, *not* of results, goods, performance, or abilities. Hence, we must distinguish between just and unjust inequalities, a distinction that is often ignored in our entitlement-laden day.

By its intrinsic character, then, justice is the very foundation of law. And since Aristotle, moral thinkers have distinguished between what is just by nature and what is legally just—a distinction that is by no means artificial. How do human beings establish what is just by nature— that is, what is intrinsically and unalterably just? The Christian responds that morality must have a transcendent source—not the mere conditionality of a particular culture—if justice is truly just; hence, the importance of the natural law, as embedded in creation. Moral law exists prior to jurists and legal theorists. They do not create law; inversely, law—that is, *moral* law—is the *precondition* of the legal profession. We may, therefore, insist that moral law is prelegal and prepolitical, and for this very reason it exists to guide and protect human life. Without morality, law becomes

---

35. So Thomas Aquinas, *Summa Theologica* II-II Q. 58, a. 5.

unjust. And without justice, as Augustine rightly observed, there is no distinction between the state and organized bands of robbers.[36]

Because of human nature, every human community needs to be ordered by some form of authority. Human society cannot be ordered and cannot flourish without a legitimate authority that safeguards its basic institutions. The role of public authority, then, quite simply, is to ensure the common good of society.[37] While a diversity of political regimes is morally permissible, those that deny basic natural-law-informed realities such as human dignity and human rights cannot achieve the common good, and hence are illegitimate—or, in Augustinian terms, "robber bands."

Law and the Common Good

The historic Christian tradition has classified law according to three types—divine, natural, and human or civil.[38] Divine law, that "eternal and immovable" judgment "impressed on human minds," is given with the purpose that it "directs what we are to be like, what we are to do, [and] what we must omit." Human law, by contrast, only "demands or forbids external works." Humans, Aquinas insisted, participate in divine law, and they do so in two essential ways. First, human nature inclines us to act in particular ways that are characteristically "human."[39] Second, human nature—and ordered human behavior—presupposes the existence of a transcendent moral order, which the Creator in his wisdom has ordained. Thus seen, we "participate" in divine law by means of the natural law. The natural law is "the natural knowledge of God and of the governance of our conduct," "grafted into the nature of man" as a result of our creation "in the image of God"; this knowledge therefore is part of "the likeness of God." In its essence, this moral knowledge is self-evident, inform-

---

36. Augustine, *City of God* 4.4.

37. On this see the *Catechism of the Catholic Church*, nos. 1897–1904; cf. Rom. 13:4.

38. What follows in this section is extracted from Article 6, "The Divine Law," in the 1543 edition of Philip Melanchthon's *Loci Communes*, trans. J. A. O. Preus (St. Louis: Concordia, 1992).

39. *Summa Theologica* I-II Q. 94; cf. also I-II Q. 29. The citations of Aquinas that follow in this section are drawn from *Summa Theologica* I-II QQ. 90–108.

ing all human beings of the difference between what is honorable and shameful, good and evil, just and unjust. This moral judgment is "implanted" within human understanding, just as our knowledge of numbers and mathematics has been divinely implanted in the human mind. The voice of the natural law has sounded "from the beginning of the world," based on our being created in the divine image. For this reason, the writer of Ecclesiastes asserts that God has set "eternity" in the hearts of men (Eccl. 3:11). Eternity in the hearts of human beings—this formulation corresponds with what Paul calls the law "written on their hearts" (Rom. 2:15 NIV), the natural law, which gives an awareness of our moral obligations to God and to others. The fundamental structure of human nature *does not* change. This explains why the commandments against murder, theft, defrauding others, and adultery are immutable.

When seeking to preserve the common good of society, Christians of every age must be able both to conceptualize and to articulate a shared or common nature that unites all people. While natural law does not pretend to offer an exhaustive account of ethics with a set of detailed prescriptions, it does presuppose basic inclinations—which is to say, certain universal, cognitive foundations of the moral life that must be cultivated in the direction of virtue and away from vice. Ethicists and theorists—and Christians—who reject natural-law thinking lack the ultimate grounding for an account of morality in the public sphere. To reject or dispense with natural-law thinking, therefore, is to undercut our ability to argue for any sort of common morality.

Offering a public account of morality, of course, will not be easy, given the moral obtuseness of the post-consensus cultural climate in the West and the lack of moral seriousness that we see everywhere around us in American culture. But natural-law reasoning will impel us, in the marketplace, to contend that human beings have a particular design, in accordance with their fundamental nature. And to contravene this nature—at the biological level, at the psychological level, at the sexual level, at the relational level—is to incur the wrath, as it were, of our inherent design and nature. In past generations, of course, this acknowledgment would have been wisdom and common sense. Today, however, wisdom and common sense have become contraband.

A Test Case for the Human Person and Society: Justice, Natural Law, and Humanitarian Intervention

To illustrate the public character of justice and how natural-law thinking might inform matters of public policy, I will consider humanitarian intervention at the international level. Many people are unfamiliar with a rich and living tradition that extends over roughly two millennia and assists nations in discerning the relative justness of intervention. Here I am referring to the just war tradition, so called not because any war or intervention ever is perfectly just but because it helps establish the relative justness of such a task. Just war moral reasoning establishes moral criteria by which to judge how to respond to injustice, criminal behavior, and sociopolitical evil. In fact, the principles for criminal justice as we know it, humanitarian intervention, and entering war all rest on the same foundation. Why? Because justice—that nonnegotiable of the human species—is nonfluid and universal in its constitution.

To intervene or not intervene should always be a difficult question. The just war tradition severely qualifies both *whether* to intervene (known by the Latin *ius ad bellum*) and *how* to proceed in intervention (known by the Latin *ius in bello*). (In recent years, a third category, what justice requires *post*-intervention, has entered public discussion and debate.) What are the traditional moral criteria for whether to intervene? Some of these are doubtless familiar: just cause, legitimate authority, right intention, and last resort. The chief moral criteria concerning how to proceed in intervention are noncombatant immunity (or discrimination) and proportionality.

It is significant that the just war tradition has been chiefly developed and refined within the Christian moral tradition over the last two millennia. Important thinkers contributing to the tradition include Ambrose, Augustine, Thomas Aquinas, Luther, Calvin, Hugo Grotius, and John Locke, as well as modern thinkers such as Paul Ramsey, William V. O'Brien, James Turner Johnson, Jean Bethke Elshtain, and Michael Walzer. (Walzer is the only one of these who is not Christian in orientation.) An important theme among all these thinkers is that war and coercive force may be an expression of neighbor-love and justice. While war and coercive force typically are *not* such expressions, the mainstream of the Christian moral tradition insists that they *may* be. The wedding together of neighbor-love and justice caused ethicist Paul Ramsey to speak of an "ethics of protection" for those who stand in dire need, due to genocide, political oppression, or moral atrocity.[40] Charity and justice wed together are an expression of the Golden Rule—do unto others what you would want done to yourself, and do not do to others what you would not want done to yourself. Yet a further application of the Golden Rule makes for responsible policy at the international level in terms of humanitarian intervention: namely, *do not allow to be done to others what you would not want done to yourself.* The Golden Rule, it needs emphasizing, is quite simply the natural law at work within.

Conclusion

In concluding I would like to offer several final thoughts on why a Christian anthropology, with its constrained and realistic vision, is so important not only for Christian doctrine but for society as a whole, to which Christians are called in service. It is a general pattern that a renewal of natural-law thinking often accompanies sociocultural upheaval or the totalitarian threat in the world. Based on a proper view of the human person, cultural stewardship depends on wise, creative, and faithful involvement in society. First, let us turn to the linkage between natural-law thinking and cultural upheaval.

The Recurrence of the Totalitarian Option: Natural-Law Renewal and Sociocultural Upheaval

We observed in the previous essay that Alexis de Tocqueville, in his important work *Democracy in America*, acknowledged two types of tyranny—that of the minority (historically the common practice among the nations) and that of the majority (on which he reflected in light of the American context). Democracy, he worried, tends toward the latter. But regardless of its form, "hard" or "soft," tyranny results from a denial of natural law. After all, what *is* totalitarianism but brute will and power, as pirates, terrorists, and the Mafia (of any era) well illustrate? Earlier we noted the Augustinian observation that without justice kingdoms are merely great bands of robbers.

---

40. Paul Ramsey, *Basic Christian Ethics* (New York: Scribner's, 1954), 165.

Augustine surely cannot be accused of naiveté; he lived at a time when Rome, literally, was collapsing. And yet he knew full well how important justice is to any society and that there are varying *degrees* of justice, even when perverted. The Mafia, for example, maintains a certain order and "peace" in order to carry out its dreaded and deadly business. Peace, then, must be justly ordered, for it is possible that an unjust peace may reign. Therefore, society requires a *relatively just* ordering; otherwise, evil and injustice are enthroned. It is surely no coincidence that a revival in natural-law thinking occurred during the 1930s and 1940s, as both National Socialism and Communism were ascendant and literally millions of people were disappearing, being exterminated or ending up in concentration camps. Many European thinkers emigrated to the United States during those years, having been imprisoned or seeking to avoid imprisonment either by the Nazis or by Stalinists. Many of these thinkers were natural-law theorists. Relatedly, the important universal declarations on human rights during the late 1940s mirrored this reawakening of the natural law. And not surprisingly, the one pope who knew totalitarianism intimately in his native Communist Poland, John Paul II, emphasized the natural law in his encyclicals, notably in *Veritatis Splendor* ("The Splendor of Truth").

Every generation finds a fresh reason for the study (and advancement) of natural law. Perhaps the flight of European and North American cultures from their Christian heritage in our lifetime, and the resultant moral chaos that presently dominates, is impetus for another resurgence of natural-law thinking.

The Church's Responsibility for Society: Christian Faith, Cultural Stewardship, and the Common Good

It is fitting that this essay conclude with a word on cultural stewardship. A Christian view of reality historically has been founded on several doctrinal cornerstones: among these, creation, fall, and redemption. For our present purposes, several features of these important biblical doctrines have already been underscored and need reiterating: first, the fact not only of creation ex nihilo from the beginning but also of God's sovereign sustaining and continual guiding of all creation for his purposes by means of his common grace;

second, the fact of creation's inherent goodness; and third, the fact that *all things*—material and immaterial, visible and invisible—were created *by* and *for* Christ. These realities combine with a full-orbed doctrine of redemption, by which we confess that the sheer scope of God's redemptive work is not just the spiritual realm narrowly defined; rather, Christ's redemptive work extends to and affects every dimension of creation. The implications, though staggering, would seem to be clear. The Christian is called to the world. From a Christian standpoint, everything is fair game; nothing is off-limits in terms of Christian participation. This outlook, of course, places us at odds with Christians like the church father Tertullian, whose rhetorical question "What does Jerusalem have to do with Athens?" was met with the answer "very little," since, in the end, aspects of the surrounding culture do not "save."[41] After all, why study philosophy, history, literature, language, science, and the arts when culture is destined for the dustbin anyway? But the Tertullian response does not represent mainstream historic Christian thinking, even when "Tertullians" can be found in any era, past or present. Theologically, the Tertullian outlook misses the wider purpose of creation and redemption. We are stewards of *everything* in culture—unless, of course, something is inherently evil.

To presuppose a particular view of the human person from the standpoint of Christian faith is to assert the intrinsic worth or dignity of human beings, which distinguishes humans from the rest of the created order. And to presuppose this view of human beings, in turn, is to maintain a particular view of human society. If Christians are convinced of their view of both the person and society as a whole, then cultural stewardship requires that they contend for those views in the public sphere. In a day when competing visions of both the human person and human society are afoot, much is at stake.

---

41. Tertullian's famous question is found in his work *Prescriptions against Heretics*.

Three

Ethical Integrity and the Ethics of Humanitarian Intervention*

A few years ago I was invited to speak at Fort Leavenworth at the US Army's annual ethics symposium, which is part of the curriculum designed by the US Army's Command and General Staff College. My invitation was to address midlevel officers—mostly majors and lieutenant colonels—on the ethics of humanitarian intervention, arguing that moral principles and ethical integrity not only apply to individuals but to governments, societies, nations, and—yes—military personnel.

Specifically, I was asked to address the *why* and the *how* concerning humanitarian intervention, particularly given the role of the US military in foreign affairs. One need only think of catastrophic scenarios around the globe in the last twenty-five years—for example, Rwanda, Bosnia, Kosovo, Liberia, Somalia, Sudan, Iraq, and Syria. In these and more we have witnessed cases of genocidal practice or massive human rights violations by various regimes for a variety of reasons. How should relatively free nations respond? It is a question that most—if not all—Western nations tend to avoid.

---

*A version of this essay was presented as part of a senior seminar for graduating students in the engineering department at Kansas State University on April 19, 2016.

What I argued at the Army's ethics symposium, and what I argue here, is that a two-thousand-year-old conversation called the just war tradition—an approach to moral reasoning that severely qualifies the use of coercive force—provides an enduring source of moral wisdom as we face complex humanitarian emergencies in our day. The just war tradition, it needs emphasizing, is *not* some pretext for US imperialism or nationalism, by which we as a nation simply bless whatever we wish to do anywhere in the world. Quite the contrary. Sometimes the moral wisdom of the tradition confirms the need for intervention, given the massive amount of suffering going on in that part of the world (think of Rwanda in 1994[1]), and sometimes the wisdom of the tradition causes us to *refrain* from intervening. A fascinating thought is that we will never know what potential conflicts we did *not* enter because of the moral discernment emanating from just war moral reasoning.

At its heart, the tradition requires not only that a just cause for intervening be demonstrated—that is, should we or shouldn't we and *why?*—and not only that intervention be authorized by representative political authority but also that a right intention—that is, a proper motivation—be shown to protect the defenseless, oppressed, or innocent who are suffering egregiously.[2]

At bottom, just war moral reasoning assumes that moral principle and ethical integrity must guide us in all that we do. But what is integrity? It is not raw skill, talent, or power; after all, tyrants and dictators have these qualities in abundance. Central to integrity is the idea of wholeness and consistency of character. Compartmentalization

---

1. The Rwandan tragedy of 1994 simply defies imagination. In the course of approximately one hundred days, anywhere between 750,000 and 1.25 million people were clubbed or macheted to death. The slaughter arose from a history of simmering conflict between two tribes—the Hutus and the Tutsis. Estimates vary greatly on the precise number of victims during this bloodletting. The tragic lesson is that Western and relatively free nations chose to do nothing in the way of intervention and prevention, despite prior indications that a bloodbath might ensue.

2. These primary moral criteria for whether to go to war—the *ius ad bellum*—are helpfully and concisely spelled out by Thomas Aquinas in his *Summa Theologica* II-II, Q. 40, and serve as an abiding reference point for just war thinking.

or inconsistency of character ends up creating a moral fragmentation within the person or the people group, resulting inter alia in a breach of trust. With the collapse of trust—at any level—comes a collapse of the common social good. My thesis, then, is that humanitarian intervention offers us a test case of neighbor-love, for without ethical integrity we cannot love our neighbor properly—whether at the personal, societal, or international level.

Human relations are governed by the wedding of two universal virtues—justice and charity (or neighbor-love). This applies not only to daily life, the marketplace, and personal relations but also to public affairs—for example, criminal justice in domestic life and justice in international affairs. Before entering the university classroom full time I did criminal justice research in Washington, DC, and because of this season of life I have abiding interests in issues of ethics and justice broadly construed. Ethical principles cannot be fluid, can they? Consider how people react when they perceive—rightly or wrongly—that justice is sliding and of a fluid nature. People then resort to the language of "moral travesty" or "miscarriage of justice" to depict scenarios that seem inherently unjust. Why? They intuit, based on the natural moral law (i.e., that moral sense that is implanted in every human being), that justice—if it is truly just—may not be fluid. It must be the same for Kansans, Canadians, Kenyans, and Kazakhstanis. When and where ethical principle is not consistent, ethics reduces to personal preference. In the language of the streets, one man's mugging is another man's good time.

But in practice ethical relativism is an impossibility since *someone*'s ethics, *someone*'s sense of where to draw the line morally, will be imposed in the public sphere by force. The advantage of relatively free societies is that they can choose to enact laws and policies that, in relative terms, build rather than destroy the common good.

Justice and neighbor-love—these two elements are universal virtues. That is, they apply to and are recognized by all people everywhere, regardless of culture or social location. Justice, of course, is considered one of four cardinal virtues. From Aristotle to Augustine to Aquinas, *justice* has been defined as rendering to each person what is due—a rendering based on the commonality, dignity, and worth of each person. Notice that justice is presumed to be an intrinsic or inherent commodity; it is not based on performance or giftedness or status.

If justice, as we have emphasized, differs from person to person, from people group to people group, or from nation to nation, then it is not truly justice. As a universal virtue, justice may not be fluid.

Charity, or neighbor-love, is perhaps best and most universally defined by the so-called Golden Rule as taught by both Plato and Jesus: Do to others as you would have them do to you. Its negative corollary applies as well: Do not do to others what you would not want done to you. The universality of this moral principle is confirmed by the fact that *everyone expects it* and lives by it (whether consistently or inconsistently). We can extend its negative corollary even one step further, and this truth is what undergirds the occasional and tragic necessity of humanitarian intervention: Do not allow to be done to others what you would not want done to you.

Sadly, it is often the case in contemporary ethics—whether in popular thinking or among professional ethicists and philosophers—that there is a divorce or separation between justice and charity. It is often thought or presupposed that the two stand in tension or even in opposition, as if justice is somehow cold, harsh, impersonal, and demeaning, whereas charity is compassionate, relational, and relevant. But this is a false dichotomy. Charity is not moral spinelessness or sentimentalism; neither is it based on kinship or like-mindedness. If charity has moral fiber (and it *must*), it will always seek to do what is right and just for others. And justice, if it is truly just, will always be motivated by the intent to dignify human beings as moral agents, which is why not only acts of kindness but punishment properly applied and motivated confirm rather than undermine human dignity.[3] For example, the parent who refuses to discipline little Johnny for his tantrums or outbreaks of disobedience ensures that little Johnny will become a hellion and a menace to society. To fail to apply appropriate discipline is to fail to love properly the other for whom we

---

3. Few writers have pressed this point with greater clarity than C. S. Lewis in his essay "The Humanitarian Theory of Punishment" (1949), in *God in the Dock: Essays on Theology and Ethics*, ed. Walter Hooper (1970; repr., Grand Rapids, MI: Eerdmans, 2002), 287–300. Lewis's argument is straightforward, though in our day offensive: we punish fellow human beings—and we do so proportionately—*precisely because* they are moral agents and know better.

are accountable. This is as much a failure to love one's neighbor as failing to offer a cup of cold water to someone in dire need.

A memorable picture of the wedding or symbiosis of justice and charity is the parable of the good Samaritan from the New Testament (Luke 10:25–37). Set in a Middle Eastern cultural milieu, an ethnic "enemy" comes across someone who has been beaten, robbed, and left for dead. And he comes after religious leaders who are ethnically akin to the victim have seen him but pass by out of indifference. The Samaritan is chosen in this teaching opportunity by Jesus as a powerfully relevant example for any first-century Jewish audience. Samaritans were despised by most Jewish people for interlocking religious and ethnic reasons—factors that derive from the Assyrian captivity of the Northern Kingdom of Israel in the late eighth century. As the incident recounted in the fourth gospel indicates (John 4:1–42), most biblical commentary assumes that Jews and Samaritans had little contact. The context in Luke in which the parable of the good Samaritan occurs is instructive: Jesus is engaging a lawyer on the matter of what true religion requires. His answer is twofold: to love God and to love one's neighbor.

Compounding guilt on his listeners, Jesus's telling of the parable implies that regardless of the Samaritan's values, beliefs, or racial views, the Samaritan recognized the presence of human need in the course of his journey (a journey that, from a Samaritan standpoint, would have been considered unwise). In Jesus's telling, the Samaritan loved his "neighbor," and thus he was manifesting the "good." The concrete expression of neighbor-love—that is, an awareness of the dignity of the human person—moved the Samaritan to act in a manner that was consistent with what Christian disciples hold to be true: because people are created in the *imago Dei* we treat them as such, and hence we respond to extreme human need when and where it falls within our orbit of influence. What is more, the Samaritan, though not legally required, manifested neighbor-love to the extent of going the "extra mile," applying first aid, transporting the victim to the inn, and taking care of him. Not only that, he provided financial means for the victim's care after his departure with the promise to cover any expense at his return.

What is the teaching of the parable? It is that sometimes my neighbor is whoever might stand in need—in this case dire need—and regardless of the inconvenience it may cause me to help that person. In a similar manner, just war moral reasoning proceeds on the assumption that justice and neighbor-love are wed together—with the welfare of others in mind—and that they are due the neighbor who stands in dire need. As it applies to foreign policy, discerning who our neighbor in dire need is can be difficult and exceedingly complex. To intervene or not intervene should *always* be a difficult question and produce deep hesitation within us. For this, we need moral discernment and much wisdom. Yet there will be situations—infrequent, we hope—in which we are morally obligated to intervene in order to protect the defenseless or the oppressed.

Ethical integrity requires that we respond to human need on the basis of the following factors: (1) when and where we are aware of the need; (2) when and where we have the wherewithal to help; and (3) when and where the cost to us is not unreasonable.[4] These factors would apply in the office, on the street, in the city, or in international affairs. (Again, recall the universal character of justice.)

Having made this argument, I am well aware of the concern that most of us have: Should the US police the world? Of course not. No nation can do that, and no nation *should* do that. At the same time, proverbial wisdom informs us that to whom much has been given, much is required. This, of course, is a moral law of the universe, no less certain than the law of gravity. Nations—just as individuals, just as businesses, just as any group of people possessing great resources—have an obligation, a *moral* obligation, to use their influence for good and retard evil.

I close with some thoughts from an address by South African Justice Richard Goldstone that were offered at the United States Holocaust Museum some years ago. Goldstone had been chief prosecutor of the international criminal tribunals for the former Yugoslavia and Rwanda. He had this to say upon reflection:

---

4. The frequently cited criterion of "last resort" in just war thinking needs qualification. Just as police and law-enforcement officers wait, plan, collude, share information, and strategize when extreme criminal violence is pending, there comes a time when action is needed in order to forestall or prevent gross evil—namely, *when and where catastrophic developments are clearly discerned through compelling evidence.*

> The one thing that I have learned in my travels to the former Yugoslavia and in Rwanda and in my own country is that where there have been egregious human rights violations that have been unaccounted for, where there has been no justice, where the victims have not received any acknowledgment, where they have been forgotten, where there's been a national amnesia, the effect is a cancer in the society. It's the reason that explains, in my respectful opinion, spirals of violence in the former Yugoslavia for centuries and in Rwanda for decades.[5]

Goldstone's remarks, fresh on the heels of unprecedented genocidal violence, serve to remind us that no authority on earth can withdraw charity and justice from those who need rescue from dereliction and oppression. Ethical integrity requires that we do unto others as we would have others do to us, that we render to them what is justly due. This confluence of moral principle and integrity applies not only to nations governed by political consensus as they confront international affairs and not only to military personnel who are the "spear" of political determinations at the international level but also to those of us who inhabit the marketplace and on a daily basis fulfill our vocational calling.

---

5. "War Crimes: When Amnesia Causes Cancer," *The Washington Post* (February 2, 1997), C4. In this speech, Goldstone recommended four measures for the sake of those who have suffered: (1) exposing the truth of specific guilt and avoiding general guilt; (2) recording the truth of moral atrocity for the historical record in order to counter attempts by the guilty to avoid guilt; (3) publicly acknowledging the loss of the victims, who, as terrified people, need justice; and (4) applying the deterrent of criminal justice, since human nature tends to be deterred from criminal behavior by the fear of punishment.

Four

Natural Law and Protestant Reform:
Lessons from a Forgotten Reformer[*]

Introduction

Formal Significance of the Five Hundredth Anniversary

If one does any reading of late medieval, early modern, or so-called Reformation history these days, one stumbles upon a notable tendency. Many book titles utilize the plural—"reformations"—rather than the singular. What is going on here? It would seem that more recent historiography is attentive to the fact that there was not just one reformation or reform movement in the period of 1400 to 1600; there were multiple reformations, even though many of these movements might get short shrift.

This trend in the literature forces on me the need for a disclosure: I grew up in the Anabaptist tradition. And though the "radical reformation" to which Anabaptism belongs is one of the offshoots of sixteenth-century Protestant reform, it was viewed by both Catholics

---

[*] A version of this essay was presented at the Acton Institute in Grand Rapids, Michigan, on the occasion of the celebration of the five hundredth anniversary of the Protestant Reformation. The essay also appears in *Pro Ecclesia* 28, no. 4 (Fall 2019), and is reproduced with permission.

and fellow Protestants at the time as deviant and heretical given its rejection of the church's authority *and* its frequent rejection (or perceived rejection) of civil authority.

In any case, an inescapable question presses to the fore as we consider important lessons from history: Of which reformation are we speaking? The Lutheran? The Reformed? The radical reformation? The so-called Catholic Counter-Reformation? What about "forerunners" to the Reformation? And what about the conciliar movement of the fifteenth century or even the Fifth Lateran Council of 1512–1517, whose decrees were filled with the language of *reformatio* but which had the misfortune of concluding just as the "Luther affair" was igniting? What do we do with fourteenth- and fifteenth-century reformers such as John Wycliffe and Jan Hus or with sixteenth-century reformers who remained within the Catholic Church? Take, for example, Cardinal Reginald Pole, who was appointed as one of three papal legates to preside over the Council of Trent and whose personal affirmation of justification by faith resulted in accusations of heresy.[1] Or take Erasmus; or Johann von Staupitz, the Augustinian vicar who mentored Luther; or others whose views on justification bore similarities to those of the Protestant Reformers. By many accounts, the language of reform and reformation saturated late medieval ecclesial culture. By 1500, calls for *reformatio* were not some new,

---

1. Complicating matters is the fact that prior to the Council of Trent, the Catholic Church had no common system of dogma that was *universally* accepted by *all* members of that organism. One sixteenth-century historian compares the church to "a huge edifice under whose roof a number of theological systems flourished" (E. G. Schwiebert, "The Background of the Times," in *The Reformation: Revival or Revolution?*, ed. W. Stanford Reid [New York: Holt, Rinehart and Winston, 1968], 28). On the ecclesiastical and political battles facing Pole, a remarkable example of tolerance in the mid-sixteenth century, see Thomas F. Mayer, *Cardinal Pole in European Context: A* via media *in the Reformation* (Aldershot, UK: Ashgate, 2000); Dermot Fenlon, *Heresy and Obedience in Tridentine Italy: Cardinal Pole and the Counter Reformation* (Cambridge: Cambridge University Press, 1972); and more generally, David C. Steinmetz, "Reginald Pole (1500–1558): The Loss of Eden," in idem, *Reformers in the Wings* (Minneapolis: Fortress, 1971), 53–65; cf. as well Pole's *Defense of the Unity of the Church*, trans. Joseph G. Dwyer (Westminster: Newman, 1965).

urgent problem; they were, in the words of one historiographer, "well-worn clichés."[2]

And so it is both accurate and judicious to insist that there were many reformations—many reform movements—both before and after 1517; thus, we need not be too Luthercentric, as much traditional scholarship has tended to be. The older perspective is that the fifteenth century was the quiet before the storm, with Luther inaugurating the storm. The newer perspective accentuates the social history of the period leading up to—and after—Luther's revolt, which, in my view, helps bring some balance to our own perception.

I submit to the reader a second disclosure: my own view is that of church historian Jaroslav Pelikan, who years ago described the Protestant Reformation as a "tragic necessity."[3] This is a fair assessment, I think. It was "necessary" because of the vulnerable condition of the late medieval church but infinitely "tragic" because wherever Christian unity is undercut, our witness to the world is diminished. Thus, the occasion of the five hundredth anniversary, wherever it is observed, should temper both our celebration and our lament.

Practical Significance of the Five Hundredth Anniversary

Today, as we commemorate the five hundredth anniversary of the second major schism in Christendom, where do we stand? What has changed since 1517 is broadly twofold. First, what was once considered Christendom—that is, the cultural entity coterminous with Europe—is gone. Christian Europe, quite obviously, is no more. In fact, most European nations today are competing to see who can get rid of their dreaded Christian heritage the fastest. In this regard one need only recall the debates surrounding the inclusion of religious language in the European Union's constitution in the early 2000s. Europe's religion, we may plainly state without exaggeration, is a militant secularism. Second, what has also changed, for the positive, is that Christians on both sides of the Reformational aisle are

---

2. Euan Cameron, *The European Reformation*, 2nd ed. (Oxford: Oxford University Press, 2012), 44, 51.

3. Jaroslav Pelikan, *The Riddle of Roman Catholicism: Its History, Its Beliefs, Its Future* (New York: Abingdon, 1959), 46, 48–52. Pelikan devotes a chapter to this thesis under the title "The Tragic Necessity of the Reformation."

together celebrating that we are broadly reconciled. Consider, by contrast, how one renowned Reformation historian describes the social environment "on the street" in the early sixteenth century; he writes, "Among the thousands of letters [from that time] I have read in the course of my Reformation researches, many contain a simple three-word postscript: 'Burn after reading.'"[4] What a difference five hundred years makes. In fact, let us count some of the ways:

- The Second Vatican Council emphasized, among other things, a rediscovery of the priesthood of all the baptized, an understanding of the church's work as service, and the importance of religious freedom.
- Many of us are familiar with efforts, begun in the 1980s by Lutheran and Catholic theologians on the occasion of the 450th anniversary of the Augsburg Confession, to reconsider the doctrine of justification, resulting in two important volumes: *The Condemnations of the Reformation Era*[5] and *Justification by Faith*.[6] And most of us are familiar with the Joint Declaration on the Doctrine of Justification,[7] signed by both the Lutheran World Federation and the Roman Catholic Church in 1999, which built on the 1980s groundwork.
- Catholics today, as a result, can regard Martin Luther's reforming concerns with greater openness than seemed possible earlier. This becomes evident in official statements by the Catholic Church in the 1980s (including those of John Paul II), which acknowledge Luther as a "witness to the gospel."[8]

---

4. Heiko A. Oberman, *The Two Reformations: The Journey from the Last Days to the New World*, ed. Don Weinstein (New Haven, CT: Yale University Press, 2003), xv.

5. Karl Lehmann and Wolfhart Pannenberg, eds., *The Condemnations of the Reformation Era: Do They Still Divide?*, trans. Margaret Kohl (Minneapolis: Fortress, 1990).

6. Karl Lehmann et al., eds., *Justification by Faith: Do the Sixteenth-Century Condemnations Still Apply?* (New York: Continuum, 1999).

7. Available at http://www.vatican.va/roman_curia/pontifical_councils/chrstuni/documents/rc_pc_chrstuni_doc_31101999_cath-luth-joint-declaration_en.html.

8. John Paul II's praise of the Reformer excommunicated from the Roman Catholic Church came in the form of a letter to Johannes Cardinal Willebrands,

- Benedict XVI also recognized the importance of Luther's theology in 2011 as he addressed Protestant leaders at the Augustinian Friary in Erfurt where Luther had lived for about six years.[9]
- And, of course, we would be remiss not to mention the recent document published by the Vatican, *From Conflict to Communion: Lutheran-Catholic Common Commemoration of the Reformation in 2017.*[10]
- And as if that were not enough, the Vatican announced in January 2017 that it would be issuing a stamp with a picture of Martin Luther on it![11]

This then, ever so briefly, is where we presently stand, and because of the convergence taking place in our lifetime there is much reason to rejoice.

Personal interest in the five hundredth anniversary, fully apart from my own ecumenical sympathies, is rooted in the fact that I married into German culture and hence am wed to German history. I began married life living and studying in West Germany during the 1980s. But apart from these personal attachments to German culture, I am drawn, in this season of reflecting on the five hundredth anniversary, to the "quiet Reformer," Philip Melanchthon, for several reasons. Melanchthon, it is no exaggeration to say, is a generally forgotten figure, yet it is no exaggeration to say that he is the statesman and official representative of the Protestant Reformation. Moreover, he wrote more on law and the natural law than any of the Reformers (including John Calvin, who was trained in law). Finally, it needs to be pointed out that, though Lutheran, Melanchthon had a notable

---

president of the Pontifical Secretariat for the Union of Christians, on November 5, 1983, to commemorate the five hundredth birthday of Luther.

9. Accessible at https://w2.vatican.va/content/benedict-xvi/en/speeches/2011/september/documents/hf_ben-xvi_spe_20110923_augustinian-convent-erfurt.html.

10. Accessible at http://www.vatican.va/roman_curia/pontifical_councils/chrstuni/lutheran-fed-docs/rc_pc_chrstuni_doc_2013_dal-conflitto-alla-comunione_en.html.

11. Accessible at http://www.vaccari.it/pdf/21777.file.00_Programma_2017_SCV___elenco.pdf.

irenic streak as he considered the difficult "ecumenical" task of his day, very much unlike his purist Lutheran brethren.

But before paying homage to Melanchthon, I suggest that it behooves us briefly to reflect both on the present cultural moment and the lamentable state of contemporary Protestantism. First, a brief word about the culture.

Natural-Law Study and Sociocultural Upheaval: Retrospect and Prospects

Once upon a time, one could argue that basic moral principles are the same for everyone, everywhere, and at all times. Surely not today. Quite simply, the challenge before us—socially, politically, and culturally—is that we live in a post-consensus period. Sixty years ago Catholic theologian John Courtney Murray titled the book for which he is best known *We Hold These Truths*. Today the fact is that we hold *no* truths; we profess *nothing* as a society, and those who do are designated as "hate-filled," "bigoted," and "intolerant." The questions confronting us, then, are these: What language should we use as we live and move in a post-consensus society? How do we engage in moral reasoning with our contemporaries, and in this endeavor how do we even get to first base in terms of ethics?

In response I would argue, in part, that human fallenness has marred the image of God, but it has not eliminated it. This is an important distinction. Even after the fall, good and evil, just and unjust remain self-evident. And if nothing is self-evident, then we shall need to be honest in acknowledging, morally speaking, that nothing is obligatory; and if nothing is obligatory, all conceptions of value crumble. I would, therefore, suggest that we need to develop the art of moral persuasion, and in our day we need to utilize backdoor strategies—namely, marshaling evidence in people's lives of moral reality and helping them see the contradiction of their profession over against how they *really* live their lives (or how they expect others to live theirs). For example, one does not have to be religious to intuit the reality of a moral law against murder or cruelty or theft. This principle, universally acknowledged and needing no religious justification, is, quite simply, the natural law at work within the human person.

Not just the culture in its amoral predisposition but also contemporary Protestantism, with its ethical vacuity, is in need of a brief assessment.

Natural Law and Protestant Thought

Natural Law and Contemporary Protestantism: A Pattern of Discontinuity

In notable contrast to splintered Protestantism and the countless theological fads found within her borders, contemporary Protestants, who otherwise have very little in common, do share common ground in their opposition to natural-law thinking. This opposition, moreover, encompasses both revisionist and orthodox thinkers. Across Protestantism one can find a broad consensus that rejects the natural law as a metaphysical reality through which God communicates to all apart from special revelation and that applies to everyone at all times and in all places. Among more theologically orthodox Protestants, this opposition arises from a cluster of related (and perhaps understandable) concerns. They worry that natural-law thinking fails to take seriously the condition of human sinfulness; that misguided trust is placed in the powers of human reason, which has been debilitated by the fall; that the ethical norms as mirrored in the Old and New Testaments, as well as the means of fulfilling those norms, are distinct; and that natural-law theory is insufficiently Christocentric and grace-centered.

While time and space prevent us here from analyzing a host of influential thinkers who have encouraged this rejection, it needs emphasizing that in the mid- to late-twentieth century one finds not only general disagreement but vehement opposition to natural-law thinking of the sort that is found in the thinking and writings of Karl Barth, Helmut Thielicke, Paul Lehmann, Jacques Ellul, John Howard Yoder, and Stanley Hauerwas, to name but a few.[12] For this reason one is hard-pressed to name a single major figure in twentieth-century Protestant theological ethics who has championed natural-law

---

12. For a more detailed treatment of many of these figures' views, see my *Retrieving the Natural Law: A Return to Moral First Things* (Grand Rapids, MI: Eerdmans, 2008), 126–55.

ethics.[13] Happily, there are signs in the last decade and a half that *some* Protestants are beginning to rethink their understanding of the natural law.[14] This is doubtless the fruit of meaningful ecumenical dialogue with Roman Catholics as we witness the collapse of moral norms in the West.

Natural Law and the Protestant Reformers: A Pattern of Continuity

Such dialogue is necessary in order to address the standard objections to natural-law ethics in our day that have been frequently advanced by more confessionally orthodox thinkers, not merely by theological revisionists. Opposition to natural-law ethics, it needs emphasizing, is a foremost (and relatively recent) Protestant phenomenon that issues out of a particular theological construal of the relationship between creation and redemption. Thus, it cries out for thoughtful theological and philosophical reflection that is consonant with and faithful to the Christian moral tradition. As such, this opposition might be said to mirror an inability to "think with the church" and takes several forms. Natural law, it is presumed, fails to take seriously the condition of human sin while placing misguided trust in the powers of human reason, which has been debilitated by the fall. Correlatively, those stressing the matter of human depravity typically argue that natural-law thinking is insufficiently Christocentric. Christian social ethics, thus construed, is thought to be located solely and exclusively within a particular understanding of grace. In consequence, natural-law thinking is hence thought to engender a form of "works righteousness," since it is viewed as detracting from the work of grace through Christ. These critics of natural law remain skeptical out of a concern that it is autonomous

---

13. In this regard, two notable exceptions are Lutheran theologians Carl E. Braaten and Robert W. Jenson.

14. As evidence thereof, see Stephen J. Grabill, *Rediscovering the Natural Law in Reformed Theological Ethics* (Grand Rapids, MI: Eerdmans, 2006); Charles, *Retrieving the Natural Law*; and Jesse Covington, Bryan McGraw, and Micah Watson, eds., *Natural Law and Evangelical Political Thought* (Lanham, MD: Lexington, 2013).

and somehow external to the center of theological ethics and God's providential care of the world.[15]

But however deeply entrenched the opposition to or neglect of natural law among Protestants is, it cannot be attributed to the Magisterial Reformers of the sixteenth century. Although it is true that they championed a particular understanding of grace, faith, and justification that took issue with their Catholic counterparts, this was not to the exclusion of other natural vehicles in the created order; therein they maintained continuity with Roman Catholics, as their writings indicate. It is accurate to insist that the sixteenth-century Reformation controversies, in their nature, were foremost theological and ecclesiastical, *not* ethical.

To the surprise of many, Luther, Calvin, Zwingli, Bucer, Bullinger, and others affirmed the natural law, even when it was not a major focus in their writings.[16] Part of the problem is that none of the Magisterial Reformers develops natural-law thinking in any sort of systematic way—*with one exception*, that is, and he is the "forgotten Reformer" and the focus of this essay.

Philip Melanchthon: The Forgotten Reformer

A Profile

Generally, and tragically, Philip Melanchthon is overlooked when we speak of the Protestant Reformers, disappearing in Luther's shadow. Consider various titles of scholarly works over the years: *Melanchthon: The Quiet Reformer*,[17] *Philip Melanchthon: Reformer*

---

15. Grabill, *Rediscovering the Natural Law*, 3–5, identifies what he believes to be three factors that contributed to Protestant rejection of natural-law thinking in the twentieth century: (1) the influence of Karl Barth's criticism of natural theology, with its "christocentric" and "logocentric" premises; (2) the perception that Roman Catholic moral theology does not take seriously enough the effects of sin on human reason; and (3) the antimetaphysical trajectory of much nineteenth-century German theology that left its mark on the Protestant mainstream.

16. See Charles, *Retrieving the Natural Law*, 111–25.

17. Clyde L. Manschreck, *Melanchthon: The Quiet Reformer* (New York: Abingdon, 1958; repr., Eugene, OR: Wipf & Stock, 2008).

without Honor,[18] *Der unbekannte Melanchthon* (The unknown Melanchthon),[19] or *Melanchthon: Alien or Ally?*[20] Melanchthon indeed does seem to languish in the shadow not only of Luther but of other well-known Reformers. But this, I must insist, is an injustice and simply should not be.

"It was not Luther but Melanchthon who determined fully what the exact consistency of Lutheranism was to be," stated one German intellectual historian.[21] Melanchthon was "the chief teacher and instructor, the scholarly publicist, and the theological diplomat of early Lutheranism.... It was Melanchthon who was responsible for the education of the new theological generation and for the formulation of all official utterances."[22] Despite our unfamiliarity with him, Melanchthon wrote the very first systematic treatise of Protestant theology, the *Loci communes*, some fifty-one editions of which were printed *during* his lifetime.[23] In fact, as the main public defender of Luther's cause, Melanchthon had a hand in the officially adopted confessional writings of the Lutheran Reformation, such as the Augsburg Confession (1530) and the Apology of the Augsburg Confession (1531). The Book of Concord (1580), considered the authoritative document of confessional Lutheranism, acknowledges its supreme debt to Melanchthon. And while, in the eyes of many, the "confessor" (Luther) is greater than the "professor" (Melanchthon),

---

18. Michael Rogness, *Philip Melanchthon: Reformer without Honor* (Minneapolis: Augsburg, 1969).

19. Robert Stupperich, *Der unbekannte Melanchthon: Wirken und Denken des Praeceptor Germaniae in neuer Sicht* (Stuttgart: Kohlhammer, 1961).

20. Franz Hildebrandt, *Melanchthon: Alien or Ally?* (Cambridge: Cambridge University Press, 1946).

21. Ernst Troeltsch, Vernunft und Offenbarung bei Johann Gerhard und Melanchthon (Göttingen: Huth, 1891), 58.

22. Robert Stupperich, *Melanchthon*, trans. Robert H. Fischer (Philadelphia: Westminster, 1965), 151.

23. James William Richard, *Philip Melanchthon: The Protestant Preceptor of Germany 1497–1560* (New York: Putnam, 1898), 103. Richard recounts how an Italian translation of Melanchthon's *Loci* had appeared in 1524, selling in large numbers in Rome, of all places, where it was read "with great applause"—until, that is, a Franciscan monk discovered it to be "Lutheran," whereupon all known existing copies were seized and burned (102).

the Protestant Reformation could not have been established or carried through without the latter.[24] The "forgotten Reformer" participated in almost every major theological colloquy of his day.

In terms of sheer giftedness, Philip Melanchthon was a prodigy. In the aftermath of his father's death when he was nine, Melanchthon was fortunate to have a great-uncle on his mother's side, Johann Reuchlin, a renowned Hebraist, who took great interest in him because of his linguistic talents as a child.[25] In fact, this great-uncle bestowed on Philip a new name in place of his family name of Schwarzerd (re-naming happened to be a custom among Renaissance and humanist scholars at the time). That new name was Melanchthon, the Greek equivalent of his German name, which means "black earth," indicating that Philip came from a lineage of blacksmiths and armorers.[26]

Philip would enroll at the University of Heidelberg at age twelve, where he studied literature, theology, philosophy, and science and graduated with a bachelor of liberal arts degree at the age of fourteen. He would subsequently take a master of liberal arts from the University of Tübingen at age seventeen, where he remained on the faculty for four years. In 1518, at the ripe age of twenty-one, Melanchthon arrived at the University of Wittenberg, appointed as a professor of Greek at the request of Prince Frederick and on the recommendation of his great-uncle Reuchlin.

Supremely interesting and illuminating is the fact that Luther and Melanchthon maintained the highest respect for each other through the years. Luther said of him that he was "a young man in body, but a

---

24. So correctly, in my view, Hildebrandt, *Melanchthon*, xi.

25. Eleven days after his father's death, Melanchthon's grandfather died. Since his mother was financially unable to raise the family (Philip was one of five children), he ended up living with his grandmother, whose brother was the Hebraist Reuchlin.

26. Philip's father, Georg, was a gifted blacksmith, so gifted in fact that he became known as the "Heidelberg armorer." Even the emperor Maximillian had heard of the quality of Georg's work, and in preparing for a "knight's combat" he ordered a suit of armor from Georg and ended up winning the competition, causing Maximillian to employ Georg in his services in the royal court. As it happened, Georg would die suddenly, at age forty-nine, of drinking poisoned water.

venerable old greybeard in intellect."[27] In the year of Luther's absence from the university, Luther noted of his colleague, "You surpass me in theology, and succeed me as Elisha followed Elijah, with a double portion of the Spirit," alluding to 2 Kings 2.[28] While Melanchthon learned the gospel from Luther, Luther learned the Greek New Testament and the apostle Paul especially from Melanchthon. Significantly, Luther never criticized Melanchthon publicly. And given Luther's temperament and tendencies—namely, to criticize and to break fellowship—that itself is rather remarkable. It is accurate to say that Luther's work and effect cannot be properly understood and appreciated apart from Melanchthon, who was many years his junior and in many ways his complement.

By 1525, seven years after he arrived at Wittenberg, Melanchthon had received special status at the university to teach whatever he wished; formally, he was appointed to both the liberal arts and the theological faculties. Luther worried that other universities would woo Melanchthon away from Wittenberg, given his meager pay, so he strongly encouraged Prince Frederick, the university's patron, to increase Melanchthon's salary.[29] And other universities did want him;[30] at one point Cambridge University desired to have Melanchthon become their Regius Professor of Divinity. The breadth of Melanchthon's scholarship simply defies description. He wrote textbooks on not only theology but also Latin and Greek grammar,

---

27. *Luther's Works*, ed. Jaroslav Pelikan, Helmut T. Lehmann, and Christopher Brown (Philadelphia: Fortress; St. Louis: Concordia, 1955–), 27:377 (hereinafter *LW*). Not long into Melanchthon's tenure Luther conceded, "that little Greek scholar outdoes me even in theology itself" (*LW* 48:136).

28. *LW* 48:232.

29. *D. Martin Luthers Werke. Kritische Gesammtausgabe* (Weimar: Herman Böhlaus Nachfolger, 1883–2009), *WA Br* 1:191–93; this concern is expressed by Luther in a letter dated August 31, 1518; see also *LW* 48:76–79.

30. Hildebrandt, *Melanchthon*, ix. Melanchthon was offered a position at the University of Ingolstadt, where the future nemesis of Luther, Johannes Eck, taught and happened to be chancellor. Richard poses the intriguing question, What would Christendom be today had Melanchthon gone to Ingolstadt and become the companion and supporter of Eck? (Richard, *Philip Melanchthon*, 32). Eck, of course, had established a reputation not only as a theologian but as a skilled debater.

rhetoric, philosophy, ethics, psychology, and history. He edited and offered commentary on numerous classical texts, including works by Cicero, Aristotle, Ptolemy, Virgil, Hesiod, and Demosthenes.

In his own lifetime, *not posthumously*, Melanchthon was accorded the remarkable title *Praeceptor Germaniae*, the "Teacher of Germany." This moniker is deserved for several reasons. First, his teaching style was infectious, as indicated by eyewitness accounts that his university lectures regularly drew six hundred people (this in a day when the young university had just over three hundred students total!). And on one occasion, two thousand people were said to have attended—among them princes and nobility in addition to regular students.[31] In one of his Table Talks four years before his death, Luther offered this observation: "If anybody wishes to become a theologian," he should do two things: (1) start with the Bible, and (2) "read Philip's *Loci Communes*.... No better book has been written after the Holy Scriptures than Philip's. He expresses himself more concisely than I do when he argues and instructs. I'm garrulous and more rhetorical."[32] Indeed, we might argue that Luther was bellicose; Melanchthon was irenic and far less polemical.

A second reason for his "Teacher of Germany" reputation is his sheer output. He trained hundreds of teachers, wrote textbooks and grammars (as noted above), wrote biblical commentaries, and taught

---

31. *Melanchthons Briefwechsel Texte* 1, no. 29, as cited by Richard, *Philip Melanchthon*, 44, and Manschreck, *Melanchthon*, 43.

32. *LW* 54:439–40. In a Table Talk recorded in the summer or fall of 1532, Luther notes: "Philip stabs, too, but only with pins and needles. The pricks are hard to heal and they hurt. But when I stab I do it with a heavy pike used to hunt boars" (*LW* 54:50). And in Luther's preface to Melanchthon's commentary on Colossians (*Commentaria in epistolam Pauli ad Colossenses* [1527]), Luther writes: "I am rough, boisterous, stormy, and altogether warlike. I am born to fight against innumerable monsters and devils. I must remove stumps and stones, cut away thistles ... and thorns, and clear the wild forests; but Master Philip comes along softly and gently, sowing and watering with joy, according to the gifts which God has abundantly bestowed upon him" (cited in Manschreck, *Melanchthon*, 54, and Richard, *Philip Melanchthon*, 42). The commentary appears in C. G. Bretschneider, H. E. Bindseil, et al., eds., *Corpus Reformatorum* (Halle: Schwetschke, 1834–1959), 12:691–96 (hereinafter *CR*), while the preface has been reprinted in *CR* 1:973–74, and in Robert Stupperich, ed., *Melanchthon's Werke in Auswahl* (Gütersloh: Gerd Mohn, 1951–1975), 4:210–11.

university courses ranging from Greek, Latin, and Hebrew; to astronomy, history, and philosophy; to rhetoric, poetry, and medicine; to, of course, theology. Lest this wide smattering suggest to us that he was a "butterfly," the truth is that it reveals Melanchthon's basic assumptions about theology and human knowledge: a Christian world- and life-view must be coherent, making connections to *all* of life.

A third justification for being called the "Teacher of Germany" is that Melanchthon was the architect of the German public education system, about which much might be said in another context.[33]

One of the things that Luther admired in Melanchthon was order—in his thinking, life, and theology. Order, after all, is part of creation and God's nature, whether applied to politics, war, family life, or theology. Christ redeems and restores order that is lost through sin. Therefore, law—and natural law in particular—for Melanchthon is an important part of human existence. Here Melanchthon is very Thomistic: he insists we can know of God by God's "effects" in creation,[34] and this allows us to reason back to the source, the Lawgiver, through the laws (and law) of nature.

A Comparison of Melanchthon and Luther: Convergence and Divergence

In spite of vastly different temperaments, giftings, and callings, Melanchthon and Luther were united on what they believed to be theological nonnegotiables. Melanchthon shared Luther's law-gospel distinction, his recognition of human depravity, a commitment to scriptural authority, justification by faith, and a two-kingdoms framework, with its understanding of a sort of "sphere sovereignty"

---

33. On this see, for example, Irene Dingel et al., *Philip Melanchthon: Theologian in Classroom, Confession, and Controversy* (Göttingen: Vandenhoeck & Ruprecht, 2012); Gerald Strauss, "The Social Function of Schools in the Lutheran Reformation in Germany," *History of Education Quarterly* 28, no. 2 (Summer 1988): 191–206; and Clyde Manschreck, "The Bible in Melanchthon's Philosophy of Education," *Journal of Bible and Religion* 23, no. 3 (1955): 202–7.

34. For Melanchthon, moral principle is like scientific principle and math: it is universally accessible and predictable; four plus four is always eight and cannot be otherwise.

applying to the three estates of family, church, and state. The two also shared the Pauline notion that a God-given awareness of moral reality through the natural law is implanted in the hearts of all, and that this law written on the heart (cf. Rom. 2:15) defines our basic obligations to God, neighbor, and self. Both believed that the Ten Commandments, the Beatitudes, and the Golden Rule give concrete expression to the natural law.

The two men differed theologically in several areas. For example, while both affirm the natural law and creation orders, they understand them somewhat differently. Melanchthon conceives them in more Thomistic terms; they are teleological, with our reason, capabilities, and inclinations ordered to the Creator.[35] Luther and Melanchthon also had slightly differing views of human freedom and the will. Over against Luther's bondage of the will, the older Melanchthon tended to emphasize cooperation of the will with divine grace. The two differed as well on the nature of the Eucharist and the physical presence. Melanchthon came to view Luther as overemphasizing Christ's physical presence in the bread and wine and was more open to accepting differing perspectives. Melanchthon speaks of Christ's presence in the sacraments as multivalent or multifaceted and is willing to negotiate on the mystery of sacramental form. In addition, for Melanchthon, faith and reason support each other, and while distinct, they are nevertheless symbiotic in their relationship. Melanchthon is less pessimistic than Luther, even when both affirm without equivocation the depth and scope of human sinfulness and that the natural law is part of general revelation.[36] For Luther, apart from a theology of the cross, reason is thought to be fundamentally hostile toward God.[37] "Prior to faith and a knowledge of God," Luther writes, "reason is darkness." Only for the believer, Luther insists, does reason have value; prior to faith reason is an "impediment."[38]

---

35. Cf. Aquinas, *Summa Theologica* I-II Q. 91, a. 2.

36. On occasion Luther can refer to the natural law as the law of love. See, for example, *WA* 1:502 and 2:580.

37. Well known are Luther's depiction of reason as a "whore" and "the devil's bridge." See *LW* 51:375–776 and 68:22–23. See also Luther's sermon in Wittenberg on the second Sunday of Epiphany (January 17, 1546), in *WA* 51:126.

38. *LW* 54:183.

Most of us, at one point or another, have heard his famous declaration, "The whole of Aristotle is to theology as darkness is to light."[39]

Yet another difference between the two, ecclesial in nature, is the matter of the church's unity. Luther the prophet views reconciliation as compromise; Melanchthon, by contrast, wishes to see concord and healing, though without compromising. One last difference—a significant one—is good works. Luther acknowledged the necessity of good works in terms of obedience, but, significantly, he rejected the message of the epistle of James while Melanchthon affirmed it. James, for Luther, is a "right strawy epistle" and does not deserve a place in the New Testament canon.[40] Why? Because of two perceived deficiencies: a lack of Christ-centeredness and, most importantly, its opposition to the Pauline teaching of justification by faith alone.[41] Melanchthon refuses to pit James against Paul, bringing the necessary corrective to Luther.[42]

---

39. Martin Luther, "Disputation against Scholastic Theology," in *LW* 31:12; here Luther adds: "Virtually the entire *Ethics* of Aristotle is the worst enemy of grace." It is, however, noteworthy that at the beginning of his teaching career at Wittenberg, Luther had lectured on Aristotle's *Nicomachean Ethics*.

40. *LW* 35:362. In 1522 Luther wrote a general introduction to the New Testament in which he contrasted James with other New Testament writings. This contrast led him to the "epistle of straw" conclusion even when he acknowledged some merit in it as a work. In terms of its canonical placement, Luther would remain doubtful about James, as well as Hebrews, Jude, and Revelation.

41. In *The Babylonian Captivity of the Church*, Luther is less tendentious: "Many assert with much probability that this epistle is not by James the apostle, and that it is not worthy of any apostolic spirit" (*LW* 35:362). In the end, Luther believed that James does not deserve a place in the New Testament canon and expressed the wish as late as 1540 (six years before his death) that James should not be taught at Wittenberg.

42. For Melanchthon, good works verify authentic faith, over against a wrong or distorted view of merit. Commenting on James's declaration "You see [then] that a man is justified by works and not by faith alone" (2:24 NASB), Melanchthon responds that James 2:19 indicates it is possible to have knowledge yet stand under condemnation; demons, after all, know yet tremble. James "is not in conflict with Paul"; rather, he is refuting the error of those "who imagine that they are righteous on account of their profession of…dogmas" (*Loci Communes* [1543], Locus 9: "Good Works"). I am relying here on the translation by J. A. O. Preus (St. Louis: Concordia, 1992), 111.

In terms of personality and temperament, Melanchthon and Luther could not have been more different. While complementary, the two were "unequal yoke-fellows."[43] One was vehement, the other pacific. One was pastoral, the other more scholarly. One was an apostle to the commoner, the other an apostle of higher education. One was militant, the other moderate and conciliatory. One was a prophetic innovator, the other a systematician. One was obstinate, at times rude, coarse, even uncharitable; the other restrained and judicious, even willing to dialogue with his enemies and those who disagreed with him.[44] Luther's own somewhat immodest assessment of how the two differed in temperament is captured in a Table Talk of May 1539:

> In the Acts of the Apostles you have a description of us [i.e., Melanchthon and Luther]. James is our Philip, who in his modesty wanted to retain the law voluntarily [Acts 15:13–21]. Peter signifies me, who smashed it: "Why do you put a yoke on the neck of the disciples" [Acts 15:10]? Philip lets himself be devoured. I devour everything and spare no one. So God accomplishes the same thing in two different persons.[45]

Theology, Philosophy, and Law in Melanchthon

As already noted, Melanchthon devotes more attention to law and moral philosophy than any other Reformer. There are several reasons for this. First, this is part of his integrated thinking as a true Renaissance man devoted to the liberal arts. Second, as "the ethicist of the Protestant Reformation,"[46] Melanchthon saw the need to keep theology and philosophy wed. In addition, he constantly wrestled with finding a middle way between the poles of antinomian (or law-denying) controversy on the one hand (as found, e.g.,

---

43. Owen Chadwick, *The Reformation* (Middlesex, UK: Penguin, 1964), 66.
44. Not a few commentators, wrongly in my view, tend to interpret these inclinations in Melanchthon as weakness.
45. *LW* 54:355.
46. Wilhelm Dilthey, *Gesammelte Schriften* (Leipzig: Teubner; Göttingen: Vandenhoeck & Ruprecht, 1921–1974), 21:193, cited as well by John Witte Jr., *Law and Protestantism: The Legal Teachings of the Lutheran Reformation* (Cambridge: Cambridge University Press, 2002), 122.

among the "radicals" and Anabaptists) and works righteousness on the other hand.

While philosophy and reason alone cannot justify a person before a holy God, Melanchthon believed that they *can* explain law and our innate awareness of it. In this vein, the events of the 1520s, so foreign to us who are some five hundred years removed, well illustrated for Melanchthon the tragedy of a lawless view of Christian faith. We refer here to the period of multiple peasant uprisings in Germany that had been fanned by Reformation teachings. These persuaded Melanchthon of the need to teach and write on law and authority as necessary societal restraints on human nature and sin, on sectarian fragmentation, and on social turbulence.[47] Melanchthon worried much throughout his career about antinomian tendencies that accompanied new outbreaks of religious enthusiasm. Liberty can be perverted, and obedience may call for self-denial. Both in Melanchthon's day and ours, the mistaken attitude is widespread that Christian faith is free from the law. And, of course, there are two brands of lawless Christianity: on the one side there is the ascetic denial of or withdrawal from the world and a denial of the legitimacy of social institutions, but on the other side one finds license and the wrong use of freedom.

Melanchthon's—and Luther's—response was that both law and gospel continually need to be preached. Law, then, is not only a necessary preamble to the gospel (which it indeed is); rather, it continues to awaken within believers a consciousness of sin, without which true piety and virtue cannot take root. For this reason, as Melanchthon is well aware, Jesus reminds his audience, "Do not suppose that I have come to abolish the law; I have not come to abolish but to fulfill it" (Matt. 5:17). Also, Melanchthon joins Luther and Calvin in distinguishing between three types of law in the Old Testament: ceremonial, judicial, and moral. All three Reformers enunciate that while ceremonial and judicial law are associated with theocratic Israel and thus pass away, moral law is abiding, as the Decalogue illustrates.

---

47. See Gerald Strauss, *Luther's House of Learning: Indoctrination of the Young in the German Reformation* (Baltimore: Johns Hopkins University Press, 1978).

Melanchthon on the Natural Law: Loci communes theologici

In his *Loci communes*, Melanchthon acknowledges that while a person cannot keep the Ten Commandments perfectly, reason, which belongs to humanity by nature (what Melanchthon frequently calls the "natural light"), informs a person that external compliance is demanded by human social life.[48] The complementary relationship of reason and revelation, for Melanchthon, informs the relationship between theology and philosophy. Theology enlarges and completes our natural knowledge of the Creator.

Consistent with most of the Reformers, Melanchthon classifies law according to three types—divine, natural, and human or civil.[49] Divine law, that "eternal and immovable" judgment "impressed on human minds," is given with the purpose that it "directs what we are to be like, what we are to do, [and] what we must omit." Human law, by contrast, only "demands or forbids external works." The natural law is "the natural knowledge of God and of the governance of our conduct," "grafted into the nature of man" as a result of our creation "in the image of God"; this knowledge therefore is part of "the likeness of God." In its essence, this moral knowledge is self-evident, informing all human beings of "the difference between honorable and shameful behavior," a judgment "implanted" within, just as our knowledge of numbers and mathematics has been divinely implanted in the human mind. The voice of the natural law has sounded "from the beginning of the world," Melanchthon notes, even "before the time of Moses," and it will "remain in force forever and apply also to the gentiles."

Several things are noteworthy about Melanchthon's presentation of natural law. One is its being anchored in the *imago Dei*, which—though marred—cannot be eliminated. That human beings have suppressed this knowledge is no argument against the natural law, as Paul in Romans 1 makes clear. It is true that the image of God in us is corrupted and "deformed," Melanchthon acknowledges, yet "the knowledge does remain" and "is not entirely extinct," which

---

48. Melanchthon will utilize this language frequently in Loci 5–8 in particular. See *Loci Communes*, ed. Preus, 47–96.

49. What follows in this section is extracted from Locus 6, "The Divine Law," in *Loci Communes*, ed. Preus, 57–80.

has enormous ramifications for how believers engage unbelievers. If there is no common human nature, no divine image, then any attempt at moral persuasion is absurd, if not impossible. If, however, there *is* a common nature, then the natural law serves as a bridge as we attempt to engage society around us. Therefore, Melanchthon insists, civil life *can* be regulated according to this "natural light."[50]

Another important feature is his accent on the "pedagogical" function of the natural law. That is, moral law not only restrains; it guides, protects, and assists us in cultivating virtue.[51] Yet a third feature unique to Melanchthon among the Reformers is his development of the three purposes of the natural law for civil use and criminal justice: it is retributive, deterrent, and rehabilitative in its character and function.[52] Significantly, these three functions were adapted by early modern English and American approaches to criminal justice.

Given Melanchthon's attention to law, the natural law, and moral philosophy, as well as his influence as an educator, Melanchthon's role as a Reformer is surely noteworthy. So we should ask, What might we learn from the forgotten Reformer?

Lessons from the Forgotten Reformer

The Importance of Theological Foundations

First, what is utterly fascinating is that Melanchthon was not trained in theology; rather, he learned the theological enterprise and,

---

50. In his *Commentary on Romans*, Melanchthon argues similarly. Gentiles possess "natural knowledge about morals that distinguishes what is honorable and what is shameful." Evidence of this, according to the apostle, is that "they have a conscience that accuses or excuses." Moreover, notes Melanchthon, the Gentiles do this "by nature"; therefore, moral knowledge is "a work of God" and known to all through the natural law (Philip Melanchthon, *Commentary on Romans*, trans. Fred Kramer [St. Louis: Concordia, 1992], 76, 89).

51. Luther had developed two uses of the law: (1) it restrains human nature and thus has a civil function, and (2) it reveals sin and thus functions theologically. Melanchthon adds a third: the law reveals the will of God and the contours of Christian freedom and obedience.

52. On this see John E. Witte Jr. and Thomas C. Arthur, "The Three Uses of the Law: A Protestant Source of the Purposes of Criminal Punishment?" *Journal of Law and Religion* 10, no. 2 (1993/4): 433–65.

in time, became *the* systematician, representing the Reformation cause at official meetings. This sense of theology's importance is praiseworthy. In the classroom, over the years I have attempted to convince my students that theology, literally, is a matter of life and death. At first my students will tend to laugh, thinking that I am being melodramatic. By the end of the semester, however, very often I find that their thinking has changed. Upon reflecting on our contemporary cultural situation, we might encounter a sobering—and disturbing—thought: Is it possible that Muslims care more about theology than most Christians do, given the standard fare today from the pulpit, whether it is a brand of health and wealth gospel, pop psychology, or a caving in on matters sexual?

The Importance of an Ecumenical Spirit

Second, among historians of the Protestant Reformation, there are two predominant views of Melanchthon: either he was weak and lacked the backbone that Luther had (the dominant view), or he was more temperate and sought unity where possible. In reading Melanchthon, one becomes convinced of the latter view. In this regard, the well-known maxim, it would seem, is ever relevant, particularly as we reflect back on five hundred years: In essentials, unity; in nonessentials, diversity; in all things, charity. Melanchthon kept alive a burden for the unity of the entire church, based on John 17, to his dying days—something that sadly escaped Lutheran purists of his own generation and beyond.[53]

The Importance of Effective Communication, Vision, and Moral Persuasion

Third, something in Melanchthon was clearly infectious if six hundred people routinely attended his lectures and two thousand were known to attend on one occasion. What was it that drew people to Melanchthon's lectures? Vision, we often hear, is caught, not taught; that is to say, it is infectious. But it must be a vision that is committed

---

53. Following Luther's death in 1546, Melanchthon became more active in seeking dialogue with Roman Catholics and other Protestants. Unfortunately, he was often hampered by fellow Lutherans—former colleagues and former students who viewed this as compromise.

to the hard work of cultural renewal, and this will require the difficult task of moral persuasion, done in creative and winsome ways. This hard work may take very different shapes. Sometimes God calls us to undertake something entirely new, never before in existence; sometimes, however, he calls us to operate within the existing social and institutional arrangements. The University of Wittenberg was only a few years old when Melanchthon arrived, but it became a trendsetter. Archival evidence indicates that between 1520 and 1560, the year Melanchthon died, at least 16,300 students were enrolled at Wittenberg. Melanchthon would be responsible for helping design the curriculum at the new University of Marburg, founded in 1527, and he was instrumental in helping change curricula at the universities of Tübingen, Leipzig, and Heidelberg some years later.[54] One could argue that without Melanchthon German universities would not have become what they were by the nineteenth century. Both his writings and those influenced by his teaching indicate that Melanchthon was a remarkable communicator and learned not only the importance of theology but the art of ethical persuasion.

The Importance of a Comprehensive and Coherent World- and Life-View

Fourth, knowledge, as Melanchthon knew, is not fragmentary in the Christian scheme of things; rather, it is unitary, and we begin with the whole. This conception of education, it goes without saying, stands in great contrast to how education today is conceived and presented. But Melanchthon intuited and embodied this unity, even when he did not use the language of "worldview" (*Weltanschauung*), which was a nineteenth-century development. Human nature, math and science, history, and ethics are all intelligible because they have a unity.[55]

---

54. See, for example, Richard L. Harrison Jr., "Melanchthon's Role in the Reformation of the University of Tübingen," *Church History* 47, no. 3 (1978): 271–78.

55. This is why Christian liberal arts education, understood in the widest and best sense, is so important. It prepares students for life.

The Importance of Keeping Faith and Reason Wed

Fifth, reason supplements, and is not abolished by, revelation. The two, though distinct, must not be divorced; otherwise either one can become stunted. In certain contexts, Luther considered reason a whore, while for Melanchthon it was a source of wisdom. In this regard we do well to recall the opening sentence of John Paul II's important 1998 encyclical, *Fides et Ratio*, with that wonderful image of the bird ascending in flight, observing that faith and reason in their pursuit of truth are like two wings of a bird in its ascent.[56] On this score, not Luther but Melanchthon had it right.

The Importance of Keeping Faith and Concern for the Culture Wed

Sixth, in asking why the focus on natural law in Melanchthon's work was so prominent, one is left to conclude that, given the acknowledgment that moral law is implanted within us by way of the image of God, Melanchthon intuited that without discerning the moral underpinnings of law, the common good collapses and civil society is impossible. In his calling, Melanchthon used his influence to inform social and political change. Doubtless a temptation for many Millennial believers today, given the political disenchantment of our time, is to withdraw from political engagement. Philip Melanchthon would have none of it. With wildly popular ethicists, on the one hand, whose effect is to remove Christians from responsible cultural participation,[57] and an increasing number of evangelically minded believers, on the other hand, calling for a wholesale withdrawal of Christians from politics and the world, we need voices such as Melanchthon's. Law, politics, and policy are important callings from God, too.

---

56. John Paul II, Encyclical Letter on the Relationship between Faith and Reason, *Fides et Ratio* (September 14, 1998), http://w2.vatican.va/content/john-paul-ii/en/encyclicals/documents/hf_jp-ii_enc_14091998_fides-et-ratio.html.

57. Here one thinks, for example, of individuals such as Stanley Hauerwas and his mentor in many ways, John Howard Yoder.

The Importance of Keeping Charity and Justice Wed

A final application has enormous ethical ramifications for our day. There is a tendency among religious people to view charity as standing in tension with—or in outright opposition to—law and justice. But to separate the two, ethically and politically, is to breed disaster. Often it is thought that law and justice are cold, harsh, and impersonal, while love is compassionate, humane, and forgiving. This is a false dichotomy. Melanchthon would remind us, just as both Paul and James do in their New Testament letters, that love *fulfills* the law; the two are not to be viewed as standing in conflict or tension.[58]

Concluding Reflections

Post-Secular Possibilities: On the Pre-Political Foundations of Law, Politics, and the State

About a decade and a half ago, there took place one of the most remarkable dialogues that most people have never even heard about. I refer to an encounter in January 2004, sponsored by the Catholic Academy of Bavaria, between one of the most influential contemporary philosophers, the German Jürgen Habermas, and Joseph Cardinal Ratzinger, who was soon to be elected Pope Benedict XVI. Many commentators, at the time and since, expressed bewilderment at the meeting of these two intellectual antipodes. Their assignment? To debate the topic "The Pre-Political Moral Foundations of a Free Society."

Habermas, who describes himself as "tone deaf in the religious sphere,"[59] surely surprised many by insisting that secular society must acquire a new understanding and appreciation of religious conviction. Of course, Ratzinger was well positioned to respond to Habermas and enunciate, from a classically Christian standpoint,

---

58. On this see J. Daryl Charles, "Toward Restoring a Good Marriage: Reflections on the Contemporary Divorce of Love and Justice and Its Cultural Implications," *Journal of Church and State* 55, no. 2 (2013): 367–83.

59. Jürgen Habermas and Joseph Ratzinger (Pope Benedict XVI), *The Dialectics of Secularization: On Reason and Religion*, ed. Florian Schuller, trans. Brian McNeil (San Francisco: Ignatius, 2006), 11.

the "pre-political moral foundations of a free society." The result was a rather remarkable debate, with a surprising area of agreement between the two on post-secular possibilities. Ratzinger helpfully summarized aspects of the two men's agreement by observing that there are pathologies of religion and pathologies of reason when the two realms are divorced, as they have been in the Western context. Further, freedom without law, he noted, equates to anarchy, and law without the religious-moral impulse inevitably becomes unjust and totalitarian. Hence, Ratzinger concluded, the importance of the natural law in bridging church and society in order to have a common moral grammar by which to debate and discuss the "permanent things."[60]

Natural-Law Renewal and Sociocultural Upheaval

In periods of sociocultural upheaval, there is often a renewal of natural-law thinking. Every generation finds a new reason to study and advance the natural law. Philip Melanchthon and others in the Protestant Reformers' generation did so (even when it was not their chief focus). In fact, there were others of that generation who did focus on the natural law, including the Spanish Dominican theologian Francisco de Vitoria, and this in the context of New World discoveries. Right about the time that the University of Wittenberg was being founded (the first decade of the 1500s),[61] reports were reaching Spain of "human rights" abuses in the New World. Vitoria had the audacity to declare that neither the pope nor the king may make war on the Native Americans, nor may they enslave them (as both Spain and Portugal were doing), nor may they force Native Americans to convert to Christianity. On what basis did Vitoria argue this? The natural law. Vitoria's message, it needs emphasis, was radical—indeed, heretical—in his day, and yet it constituted the beginnings of what we call international law. In the next generation the Dutch

---

60. Habermas and Ratzinger, *The Dialectics of Secularization*, 77–80. The German original of this volume, *Dialektik der Säkularisierung: Über Vernunft und Religion*, was published in 2005 by Herder.

61. The university at Wittenberg was established by Prince Frederick (the Wise), Duke of Saxony, and opened on October 18, 1502.

legal theorist Hugo Grotius advanced natural-law thinking against the backdrop of the exceedingly tragic Thirty Years' War.

The founders and framers of our nation and their generation found a fresh reason to advance natural-law thinking. For them, the reason was twofold: a commitment to avoid tyranny in this "experiment of ordered liberty" and a growing commitment to promote religious tolerance. Closer to our time, the generation of the Holocaust found a new reason to rediscover natural law, which led to the important universal human rights declarations of the late 1940s that we take for granted today. The present generation needs to rediscover natural-law thinking as well, against the backdrop of the West's post-consensus, post-everything cultural climate and the moral bankruptcy of secular fundamentalism. Today the words of George Orwell apply as much as ever: "We have now sunk to a depth at which re-statement of the obvious is the first duty of intelligent men."[62]

Ecumenical Dialogue on the Natural Law

Indeed, every generation must rediscover the moral foundations of law, politics, and civil society, which are owing to the natural law. When these foundations are neglected or denied, civil society (at least as we know it) collapses and some form of tyranny sets in. Though he was no prince or politician, Philip Melanchthon understood the relationship between natural-law thinking and the common good. He understood that the foundations of politics, law, and government are indeed pre-political and pre-legal. Sadly, many—if not most—of his Protestant offspring, to the present day, are unaware of this connection. This is why ecumenical dialogue on the natural law is so important in our time.

Earlier in these reflections I alluded to having married into German culture. My German father-in-law served all five years of the Second World War in Poland, working for the *Bundesbahn* (the German railroad), where he served as a railroad-car switcher. Some of the most important natural law theorists of the twentieth century were part of my father-in-law's generation, intimately acquainted with evil and totalitarianism. Because of these theorists' work and writings, the

---

62. George Orwell, review of *Power: A New Social Analysis*, by Bertrand Russell, *Adelphi* (January 1939): 375.

world is a better place. In our time it needs emphasizing that unity between Catholics and Protestants on theological essentials and moral first principles, five hundred years removed, in the end is no luxury but rather an absolute necessity as we attempt to demonstrate a robust and faithful Christian presence in a hostile cultural environment—today and in the years ahead. Philip Melanchthon serves as a helpful reminder of the importance of those moral first principles.

Five

The Kuyperian Option: Cultural Engagement and Natural-Law Ecumenism*

Considered a century removed, Abraham Kuyper (1837–1920) lived a life that defies categorization. He was a parliamentarian, a prime minster, a pioneer and founder, an administrator, an editor, and an educator. Perhaps most significantly, Kuyper was a public theologian, and in some quarters of Protestant Reformed Christianity, his legacy endures with surprising potency.

Kuyper is best known for three emphases: sphere sovereignty, antithesis (between faith and the world), and common grace. In contrast to antithesis, common grace (*de gemeene gratie*) places an accent on our shared humanity and common moral ground, and hence on public participation and social responsibility. Common grace may be summarized as God's preserving and sustaining work in the created order. In Kuyperian thought, common grace both justifies and bridges the antithesis.

---

*This essay originally appeared in *Touchstone* (May/June 2018), pp. 22–28, and is reproduced with permission. A version of the essay was presented in April 2017 at the conference on Abraham Kuyper and Public Theology at Princeton Theological Seminary.

That is to say, common grace does not work against special or saving grace, despite the tendency in contemporary Reformed circles to pit one against the other. The two work together, in the same way that grace builds on and completes nature. This represents the complementarity of general and special revelation. Common grace, as Kuyper understood it, is not some sort of modern theological innovation; rather, it prevents a culturally irrelevant and ineffectual Christianity insofar as it understands that God has gifted everyone to contribute to the common good.

Kuyper and the Moral Order

Morality, Kuyper insists against the modern—and, we might add, ultramodern—ethos, cannot be *"created by us* at will";[1] it must transcend us. The eternal principles of God's character apply to the sociopolitical realm, not "directly" or "by the pronouncement of any church," he adds, but through conscience and an awareness of divine ordinances.[2] How does Kuyper understand "divine ordinances"? In his second Princeton lecture, part of the 1898 Stone Lecture Series at Princeton Theological Seminary, he observes: "All created life necessarily bears in itself a law for its existence, instituted by God Himself. There is no life outside us in Nature, without such divine ordinances—ordinances which are called the laws of Nature."[3]

But a qualification is in order: the term "nature," he cautions, is acceptable *provided* that we understand thereby "not laws originating *from* [or in] Nature but laws imposed [from the outside] *upon* Nature."[4] Based on his comments regarding common grace and science, Kuyper appears to be offering this caveat in response

---

1. Abraham Kuyper, *Ons Program*, 2nd ed. (Amsterdam: J. H. Kruyt, 1880), § 6. I am dependent on the English translation: Abraham Kuyper, *Our Program: A Christian Political Manifesto*, trans. Harry Van Dyke (Bellingham, WA: Lexham Press, 2015), 4 (emphasis in original). Further references in this essay to *Ons Program* will cite the section or the article number (as appropriate) and the page number of the English edition.

2. Kuyper, *Program*, art. 3 (p. 29); Abraham Kuyper, *Lectures on Calvinism* (repr., Grand Rapids, MI: Eerdmans, 1987), 70–72.

3. Kuyper, *Lectures*, 70.

4. Kuyper, *Lectures*, 70.

to the regnant metaphysical materialism that proceeded from the Darwinism of his day, which, he points out, "leads to atheism" and "denies that we are formed according to the image of God."[5]

What precisely is the character and constitution of these divine ordinances? They are the "servants of God" in that they regulate every aspect of creation—material and nonmaterial. "Moral life," Kuyper observes, "just like physical life, is subject to laws and influences that are determined by God, not man. We are all obliged to follow these laws and obey those influences."[6] There are ordinances "in logic" that regulate our thoughts, ordinances "for our imagination" in the domain of aesthetics, and indeed ordinances "for the whole of human life in the *domain of morals*."[7] These moral ordinances, moreover, govern "the mightiest problems and the smallest trifles" and are "urged upon us as the constant will of the Omnipotent and Almighty God, who at every instant is determining the course of life, ordaining its laws and continually binding us by His divine authority."[8]

And lest the Christian believer wrongly assume that these "general moral ordinances," expressed in the "Law of Sinai," differ in any way from "more special *Christian* commandments," Kuyper is adamant that such a distinction is "unknown" to God, since they are part of creation.[9] Kuyper is quick to address the false assumption, perhaps in his day held by many Christians, that the moral law does not exist for all time and that it is superseded by Christ. With rhetorical force he asks:

> Can we imagine that at one time God willed to rule things in a certain moral order, but that now, in Christ, he wills to rule it otherwise? As though He were not the Eternal, the Unchangeable, Who, from the very hour of creation, even unto all eternity, had willed, wills, and shall will and maintain, one and the same firm moral world-order![10]

---

5. Abraham Kuyper, *Wisdom and Wonder: Common Grace in Science and Art*, ed. Jordan J. Ballor and Stephen J. Grabill, trans. Nelson D. Kloosterman (Grand Rapids, MI: Christian's Library Press, 2011), 99.

6. Kuyper, *Program*, §20 (p. 21).

7. Kuyper, *Lectures*, 70 (emphasis in the original).

8. Kuyper, *Lectures*, 70–71.

9. Kuyper, *Lectures*, 71.

10. Kuyper, *Lectures*, 71.

And while Christ "has strengthened in us the ability to walk in this world-order with a firm, unfaltering step," the world-order itself, Kuyper notes, "remains just what it was from the beginning."[11] In fact, it lays full claim "not only to the believer (as though less were required from the unbeliever)" but "to every human being and to all human relationships."[12]

Kuyper wishes to be clear: "All ethical study is based on the Law of Sinai, not as though at that time the moral world-order began to be fixed, but to honor the Law of Sinai, as the divinely authentic summary of that original moral law which God wrote in the heart of man, at his creation, and which God is re-writing on the tables of every heart at his conversion."[13]

This is none other than the natural law.

Kuyper and Roman Catholicism

Kuyper is well known for his strong disagreements with the Roman Catholic Church—disagreements that are delineated in considerable detail in his Princeton lectures. In his first lecture, "Calvinism a Life-System," he says that Calvinism posits "no mediate communion between God and creature, as Romanism does."[14] The problem with Rome is that it places itself "between the soul and God."[15] Elsewhere Kuyper offers a similar criticism of the Roman Catholic Church: it does not aid and build the layperson in terms of personal faith; it imparts, rather, an "implicit faith," which fails to anchor Christian doctrine.[16]

Relatedly, Romanism places every human relationship in a hierarchy, almost a religious caste system.[17] What is more, as developed in the medieval period, the Church dominated and guarded every aspect

---

11. Kuyper, *Lectures*, 71.
12. Kuyper, *Lectures*, 71–72.
13. Kuyper, *Lectures*, 72.
14. Kuyper, *Lectures*, 21.
15. Kuyper, *Lectures*, 21.
16. Abraham Kuyper, *The Antithesis between Symbolism and Revelation* (Edinburgh: T&T Clark, 1899), 19.
17. Kuyper, *Lectures*, 26–27.

of social life, thereby becoming an obstacle to social development.[18] And where escape from the world has been chosen, it has often been monastic or clerical in nature.[19]

In his second Princeton lecture, "Calvinism and Religion," Kuyper insists that Roman Catholicism encourages the sacred-versus-secular dichotomy, as opposed to emphasizing the priesthood of all believers and the nobility of nonecclesial callings.[20] Furthermore, it encourages an unhealthy mysticism rather than public theology. "Not Bernard of Clairvaux but Thomas of Aquino, not Thomas à Kempis but Luther … have ruled the spirits of men," he retorts.[21] For by its very nature, mysticism "strives rather to avoid contact with the outside world."[22]

In terms of the *cultus*, as Kuyper sees it, Roman Catholicism's preoccupation with sacrifice, the altar, and priesthood together take away from their eternal expression through Christ, resulting in an unhealthy sacerdotalism.[23] In measuring various social, economic, and political developments on several continents around the globe, Kuyper laments the backwardness and underdevelopment of the nations of the south, whether in southern Europe or in Latin and South America, where the Catholic Church "has full sway."[24] Finally, and perhaps most severely, Kuyper declares, "Rome says 1517 led to 1789 [i.e., the French Revolution]. We say Roman Catholicism is responsible in church and state for 1789, as an illegitimate mother. Thus[,] we cannot join Rome."[25]

Kuyper and Common-Cause Cooperation

These are strong words. And yet in his critique of "Romanism," Kuyper makes some rather remarkable concessions that require our attention. Despite his harsh (and many) criticisms, in surprising

---

18. Kuyper, *Lectures*, 29.
19. Kuyper, *Lectures*, 29.
20. Kuyper, *Lectures*, 49.
21. Kuyper, *Lectures*, 188.
22. Kuyper, *Lectures*, 188–89.
23. Kuyper, *Lectures*, 60.
24. Kuyper, *Lectures*, 184–85.
25. Cited in James E. McGoldrick, *Abraham Kuyper: God's Renaissance Man* (Auburn, MA: Evangelical Press, 2000), 260n25.

though select ways he identifies elements of Roman Catholicism that are "commendable" and have "our warm approval."[26] Kuyper is able to praise Catholicism for its unity and coherence as a "life-system," much in contrast to Protestantism, which for him is splintered and moving "without aim or direction."[27]

He is impressed by the "marvelous energy displayed in the latter half of this century by Rome."[28] This is doubtless a reference to Pope Leo XIII's important 1891 social encyclical *Rerum novarum*, in which the pontiff addresses "the social question." The pope and Kuyper share important common ground—namely, a similar vision of humanity and society as well as an antipathy toward the socialist/collectivist "solution" being offered in their day. Elsewhere, in *The Problem of Poverty*, Kuyper writes, "We must admit, to our shame, that the Roman Catholics are far ahead of us in their study of the social problem. Indeed, very far ahead. The action of the Roman Catholics should spur us to show more dynamism." And here he acknowledges explicitly that Leo's encyclical "states the principles which are common to all Christians and which we share with our Roman Catholic compatriots." Hence, Kuyper asks of his fellow Reformed that they "not too hastily dismiss this question" of common ground with Roman Catholicism. In his sixth Princeton lecture, he insists:

> Though the history of the Reformation has established a fundamental antithesis between Rome and ourselves, it would nevertheless be narrow-minded and short-sighted to underestimate the real power which even now is manifest in Rome's warfare against Atheism and Pantheism. Only ignorance of the exhaustive studies of Romish philosophy and of Rome's successful efforts in social life ... could account for such a superficial judgment.[29]

What needs emphasis is Kuyper's concession that *two specific realms*—creedal confession and morals—are "not subject to contro-

---

26. Kuyper, *Program*, § 13 (p. 12).
27. Kuyper, *Lectures*, 18.
28. Kuyper, *Lectures*, 183.
29. Kuyper, *Lectures*, 183.

versy between Rome and ourselves."[30] Moreover, "what we have in common with Rome concerns precisely those fundamentals of our Christian creed now most fiercely assaulted by the modern spirit."[31] And while on particular points of ecclesiology and theology—for example, Rome's teaching on justification, the Mass, the invocation of saints, and purgatory—Kuyper's Calvinism is "unflinchingly opposed to Rome," Kuyper can contend that these differences are "not now the points on which the struggle of the age is concentrated."[32] Rather, "the lines of battle," as he views them, are drawn as follows:

- Theism versus atheism and pantheism
- Human fallenness versus human perfectibility
- The divine Christ versus Jesus the mere man
- The cross as a sacrifice of reconciliation versus a mere symbol of martyrdom
- The Bible as inspired by God versus a purely human product
- The Ten Commandments as ordained by God versus a mere archaeological document
- The eternally established ordinances of God versus an ever-changing law and morality spun out of human subjectivity

"Now, in this [cultural] conflict," Kuyper maintains,

> Rome is not an antagonist, but stands on our side, inasmuch as she also recognizes and maintains the Trinity, the Deity of Christ, the Cross as an atoning sacrifice, the Scriptures as the Word of God, and the Ten Commandments as a divinely-inspired rule of life. Therefore, let me ask[,] if Romish theologians take up the sword to do valiant and skillful battle against the same tendency that we ourselves mean to fight to the death, is it not the part of wisdom to accept the valuable help of their elucidation? Calvin at least was accustomed to appeal to Thomas of Aquino. And I for my part am not ashamed

---

30. Kuyper, *Lectures*, 183.
31. Kuyper, *Lectures*, 183.
32. Kuyper, *Lectures*, 183.

to confess that on many points my views have been clarified through my study of the Romish theologians.[33]

What is more, Kuyper concludes, "we should not lose sight of the fact that in Christian works and devotion Rome still outstrips us."[34]

Protestant unity with Roman Catholics on basic creedal matters and on the cultural front, despite Kuyper's strong criticisms of Rome, is borne out by the Anti-Revolutionary Party's coalition with Catholic members of the Dutch Parliament, which resulted in Kuyper becoming prime minster in 1901. In fact, eleven years prior, a Protestant–Roman Catholic coalition had secured passage of the Education Act, which allowed public funding of private education. It is fair to say that by encouraging common-cause cooperation with Catholics, Kuyper was instrumental in helping dissolve some of the Protestant–Roman Catholic antagonism that had built up over the previous three hundred years.[35]

Common Grace and Common Ground

The character of common grace in Kuyperian thought is its accent on our shared humanity, common moral ground, and public responsibility based on the created order. As a theological reality, it has its roots in the absolute sovereignty of God, a sturdy doctrine of creation, and a full-orbed, all-encompassing understanding of redemption.

One domain needing greater attention among "Reformed" types in particular is that of moral law. As Kuyper and his Roman Catholic counterparts understood, moral law is the means by which God governs the universe. Kuyper understands moral law in terms of "divine ordinance," and this moral law is woven into the very fabric of creation. In *Ons Program*, published in 1879 and intended as a theological and ideological commentary on political involvement in the Netherlands, Kuyper speaks of the "natural knowledge of God,"

---

33. Kuyper, *Lectures*, 183–84.

34. Kuyper, *Lectures*, 188.

35. On this see Bernard H. M. Vlekke, *Evolution of the Dutch Nation* (New York: Roy, 1945), 365–69, wherein the author provides useful biographical sources for the Eighty Years' War and the period extending from the sixteenth through the nineteenth century.

accessible to all human beings, and "universal moral law."[36] This universal moral law, moreover, "was ingrained in man before his fall" and,

> however weakened after the fall, still speaks so sharply, so strongly, so clearly among even the most brutalized peoples and the most degenerate persons that Paul could write: "For when the Gentiles, who do not have the law, by nature do what the law requires, they are a law to themselves, even though they do not have the law. They show that the work of the *law is written on their hearts*, while their conscience also bears witness, and their conflicting thoughts accuse or even excuse them."[37]

This, of course, is none other than the language of natural law. Thus it is that Kuyper can speak of "the ordinances of God" that direct and preserve all of human life and form the underpinnings of common grace. These laws or ordinances, in turn, facilitate what Kuyper referred to as "sphere sovereignty" (*souvereiniteit in eigen kring*), or "structural pluralism,"[38] developed at some length in his third Princeton lecture, "Calvinism and Politics." Common grace, supported by divine ordinances, makes civil life possible, based on moral principle and shared morality. At bottom, justice is impossible without the moral law. In Kuyper's understanding, justice derives from divine ordinances.

In addition to Kuyper's insistence that two realms—creedal confession and morality—are the basis for Protestant–Roman Catholic unity, a further bit of evidence indicates that natural law represents common ground between Kuyper and Roman Catholicism. In 1897, on the occasion of the twenty-fifth anniversary of his editorship of

---

36. Kuyper, *Program*, arts. 28, 50, 56, and 63 (pp. 31, 59, 66, 76).

37. Kuyper, *Program*, art. 63 (pp. 76–77) (emphasis in the original).

38. On the equation of "sphere sovereignty" and "structural pluralism," see Simon P. Kennedy, "Abraham Kuyper: Calvinist, Anti-Revolutionary Politician and Political Thinker," *Australian Journal of Politics and History* 6, no. 2 (June 2015): 169–83; James D. Bratt, *Abraham Kuyper: Modern Calvinist, Christian Democrat* (Grand Rapids, MI: Eerdmans, 2013), 130–48; Kent A. Van Til, "Subsidiarity and Sphere-Sovereignty: A Match Made in …? *Theological Studies* 69, no. 3 (2008): 610–36; and James W. Skillen and Rockne M. McCarthy, eds., *Political Order and the Plural Structure of Society* (Atlanta: Scholars Press, 1991).

De Standaard, Kuyper stated what was his one great passion in life: "to affirm God's holy statutes" in all of life and "to engrave God's holy order," known through creation and Scripture, "upon the nation's public conscience."[39]

While we might wonder—quite legitimately—why the grammar of "natural law" or "the law of nature" is not part of Kuyper's vocabulary, we must recall the dominant ideological tendencies of his day—the late nineteenth century—when the influence of Darwin, Hegel, Kant, and Spencer was prevailing. Recall, too, his qualification of the term *nature* noted earlier: he was willing to accept it provided that we understood thereby "not laws originating *from* Nature but laws imposed *upon* Nature." In any event, Kuyper is at home in the natural law tradition—a tradition that is acknowledged by Calvin himself.

Two In-House Problems

In Kuyper's day there was a problem in the Christian church, as there was even in Calvin's, and as there is—it needs pointing out—in ours. This problem, developed extensively in the Princeton lectures, is the tendency either toward capitulation to contemporary, secularizing assumptions or toward isolation from the culture. Capitulation or isolation—in Kuyper's thinking, this twofold problem called for a "third way." While social liberals, in Kuyper's view, were all too ready to ignore the antithesis, Anabaptist and pietistic types suffered from a stunted view of creation and redemption, resulting in a fleeing or withdrawing from the culture in ways that discounted the church's "cultural mandate." Anabaptism, for Kuyper, "in its effort to evade the world," adopted "the monastic starting-point, generalizing and making it a rule for *all* believers."[40] Common grace, in bold contrast, should render us "duty bound to take all civil life under its guardianship and to remodel it."[41] Kuyper's social philosophy embraces everything that is a part of this present world based on creation and

---

39. John Hendrik de Vries, "Biographical Note: Abraham Kuyper 1837–1920," in Kuyper, *Lectures*, iii.

40. Kuyper, *Lectures*, 30 (emphasis in original).

41. Kuyper, *Lectures*, 31.

common grace. Redemption, therefore, entails a "creation regained," in the words of writer Al Wolters.[42]

In our day there is an additional problem, and it is also "in-house." It is the widespread tendency among Protestants—indeed, among both revisionists and orthodox types—to be suspicious of or to reject natural-law thinking. This bias seems to be rooted in a mentality that assumes that natural law is a medieval construct (and hence outmoded), or that it is chiefly a "Catholic" thing (and hence skews the nature-grace relationship while being insufficiently Christocentric), or that it doesn't account for cultural diversity and "pluralism" (and hence is "imperialistic").

What needs emphasis is that the Magisterial Reformers—Luther, Calvin, Melanchthon, Zwingli, Bullinger, and others—all affirmed the natural law.[43] Given the strong emphasis on human depravity in Calvin's theological system, many believers today assume that Calvin had a dim view of the natural law, in contrast to his Catholic counterparts. Such, however, is not the case. And while natural law is not a *major* focus of the Protestant Reformers when compared to, say, justification, Calvin is keenly aware of Paul's argument in Romans that the Gentiles "show the work of the law written on their hearts" (Rom. 2:15).

Calvin's uses of the law in his *Institutes of the Christian Religion*—ceremonial, judicial, and moral—mirror his conviction that there are aspects of human law that are both binding and nonbinding.[44] Calvin is a Thomist in assuming that, from natural instinct and our social nature, human beings are disposed to regulate themselves by moral law. The seeds of just laws, he insists, are "implanted in the breasts of all without a lawgiver." Furthermore, they remain unaffected by the vicissitudes of life, so that "neither war nor catastrophe nor

---

42. Albert M. Wolters, *Creation Regained: Biblical Basics for a Reformational Worldview*, 2nd ed. (Grand Rapids, MI: Eerdmans, 2005).

43. See J. Daryl Charles, "Burying the Wrong Corpse," in *Natural Law and Evangelical Political Thought*, ed. Jesse Covington, Bryan McGraw, and Micah Watson (Lanham, MD: Lexington, 2013), 3–34; and J. Daryl Charles, *Retrieving the Natural Law: A Return to Moral First Things* (Grand Rapids, MI: Eerdmans, 2008), 111–55.

44. John Calvin, *Institutes of the Christian Religion*, ed. John T. McNeill, trans. Ford Lewis Battles (Louisville: Westminster John Knox, 2006), 2.7.6–13.

crime nor disagreement can alter these moral intuitions."[45] Nothing can destroy "the primary idea of justice" that is planted within the human soul.[46]

How corrupt is the human heart, according to Calvin? Thoroughly. Is there any realm of human experience unaffected by sin? Emphatically not. Notwithstanding this reality, neither Calvin, nor Kuyper for that matter, can be interpreted as teaching that humans are incapable of basic moral reasoning. Calvin sides with Paul: "Natural law is that apprehension of the conscience which distinguishes sufficiently between just and unjust, and which deprives men of the excuse of ignorance while it proves them guilty by their own testimony." The Reformer acknowledges that despite "man's perverted and degenerate nature," the image of God is "not totally annihilated and destroyed"; rather, "some sparks still gleam" in human creation.[47] Kuyper would agree.

While an examination of influential post-Kuyperian "Reformed" voices that questioned or rejected natural-law thinking—for example, Herman Dooyeweerd a generation later, Helmut Thielicke, and Karl Barth—is beyond the scope of the present discussion, it does need emphasizing that an inaccurate (or outdated) account of *contemporary* Roman Catholic teaching, coupled with Protestants' worry that natural law either is insufficiently Christocentric or misconstrues nature and grace, has contributed to the Protestant dilemma to the present day. Add to this the influence of people like John Howard Yoder, Stanley Hauerwas, and other Anabaptist scholars, and Protestants remain generally suspicious of natural law ethics. Happily, in the last decade there has been something of a renewal of natural-law thinking in some corners of Protestant thought—clearly not everywhere, but here and there. This, surely, is a critically important ecumenical development. In Kuyperian terms, it is indispensable for a sturdy public theology.

---

45. Calvin, *Institutes*, 2.2.13.
46. Calvin, *Institutes*, 2.2.13.
47. Calvin, *Institutes*, 1.15.4, 2.2.12.

Kuyper and the Catholic *Catechism*

At bottom, Kuyper's concept of common grace is underpinned by his belief in a universal moral law, and this accords with Catholic—and classically Christian—teaching on the natural moral law. The *Catechism of the Catholic Church*, which represents that church's official position on matters doctrinal and social, affirms the natural law with its ramifications in part 3, section 1.[48] The broader contours of the natural law, as affirmed in paragraphs 1954 through 1964 of the *Catechism*, are as follows:

- The natural law expresses the original moral sense that allows humans to discern the good and the evil, the truth and the lie.
- It is written and engraved in the soul of each person.
- It states the first and essential precepts that govern the moral life and thus is the light of understanding placed in us by God.
- It is universal in its precepts; hence, its authority extends to all people.
- It finds its application in various ways in different cultural contexts, yet within this diversity it binds humans together by common moral principles.
- It is in conformity with our created nature, the image of God; it prohibits what is contrary to our nature and prescribes what is essential to the good and human flourishing.
- It is immutable and permanent throughout the variations of history.
- It provides the solid foundation on which human beings can build the structure of moral rules to guide their choices and moral obligations.
- It is a law that cannot be abrogated and that sin cannot efface.
- It is the basis for civil and positive law, and it prepares human beings for the reception of grace.
- It is summarized in the precepts of the Ten Commandments.

---

48. *Catechism of the Catholic Church* (Washington, DC: United States Catholic Conference, 1994), nos. 1954–1960 (pp. 474–76).

To read the Catholic *Catechism* as a Protestant is to be surprised at the convergence of Catholics and Protestants in important theological contexts, especially with respect to justification, faith, and grace, which are treated in both part 1 and part 3. This "convergence" has been demonstrated in our lifetime by several remarkable developments—not unrelated to each other—that require Protestants to reevaluate what Jarsolav Pelikan called the "tragic necessity" of the Reformation divide.[49] Such a reevaluation is fitting in 2018, the year following the five hundredth anniversary of the Reformation's beginning. Clearly, in the second decade of the twenty-first century, things are not as they were in 1517. In the words of two religious historians, "Protestants are duty-bound to try to understand the tragic dimensions of the Reformation."[50]

Consider, for example, the Lutheran–Roman Catholic dialogues on justification that extended through the 1980s, resulting in the significant document Joint Declaration on the Doctrine of Justification, published in 1999 by the Pontifical Council for Promoting Christian Unity and the Lutheran World Federation.[51] Or the Vatican's official response to the Joint Declaration, which acknowledged that while significant areas of theological difference have not been eliminated, "a consensus in basic truths of the doctrine of justification" in fact exists.[52] Or consider that both Catholic and Protestant writers of our generation are writing on the similarities of "sphere sovereignty" and "subsidiarity."[53] Or consider the many Protestant admirers of John

---

49. This phrase originally appeared in Jaroslav Pelikan, *The Riddle of Roman Catholicism: Its History, Its Beliefs, Its Future* (New York: Abingdon, 1959).

50. Thomas Albert Howard and Mark A. Noll, *Protestantism after 500 Years* (New York: Oxford University Press, 2016), 17.

51. Avilable at http://www.vatican.va/roman_curia/pontifical_councils/chrstuni/documents/rc_pc_chrstuni_doc_31101999_cath-luth-joint-declaration_en.html.

52. Prologue to Response of the Catholic Church to the Joint Declaration of the Catholic Church and the Lutheran World Federation on the Doctrine of Justification, http://www.vatican.va/roman_curia/pontifical_councils/chrstuni/documents/rc_pc_chrstuni_doc_01081998_off-answer-catholic_en.html.

53. See, e.g., Van Til, "Subsidiarity and Sphere-Sovereignty," 610–36; Henk E. S. Woldring, "Multiform Responsibility and the Revitalization of Civil Society," in *Religion, Pluralism, and Public Life: Abraham Kuyper's Legacy for the Twenty-First Century*, ed. Luis E. Lugo (Grand Rapids, MI: Eerdmans,

Paul II, not least because of the timeliness and trenchant nature of cultural criticism found in his encyclicals. Or the Evangelicals and Catholics Together initiative, birthed in the early to mid-1990s and continuing to the present day. Or the September 2011 address by Benedict XVI to the Council of the Evangelical Church in Germany, which stressed the importance of our "shared foundation" in light of worldwide challenges to the faith.[54] Or the recent document "From Conflict to Communion: Lutheran–Catholic Common Commemoration of the Reformation in 2017," crafted in preparation for commemorating the five hundredth anniversary of the Reformation.[55] Without question, the possibilities that now exist for genuine ecumenical dialogue, theological discussion, and common-cause cooperation are infinitely greater than even a generation ago.

Let it be said, as well, that the things Kuyper believed represent no mere "lowest-common-denominator" approach to ecumenical relations, which was so fashionable in much of the twentieth century. They represent, rather, an ecumenism rooted in faithfulness to the historic Christian tradition and are necessary for the cultural mandate before us.

Kuyper and the Culture

Over a hundred years removed from us, Abraham Kuyper found common ground with Roman Catholics through his teaching on common grace and universal moral law. This common ground is none other than the natural law, as both classical Christian social teaching and the Catholic *Catechism* bear witness. Kuyper was dismayed by the church's uncritical acceptance of society's increasing secularization as well as by its ineffectual social witness. In the words of Max

---

2000), 175–88; and Paul Sigmund, "Subsidiarity, Solidarity, and Liberation: Alternative Approaches in Catholic Social Thought," in *Religion, Pluralism, and Public Life*, 205–20.

54. Benedict XVI, Meeting with the Council of the Evangelical Church in Germany, September 2011, https://w2.vatican.va/content/benedict-xvi/en/speeches/2011/september/documents/hf_ben-xvi_spe_20110923_evangelical-church-erfurt.html.

55. http://www.vatican.va/roman_curia/pontifical_councils/chrstuni/lutheran-fed-docs/rc_pc_chrstuni_doc_2013_dal-conflitto-alla-comunione_en.html.

Stackhouse, Kuyper recognized that "the well-being of the soul, the character of local communities, the fabric of the society at large, and the fate of civilization [all] are intimately related and cannot be separated from theological and moral issues."[56]

As students of Kuyper are quick to point out, this remarkable man found little appeal in world-fleeing pietism, theocratic triumphalism, or social-gospel liberalism. His was a robust, active vision that avoided privatized faith, eschatological top-heaviness, and the attenuation of truth. Biographer James Bratt expresses it well: "Kuyper did not want a naked public square but a crowded one."[57] Indeed. His idea of the public square, moreover, was that of a structured pluralism, with Christians contending in the public square.

This makes rather remarkable the decision by Princeton Theological Seminary to rescind the 2017 Abraham Kuyper Prize for Excellence in Reformed Theology and Public Life, which was to have been awarded to Rev. Tim Keller at the conference "Neo-Calvinism and the Church," sponsored by the seminary's Abraham Kuyper Center for Public Theology. It was remarkable and yet predictable, given the state of the Protestant mainline. Keller, the well-known founder and pastor of Redeemer Presbyterian Church in Manhattan, was to have been honored with the award in light of his demonstrated "innovation" and "excellence" in public theology. Princeton Seminary president Craig Barnes, in announcing the reversal only two weeks before the event, claimed to be responding to protests from students and Presbyterian Church (USA) pastors who denounced Keller's and his denomination's (the Presbyterian Church in America) views on the ordination of women and on same-sex causes.

The Kuyper Prize is awarded each year to "a scholar or community leader whose outstanding contribution to their chosen sphere reflects the ideas and values characteristic of the Neo-Calvinist vision of religious engagement in matters of social, political and cultural significance in one or more of the 'spheres' of society." The recipient of the prize typically delivers the opening keynote address at the Kuyper conference. Past recipients include Congressman

---

56. Max Stackhouse, foreword to *Religion, Pluralism, and Public Life*, xiii.
57. James D. Bratt, ed., *Abraham Kuyper: A Centennial Reader* (Grand Rapids, MI: Eerdmans, 1998), 14.

John R. Lewis (2015); Nicholas Wolterstorff, Noah Porter Professor of Philosophy Emeritus, Yale University (2014); Marilynn Robinson, writer and Pulitzer Prize winner (2011); Lord Jonathan Sacks, chief rabbi of the United Hebrew Congregations of the Commonwealth (2010); Alvin Plantinga, professor of philosophy emeritus, University of Notre Dame (2009); Richard Mouw, former president of Fuller Seminary (2007); and Jan Peter Balkenende, prime minister of the Netherlands (2004).

What may be said, at the very least, of the seminary's decision is that it is un-Kuyperian in the extreme. Kuyper desired a lively and pluralistic public arena in which Christians were free to contend. Clearly, the seminary cannot tolerate such pluralism. And although it claims to tolerate—or even encourage—"diverse viewpoints" on the matter of sexual ethics, it clearly *cannot* tolerate divergence or disagreement of any kind. In truth, it is saying that disagreement on matters of gender and sexuality *dare not* be tolerated. And therewith it is declaring that historic Christian orthodoxy is unacceptable.

But Kuyper would have none of this, were his voice allowed in the public sphere today. While sexual ethics was not *the* watershed issue—and hence *the* litmus test—of his day as it is of ours, he did decry the church when and where she capitulated to the cultural *Zeitgeist*. In this regard, we very much need an Abraham Kuyper in the twenty-first century—updated and chastened, to be sure, since he was a man of his time. His courageous spirit is desperately needed in Protestant circles.

If we update Kuyper's program where needed and push it in a fuller ecumenical direction, the fruit might be rich beyond measure. And it may well be that the unity between Catholics and Protestants (at least, what faithful Protestants remain in the North American context) on theological essentials and moral first principles, in the end, is no luxury. That unity, rather, may be an *absolute necessity* and prerequisite for survival as we attempt, in the season before us, to demonstrate a robust and faithful Christian presence in a hostile cultural environment.

Six

Why Do Economic Issues Merit Moral Reflection?*

Why economic issues merit moral reflection is an important question, and a most intriguing one at that. In reflecting on the matter, one comes to realize that there is a short answer and a longer answer to the question. In response to *why* economic issues merit moral reflection, one might answer, quite simply, because *all of life* merits moral reflection, based on a theocentric view of reality. There is no domain of human existence that falls outside a Christian view of the created order. All spheres require Christian engagement.

Assuming that bottom-line premise, permit me to develop my response in a slightly longer version, utilizing a threefold rationale. The first part of my response to the question is that there is no free society apart from virtuous people.

---

*Address presented at the symposium "Toward a Free and Virtuous Society: The Moral Case for Market Economics" in New Orleans, Louisiana, May 10–12, 2018, sponsored by the Acton Institute.

The Impossibility of a Free Society apart from Virtuous People

What is the Acton Institute's motto? "Toward a free and virtuous society." There is no such thing as a free society without people who are virtuous. Neither sound economic theory nor policy directives nor "good government" can cure a sick society unless the medicine of moral renewal enters the hearts and minds of both rich and poor, upper and lower classes. Without virtue, without the moral impulse, without the ability to engage in moral reflection and make moral judgments (which contemporary culture is loath to do!), it is only a matter of time before society collapses, something that you and I have never experienced in our lifetime. At which point, were that ever to happen, matters of economic theory, policy, and the market disappear or become irrelevant.

Perhaps I exaggerate. Surely some of you doubtless are thinking that I should refrain from this sort of apocalyptic thinking. After all, that sort of societal disintegration could never happen here in American culture. In response, let me assure you that in my Christian pilgrimage I have never been an alarmist, that my eschatology is not that of fundamentalist dispensationalism, and that I despise what someone has called "lifeboat theology," whereby it is thought that since culture is going to hell in a handbasket anyway, why rearrange chairs on a *sinking* ship? While that sort of nonsense sells books, I reject it as systematic error. And while such apocalyptic thinking, wittingly or unwittingly, may have the effect of *removing* us from society and responsible cultural participation, mainstream Christian theology requires that we participate in the social, cultural, and political arrangements to which God has called us. Withdrawal is *never* an option, even when we are being persecuted for our faith.

At the same time, we must be moral realists, which means that we take culture seriously for better or for worse, and which requires that we understand various social and cultural currents since stewarding the culture is part of the creation mandate. And being stewards of the culture means that we create, develop, shape, and extend human culture with our gifts, talents, and vision, based on the image of God—that is, God's likeness—within. At the same time, it needs to be said that there is an ebb and flow to all human culture and human social development. There is *no guarantee* that a free society remains free. Democracy is procedural; it is instrumental. It does not automatically renew itself; the people who inhabit a democracy must renew themselves, and then it can work optimally. In fact, the historical record indicates that when a people loses its moral bearings, it slides into some form of anarchy, followed by some form of totalitarian arrangement.

When Alexis de Tocqueville visited America in the nineteenth century and praised the young nation for its religious freedom, he reflected with sobriety on the "democratic tendency." "Rule by the people," he worried, could result in what he called a "tyranny of the majority."[1] For if the masses are given to a prostituted or wrong view of freedom, then their laws, their government, and their institutions become a reflection of that tyranny. And whether a tyranny is majoritarian or minoritarian, people are not truly free; some form of enslavement ensues.

One of the consistent themes in John Paul II's work during his pontificate was to stress in his writings the importance of an ordered liberty, a freedom not toward license but toward a harnessing of itself to truth. John Paul is perhaps best known for critiquing what he called our "culture of death," by which he meant a corruption of conscience that was taking place in Western societies and the attendant inability to name good and evil. His comments on the current challenge to Western democracies came after the extraordinary events that took place in the former Soviet Union and Eastern Europe in 1989 and 1990. In his 1993 encyclical *Veritatis Splendor* ("The Splendor of Truth"), he worried about what he called an "alliance between democracy and ethical relativism, which would remove any sure moral reference point from the political and social life, and on a deeper level make the acknowledgement of truth impossible."[2]

---

1. Alexis de Tocqueville, *Democracy in America*, ed. Harvey C. Mansfield and Delba Winthrop (Chicago: University of Chicago Press, 2000), I.2.4, 7, 8 (pp. 180–86, 235–64).

2. John Paul II, Encyclical Letter on Certain Fundamental Questions of the Church's Moral Teaching, *Veritatis Splendor* (August 6, 1993), no. 101, http://w2.vatican.va/content/john-paul-ii/en/encyclicals/documents/hf_jp-ii_enc_06081993_veritatis-splendor.html.

Was John Paul perhaps overstating the potential for this "alliance"? His caution was that if no moral truth was acknowledged to guide and direct the activity of a society, then ideas and institutions are easily manipulated for the purposes of corrosive political power. In the end, he worries that "a democracy without values readily turns into open or thinly disguised totalitarianism."[3]

When in early 1998 the newly appointed American ambassador to the Vatican paid Pope John Paul II a visit, the pontiff reminded her that America's experiment in national self-government left the nation with a "far-reaching responsibility, not only for the well-being of its own people, but for the development and destiny of peoples throughout the world." America's founding fathers, John Paul observed, affirmed certain "self-evident" truths about the human person and human freedom, owing to "nature's God" for the purpose of maintaining an "ordered liberty."[4]

John Paul was rejecting the prevalent view of citizenship—namely, the understanding that I am free to do whatever I want; rather, he insisted on the importance of self-mastery based on self-evident truths. The conclusion to be drawn is as clear as it is offensive: national self-government is directly and inescapably linked to *personal* self-government. Without the freedom to commit ourselves to the moral ordering of our lives, there can be no genuine political and social—and hence economic—freedom.

We reiterate, then, our first chief point: there is no free society without a virtuous people. Hence, we must keep first things first, even when this message is roundly rejected in our day. Those who wish to stand for moral principle are lambasted today as hate-filled, bigoted, and intolerant. But we cannot live in the fear of what others might think, nor can we simply withdraw from cultural participation, as many are tempted to do today. Rather, based on theological and moral conviction—that is, based on our cultural mandate that is anchored in the doctrines of creation, providence, redemption, and incarnation—we are placed here on earth to be *stewards* of human culture. Which brings me to the second part of my answer. Why

---

3. John Paul II, *Veritatis Splendor*, no. 101.

4. Quoted in Michael S. Joyce, "On Self-Government," *Policy Review* 90 (July/August 1998): 41–42.

do economic issues merit moral reflection? Answer 2: because the Christian's cultural mandate consists of stewardship.

Stewardship as the Christian's Cultural Mandate

Stated with other words, economic issues entail first and foremost a *stewarding of resources*. To properly understand this task, we must begin with the doctrines of creation and providence. Our mandate, based on creation (which has not been overturned or altered), is that we cocreate (with God, based on the *imago Dei*, his likeness); that we develop, shape, and extend what God has called into being. Therein we utilize the endless and varied resources that he has placed at our disposal, in addition to our personal gifts and abilities. Principles of stewardship, it needs to be emphasized, flow from and are anchored in the doctrine of creation. According to the Genesis narrative, humankind is to develop as coregents all that God has created.

Principles of stewardship, furthermore, also derive from the doctrine of divine providence, by which we understand that all things are sustained continually by the Sovereign Lord God Almighty, the Creator. This process—what theologians call the period of the "already but not yet" (accomplished through the cross and resurrection but awaiting total fulfillment)—finds its consummation in the eschaton, at which time creation is not simply thrown on a cosmic ash heap but rather continues, though transformed. The new heavens and new earth mirror the fact that what has been called into existence by the Creator does not cease to be; rather, it continues, albeit in a transformed and glorified state. The reality of the doctrines of creation and providence undergird the important—though neglected—doctrine of judgment according to works. This doctrine neither plays on the Catholic tendency toward justification through works nor the Protestant tendency to neglect the importance of our earthly works. Rather, it underscores the economic principle of stewardship. But I get ahead of myself.

Important New Testament texts that underscore the reality of Christ as both creator and redeemer need mentioning. It is astonishing how stereotypical Christian teaching and preaching utterly misses the ramifications of both creation and redemption. The writer to the Hebrews notes, in his introduction, that the Son is the "appointed heir of all things," and that this Son "made the universe" and "sustains all things by the word of his power" (Heb. 1:2–3). Paul, in his introduction to the letter written to Christians in Ephesus, writes that, "in the fulness of time," "all things whether in heaven or on earth" were "reconciled" to Christ (Eph. 1:10). And the magisterial New Testament text, also Pauline, is found in Colossians 1, where the apostle declares that by the Son all things were created in heaven and on earth—the material and the nonmaterial, the visible and invisible—and that not only were all things created *through* him but *for* him. As if that were not enough, in the same pericope Paul repeats this staggering truth: *all things have been reconciled to Christ* (vv. 16–20).

What is typically absent from contemporary teaching and preaching is a fuller awareness of the ramifications of a fourth doctrine: the doctrine of incarnation. Consider how the Creator interacts with—and transforms—his own creation, noted in the prologue to the Fourth Gospel: "In the beginning was the Word, and the Word was with God, and the Word was God.... Through him [i.e., the "Word"] all things were made; without him nothing was made that has been made" (John 1:1–3 NIV). Let us consider these remarkable pronouncements. The "Word" (i.e., the Logos, which can legitimately be translated "word," "communication," "reason," or "logic") was divine, God himself. Moreover, that "Word" was incarnated; he "became flesh and made his dwelling among us," we read a few verses later (v. 14 NIV). As the enfleshment of the Creator, the "Word" continues to advertise himself in the world that he himself created.

The question I would like to pose is this: *By what standards* does he advertise himself in the world that he himself created? Are we not exceedingly glad that God did not communicate in a second-rate way? He gave his best. And we should too, incarnating his life in our cultural surroundings. Furthermore, God is the "Word," the master communicator. Where, we may ask, are Christians who aspire to become journalists, writers, policy writers, and gatekeepers in our contemporary world? Based on my three decades of teaching mostly in a Christian liberal arts environment, I am sad to say that relatively few seem motivated to go into these strategic realms of influence. To reiterate: God incarnate is first and foremost the Logos, the Word, the master communicator. Let us, having grasped his incarnate nature, be excellent communicators in and to the world. This understanding of incarnation is central to a right understanding of stewardship.

Stewarding of creation, then, and stewarding of the culture in particular lies at the heart of economics, and the doctrines of creation, providence, redemption, and incarnation anchor this stewarding. Not surprisingly, the notion of stewardship surfaces in our Lord's teaching and specifically in his use of the wisdom tradition and parables. Very briefly, I would like us to consider one of those parables, commonly referred to as the parable of the talents, found in Matthew 25.

Before we do, however, a quick word is in order on the rules of parabolic teaching and storytelling in the ancient wisdom tradition and in wisdom literature. First, parables arise from daily, real-life situations, unlike allegories; they represent personal encounters with people in typical situations, challenging the hearer in ways that abstract talk simply does not. Second, they always involve contrast, pitting the wise against the foolish, virtue against vice, or similar. Third, they almost always employ the rule of the three—for example, three travelers in the parable of the good Samaritan, three excuse-makers in the parable of the great supper, and in our case three stewards who are given various "talents" and realms of investment. Fourth, they follow the rule of climax, whereby the spotlight falls on the last person or action (as is especially the case in the parable of the talents). And finally, parables always *strike for a verdict*, seeking to evoke a response, such as "What do you think?" or "He who has ears to hear, let him hear" or "See, judge for yourselves."

With this, let us consider the parable of talents itself (Matt. 25:14–30). In New Testament times, it should be noted that a talent was a unit of coinage and meant a lot of money. In present-day value, a talent would be worth much. The five-talent person might be worth anywhere between $25,000 and $250,000; the two-talent person between $10,000 and $100,000 dollars; and the one-talent person between $5,000 and $50,000 dollars, depending on how the stock market and local economies are acting. The precise amounts do not matter, however, and are only illustrative, since the parable is about faithfulness as a steward, not simply finance.

If we consider the parable through the eyes of the wisdom technique being used by Jesus, any number of lessons strikes us as relevant and applicable:

- The master gives differing gifts; human beings as stewards have different talents; and note the language: the master calls them and entrusts to them—he puts them in charge of—various realms. The same is true of God.
- The master goes away for an extended, unspecified time; the servants do not know when he will return, but it is assumed that his return is *not* imminent.
- What matters is not the gift or talent per se or the number; what matters is how the steward uses it.
- The master does not require from a person what that person does not possess; what he does require is that each person use to the fullest the talent and ability that have been given. The same is true of God.
- Serving is the guiding motivation for use of the various gifts and talents; serving is the essence of being a steward.
- Two of the three stewards receive commendation and rewards for their work or service that is "well done"; this indicates that the master himself receives great joy when investments are made, and it suggests a doctrine of accountability and rewards. God both receives great joy and rewards people accordingly.
- Part of that reward is being given more work or more responsibility; to those who have been faithful in investing, more is given.
- No investing or multiplying of our abilities or talents—that is, no act of stepping out in faith—displeases the master; what *does* displease him is an unwillingness to take risk and invest. The same might be applied to God.
- The third steward clearly is worried about risk, change, and liability; interestingly, he has a distorted view of the master and consequently does nothing. Many people have a distorted view of God.
- This one-talent steward did not "lose" his gift during the master's absence; he simply did nothing with it, which resulted in the master's displeasure.

- To not use or "invest" what has been given is, in the end, to lose it, however, and this is the note on which the parable concludes.

What we might say of this parable is that, far from being a harmless or entertaining story, it is a spear thrust into the side of the hearer, so to speak—or a punch in the face—because of the truth that it bears. It asks of the listener not *How much do you have?* but *What are you doing with what you have been given?* While it is true that human beings are created equal in terms of their worth and dignity, *not all* are equal in terms of their motivation, resolve, taking initiative, willingness to take risk by faith, and desire to serve.

The stewardship lessons that the parable of the talents teaches are many (and doubtless other readers of the parable will detect things in it that I do not). But all these lessons are expressions of a central law in the universe—a law that is as true and constant as the law of gravity. It is the law of sowing and reaping. *We reap what we sow.* This is true in both the material and the spiritual world, in economics and morality, in private and public life; there is simply no avoiding this law. Permit me to note its corollary: *faithfulness in the small leads to faithfulness in the greater.*[5] Consider the converse as well: unfaithfulness in the small will result in unfaithfulness in the greater. If someone cannot be entrusted with smaller entities, goods, or wealth, how can he or she be entrusted with greater responsibilities or greater wealth? It should be remembered that the loss confronting the unwilling steward in the parable of the talents is not merely a threat; it is a material and spiritual law. That is, if we neglect using our gift, it will vanish, disappear. The implication is that in not investing our talent in God's service we must live with the torment of knowing that we wasted or depreciated the gifts God has given. At minimum, then, the parable behooves us to respond, and with wisdom, courage, and supreme energy to invest what God has entrusted to us.[6]

---

5. Cf. Job 4:8; Prov. 11:18; 22:8; Matt. 24:47; 1 Cor. 9:11; 2 Cor. 9:6; and Gal. 6:7.

6. Consider a parallel admonition from wisdom literature: "Whatever your hand finds to do, do it with all your might" (Eccl. 9:10 NIV). This carpe diem

This brings us to our third and final answer to the question, Why do economic issues merit moral reflection? Our response is that not just *outcomes* but *how we arrive* at outcomes—which is to say *process*—is paramount.

Process over Outcomes

Moral reflection suggests that *how we live* our lives is important. Not merely outcomes but how we arrive at outcomes is what matters. How to live is the overriding theme of a particular genre of literature—in fact, a genre of biblical literature—that, sadly, is neglected in our day. I refer to wisdom literature. The wisdom tradition is a venerable tradition that is found in much of ancient Near Eastern culture, not only in Israel. Any number of cultures had their own wisdom literature. Belonging to the canon of Old Testament Scripture are three wisdom books—Job, Proverbs, and Ecclesiastes—with several psalms containing wisdom features as well (e.g., 1, 34, 37, 49, and 73).

Wisdom literature is an invaluable resource of perennial, cross-cultural truth. Like another cardinal virtue, justice, wisdom is accessible to all people; one does not necessarily need religious faith to demonstrate wisdom. Wisdom is part of what, in theological terms, we might call common grace or general revelation; it is accessible to all. And the fact is, until modern Western culture dispensed with it, that wisdom was venerated by most cultures. To illustrate the cross-cultural nature of the wisdom tradition, consider several proverbs—or wisdom sayings—drawn from African culture. And notice that no one needs to translate or explain these; anyone from a different culture *immediately* understands them, demonstrating that wisdom is indeed universal and cross-cultural.

---

imperative is one of six recurring refrains throughout Ecclesiastes that implore the reader to receive enjoyment in life as a gift of God from the hand of God. See chapter 9 below ("Wisdom and Work: Perspectives on Human Labor from Ecclesiastes").

- It is patience which gets you out of the net.
- No polecat ever smelled his own stink.
- The strength of a crocodile is in the water.
- A butterfly that flies among thorns will have torn wings.
- When it rains, the roof always drips the same way.
- He has the kindness of a witch.
- A woman quick to love means a woman who does not love.
- A chief is like a dust-heap where everyone comes with his garbage and deposits it.
- The sons of a king do not need to be taught about power.
- When you marry a beautiful woman, you marry problems.
- Two wives are two pots full of poison.[7]

In its essence, wisdom is accumulated in nature; that is, it is *acquired*, accruing as a deposit of moral insight. How precisely is wisdom acquired? Wisdom literature itself indicates or suggests several ways in which wisdom grows. One way is through observation and reflection on the human experience. This is one of the purposes of the book of Ecclesiastes, which tends to confound most readers. While it is not impossible for a child or a teenager to be wise, such a development would be rather remarkable. For this reason a proverb states, "The glory of young men is their strength, [and] gray hair [is] the splendor of the old" (Prov. 20:29 NIV). Wisdom is the product of observation and reflection on life's experience.

A second source of wisdom, according to wisdom literature, is observing and reflecting on nature. Often in wisdom literature you read something like this: "Go consider the ant," which stores up food in a particular season; or, "Consider the lilies of the field or the birds of the air ..., and yet your heavenly Father," as Jesus says. And indeed such is the case. Whenever we take the time to closely observe something in nature, it often has a striking and usually pedagogical effect on us. Take any one of the multiple proverbial

---

7. Claus Westermann, *Roots of Wisdom: The Oldest Proverbs of Israel and Other Peoples*, trans. J. Daryl Charles (Louisville: Westminster John Knox, 1995), 145–46.

sayings recorded in Proverbs 30 as an example. Proverbs 30:24–28 (NIV) is a case in point:

> Four things on earth are small,
>> yet they are extremely wise:
> ants are creatures of little strength,
>> yet they store up their food in the summer;
> hyraxes are creatures of little power,
>> yet they make their home in the crags;
> locusts have no king,
>> yet they advance together in ranks;
> a lizard can be caught with the hand,
>> yet it is found in kings' palaces.

A second source of wisdom, then, is observing and reflecting on nature.

Yet another source of wisdom needs to be identified before we close, even when it is not readily acknowledged—in fact, people do everything they can to avoid mentioning it. I refer to the element of suffering. Of course, many people would respond by saying that it is *not* true that we must know suffering in order to be wise. At this point I would simply pose a question. In our own experience, have we encountered people who have suffered much and yet who are not bitter or angry? These are people who, quite obviously, have a deep faith. There is a manifest beauty in their lives—a quality that resembles a sweet fragrance—that defies categorization. Among other things, invariably, these people are wise. It goes without saying, of course, that we never hear about the linkage between suffering and wisdom from the pulpit; after all, suffering does not preach well. The message "Do you wish to be wise? Then come and suffer" is not exactly the most inviting call for the average Christian. Nevertheless, it contains important truth. As Christians we must "take up our cross." This does not mean constant suffering—that is not my argument—but it does mean that there are changing seasons of our lives in which God works in different ways. As Ecclesiastes reminds us, there is a time and season for everything under heaven (Eccl. 3:1–14). And there are seasons in which we must walk through sorrow and deep valleys. Suffering, it should be noted, is an economic principle—that is, we endure short-term pain, difficulty, and challenges for the sake of long-range gain and outcomes.

While much more could (and should) be said about this fascinating and crucial topic, the broader point being argued is that process—namely, how we live our lives—is more important than outcomes. This is both an economic and a spiritual principle.

Conclusion

The question placed before us is, Why do economic issues merit moral reflection? I have attempted to offer three perspectives in response. One response is anchored in a Christian understanding of human nature and the common good: there is no free society apart from virtuous people. There is no such thing as a free society if people are committed to a lifestyle of vice rather than one of virtue and upholding the common good. All social, economic, and marketplace questions are *moral* questions. Our calling, then, as Christians, is moral persuasion in the marketplace.

A second response to the question expresses the heart of Christian presence in the world. The Christian's cultural mandate consists of stewardship. Based on the doctrines of creation, providence, redemption, and incarnation, we are to steward the culture and all resources given to us by God, with no aspect of the created order being left out. Any theological framework that calls us away from the world, society, or the marketplace is aberrant and a denial of historic Christian theology.

Our third answer to the question concerns the matter of the development of Christian character. What is true of economic reality is true in the spiritual and ethical realm. Not simply outcomes but how we arrive at outcomes is what really matters. That is to say, the process by which we ultimately arrive at particular outcomes is all-important. This process, which is designed in the context of divine providence, is meant to inculcate wisdom in the believer's life. There exist, however, no shortcuts to finding wisdom, for wisdom grows only as a result of the accumulation of varied life experiences, part of which will entail—though by no means be limited to—seasons of suffering, personal need, and identifying with the needs of others. In fact, we find absolute empathy in Christ our Lord, who as our faithful and merciful high priest is touched by our infirmities and sorrows. That empathy, which he desires to instill in his disciples, is exhibited because he himself identified with humans in every manner and suffered as we human beings do.[8]

In conclusion, may we all extol the virtue of being virtuous, on which a truly free society depends but which—it needs emphasizing—is neither legalism, nor rules and regulations, nor dead religion. To the contrary, authentic virtue, rooted in genuine faith, makes us truly free as persons, by which we then can influence the culture and work for the common good. And may we be good stewards of the gifts, talents, and burdens that God has given us, aware that the fruit of our endeavors in this temporal life—a life anchored in the rich doctrines of creation, providence, redemption, and incarnation—are enduring. And may the quality of our lives, not merely what we have achieved in the way of performance, mirror those realities that transcend human limitations and glorify our Father who is in heaven.

---

8. See Phil. 2:8 and Heb. 4:15–16.

Seven

Take This Job and Shove It: Theological Reflections on Vocation, Calling, and Work*

Introduction

At this stage of life I find myself reading—and rereading—the book of Ecclesiastes, which is part of what is called wisdom literature. Wisdom literature is a literary genre that, fascinatingly, is found throughout ancient Near Eastern culture, including ancient Israel. Ecclesiastes joins Job, Proverbs, and assorted psalms as Old Testament evidence of the importance of this genre. Reading Old Testament wisdom literature, with the timeless truths that it teaches, is a sobering reminder of what we miss if we neglect the insights of wisdom, especially in a foolish age such as ours.

Wisdom literature can assume any number of forms—for example, proverb, allegory, parable, or philosophical reflection—and Ecclesiastes belongs to the latter, often to the reader's befuddlement. The writer's continual cry throughout this treatise is the meaninglessness of all things "under the sun."

---

*A version of this essay was presented in June 2018 at the Acton Institute's annual conference, Acton University, in Grand Rapids, Michigan.

Meaninglessness, however, is not applied to life or to human endeavor per se; it is applied to anything *outside of* a theistic outlook.[1] Hence, meaninglessness is the fruit of a worldview of under-the-sun secularism. This stands in bald contrast to the writer's acknowledgment that the Creator "has made everything beautiful in its time" and has planted "eternity in the human heart," even when they cannot penetrate divine providence (Eccl. 3:11 NIV). This awareness of the eternal corresponds to the natural law and what the apostle Paul calls the law "written on their hearts" (Rom. 2:15 NIV), whereby human beings have a minimum knowledge of the Creator, of the self, and of moral accountability.

A startling statement follows in Ecclesiastes. The writer observes "that every man may eat and drink and *find satisfaction in his work*—this is a gift of God" (3:13, my paraphrase, emphasis added). He then concludes with these words: "So I saw that there is nothing better for a man than to *enjoy his work*, because that is his lot" (3:22, emphasis added). This theistic conclusion is strengthened later in Ecclesiastes with the statement that "when God gives any man wealth and possessions and enables him to enjoy them, to accept his lot and *be happy in his work*—this is a gift of God ... because God keeps him occupied with gladness of heart" (5:18–20 NIV, emphasis added). And as if this were not enough, the reader is informed later in the treatise that "joy will accompany [the believer] *in his work* all the days of the life God has given him under the sun" (8:15, emphasis added), despite human inability to comprehend what God does.

Viewed from one standpoint, a brief summary of my thesis might end here with a wisdom perspective on life and human activity. More needs to be said, however, for Ecclesiastes, while it furnishes a much-needed perspective on human activity, does not address many of the specific questions that religious people have about vocation, calling, and work.

Several months ago I stumbled quite accidently upon Viktor Frankl's deceptively brief but important—indeed, classic—work

---

1. Six times in Ecclesiastes the reader encounters the admonition to revere God (3:14; 5:7; 7:18; 8:12 [twice]; 12:13).

*Man's Search for Meaning.*² Frankl, it will be remembered, was a survivor of two of the Nazis' most notorious death camps—Auschwitz-Birkenau and Dachau. His own family was sent to the gas ovens, with the exception of a sister. Yet despite the bestial conditions to which he was subjected, quite miraculously Frankl lived to reflect on these experiences and then, after the war, practice psychotherapy in Vienna (he was a student of Freud). Frankl notes that in his practice he would sometimes ask his patients who were suffering from various forms of torment why they simply did not commit suicide. From his patients' answers he would then derive a particular therapeutic strategy that best suited them in the consulting room. Frankl observed three general types of reasoning among his patients. For some, love of their family members prevented them from taking their lives; for others, lingering memories of the past served as an obstacle; but for yet other patients, there was a sense of responsibility to use their talents in this life. Frankl was especially intrigued by this third answer: life seemed to be worthwhile where hope, meaning, and purpose were identified. This accorded with his own observations as a prisoner: survival was made possible not only by relationships but by finding meaning in present suffering, which prisoners had to discover individually for themselves.

As one who has spent most of his career teaching in a Christian liberal arts environment, I must say that the Christian community generally has not done a good job in helping adults who wrestle with doubt, depression, and despair leading toward suicidal tendencies. More often than not, we have been quick to blurt out Bible verses or suggest that Christians should not battle with such tendencies. But in truth, we all wrestle with the deeper ramifications of meaning in life. We all experience seasons of suffering, sorrow, and doubt that try our faith and reduce us on occasion to agony and despair. *Why not* commit suicide after all? *Why not* end it all, since I see no way out of my present suffering and despair of the soul? Or, expressed in terms less extreme but every bit as practical, *Why not take this*

---

2. Viktor E. Frankl, *Man's Search for Meaning* (Boston: Beacon Press, 1959). The title of the German original in 1946 was *Ein Psychologe erlebt das Konzentrationslager* ("A psychologist's experience in a concentration camp").

present job and throw it in the toilet, given its utterly dissatisfying and unfulfilling nature?

The present argument, however, does not concern counseling or therapy, nor is it about suffering per se; rather, it concerns our attempts as Christian men and women to find clarity regarding our vocation or calling. After nearly thirty years of teaching and in related conversations, counseling myriads of students of differing ages, I have found one particular conversation to be recurring through the years: the pursuit of clarity regarding vocational calling. It is a topic that often goes unanswered or unaddressed by pastors, our churches, and most preaching and teaching—a topic that desperately needs to see the light of day. With this need in view, my thesis is essentially twofold: (1) life is either meaningful or meaningless to the extent that we are aware of our vocational calling; and (2) vocation, calling, and work are interlocking concepts that need to be viewed together. A basic assumption that I am making is that an awareness—and hence an embrace—of our vocation or calling and our work is a foremost *theological* matter. Our first order of business, therefore, is to define each of these concepts in terms of Christian theology and understand their interconnectedness.

The Relationship between Vocation, Calling, and Work

Etymologically, the English words that derive from the Latin *vocatio* show their root to be rich with meaning and ramification—*voice, vocalize, vocation,* and by extension, *call, summons, bidding, invitation.* (For the sake of clarity, let me note that throughout this essay I am using *vocation* and *calling* interchangeably.) Christianity is unique in its conviction that the ordinary in daily living is holy or set apart. It is also unique in its conviction that God's calls on our lives are discernible, perceivable, and to some degree accessible. This is in accordance with God's fundamental nature: he speaks, he communicates, he reveals, he initiates, he prods, and he confirms, even when we must concede that *how* he does this remains something of a mystery.

The implication of God's speaking, initiating, calling, and drawing is that we ought to respond to God as best we know how, with all our energies, talents, and capacities.[3] We do this, of course, not merely out of blind obedience, important as obeying is, but out of gratitude. Moreover, Jesus, the incarnate God and Creator, indicates to his disciples how gratitude will translate and advertise itself in the world, with other people watching: "Let your light so shine that men [and women] may see your good works and glorify your Father in heaven" (Matt. 5:16).

What is tragic—despite mostly lay-led developments that loosely identify themselves as part of the "faith and work" movement—is that the Christian church and Christian leaders for the most part have not grasped the importance of the Christian doctrine of vocation. And where the subject is treated, it is normally misperceived in a sort of bifurcated way that *encourages rather than collapses* the insidious sacred-versus-secular dichotomy that has plagued the church since time immemorial. When and where the language of *vocation* is employed in the wider culture, it typically is used in the sense of vocational training—that is, job assistance, vo-tech education, and employment enhancement; it has become a synonym for *job*, *occupation*, or *employment*. Or, it ends up morphing into best-selling self-help[4] volumes such as Stephen Covey's *The Seven Habits of Highly Effective People* or his sequel, *The Eighth Habit: From Effectiveness to Greatness*.[5] And in the Christian community where the term *vocation* is used, it more often than not presupposes a separation between calling and our work. Contemporary religious understandings of

---

3. The "responsive" nature of the Christian's vocation and work are admirably treated in David H. Jensen, *Responsive Labor: A Theology of Work* (Louisville: Westminster John Knox, 2006).

4. Here I am reminded of comedian George Carlin's comment, the source of which escapes me, but which essentially runs something like the following: "If you're looking for self-help, why read a book written by somebody else? That's not self-help; that's help!"

5. The two Covey volumes were published in 1989 and 2004, respectively. Consider as well other representative titles—for example, *The Management Method of Jesus*, *The Seven Spiritual Laws of Success*, *Chicken Soup for the Soul at Work*, *The Corporate Mystic*, *A Passion for Success*, and *Jesus CEO*. To the extent that God *does* enter discussions among self-help gurus, he is often merely "the guarantor of the authenticity of the self" (Jeffrey Scholes, "Vocation," *Religion Compass* 4, no. 4 [2010]: 217).

vocation—be they Catholic, Orthodox, or Protestant—sadly tend to call us *away* from our work in the marketplace and toward church work, Christian service, prayer and Bible study, or week-long mission trips (not that there is anything inherently wrong with these).[6]

The problem, then, is not that the concept of vocation has suffered and largely disappeared merely because of the secularization of culture; that is part of the story but surely not the whole. The disappearance of the notion of vocation—or at least its misperception—is more tragically the result of *religious thinking* that has dominated our own circles, in our own churches. Thus, we are in desperate need of rediscovering the concept of vocation, rightly understood, given its centrality in Christian theology. A return of this biblical concept to its proper place will require several things. For one, it will require, at least in the Protestant context, that pastors, teachers, and preachers in our congregations repent of our making idols of church growth, seeker friendliness, performance orientation, numerical measurements of success, and business as usual. Among Catholics and Orthodox it may mean actively working against the clergy-laity distinction that for centuries has been a part of their churches.[7] Where this recognition occurs, it will then need to be followed by a vision and willingness to train and equip our parishioners and congregants *for the marketplace*, in the awareness that our real work is *in the marketplace*, since most of us are called *to the marketplace*. After all, that is where we spend most of our lives—at least most of our waking hours. Where, we may ask, is the vision to better equip businesspeople, lawyers, social workers, government employees, medical professionals, economists, technologists, teachers, and all sorts of craftspeople to serve well *in the marketplace*? That, after

---

6. Gene Edward Veith, "Vocation: The Theology of the Christian Life," *Journal of Markets and Morality* 14, no. 1 (Spring 2011): 119, writes that of the three major teachings characterizing the Protestant Reformation—justification by faith, scriptural authority, and vocation—the first two remain while the third is lost.

7. Pope John Paul II, however, contributed to an important shift through two major encyclicals during his pontificate—*Laborem Excercens* ("On Human Work") in 1981 and *Centesimus Annus* in 1991, on the one hundredth anniversary of *Rerum Novarum*.

all, is where our social witness will be felt.[8] In addition, of course, changes will need to occur at the seminary level, since this is where most of our pastors, priests, and religious leaders are trained. But that is a topic for another day.

The specific topic of work will be the focus of our discussion below, but first we might benefit from being reminded of the centrality of *vocatio* in the Christian tradition.

A Theology of Vocation

It has been standard in Christian circles for much of the church's history to speak of three general types of calling—a calling to Christ, a calling to a specific task or service, and a calling to one's daily obligations. The Puritans—and many "Reformed" types who followed suit in the Protestant tradition—tended to emphasize two callings—a general and a special calling. Out of the general calling to Christ and his lordship, specific avenues and types of service are assumed, suggested not only by New Testament texts such as Romans 12[9] but also by the Protestant Reformation context wherein Luther, for example, speaks of various life "stations."[10] Vocation, properly under-

---

8. I am well aware that some readers will object that I am making work an idol—doubtless a severe problem in contemporary Western culture. For the sake of emphasis, however, in this essay I am addressing an opposite extreme—namely, the inability to see value and find satisfaction or contentment in the *doing* of our work for the glory of God and in service to our neighbor.

9. In Romans 12, various attitudes are identified by Paul as befitting the Christian in terms of public witness—among these, moral integrity, service orientation, continual transformation of the mind, the ability to "test" and discern, sober judgment, humility, and the awareness of gifts given graciously by God to every person. Cf. 1 Cor. 12–14 and Eph. 4.

10. The relevant literature is not agreed on either the meaning or the contemporary application of Luther's "stations," based on the Reformer's treatment of 1 Corinthians 7. The relevant Pauline prescriptions in that text are v. 17, "Each one should retain the place in life that the Lord has assigned to him and to which God has called him," and v. 20, "Each one should remain in the situation which he was in when God called him," as well as v. 24, "Each man, as responsible to God, should remain in the situation God called him to" (NIV). What frequently is ignored in much commentary is the immediate context: "Now concerning the matters about which you wrote" (v. 1). The material that follows in Pauline

stood, encompasses the totality of our lives, not merely our career, occupation, present job, or so-called retirement—although vocation does encompass *all of those, yet more*. Because of the overarching nature of our calling to follow Christ, it makes sense that this calling is expressed through our careers, our occupations, and our jobs.[11]

Moreover, everyone has a calling, even when many do not have a clearly defined career or occupation. In other words, my work, my job, or my career might come to an end, but my calling (my *vocatio*), which is all-encompassing and broader, does not. In addition, there might be different seasons within my calling—seasons that seem to involve unrelated jobs, responsibilities, or duties—yet all this occurs within my wider calling. We may encounter detours, changes, or transitions, so that the sheer mystery of walking by faith requires that we employ basic discernment—a discernment that will stabilize us in an awareness of our wider calling and in God's providential care. And because calling operates on the basis of our response, through *affection* rather than *coercion*,[12] it follows that we can deny or resist our calling. This can occur by several means—for example, insensitivity, indifference, or disobedience.

---

thought, in fact, concerns the question of being married, getting married, or remaining married, based on the individual's specific situation as a believer. What is invariably missed or ignored by much commentary on this text is the undergirding premise of Paul's response—namely, *contentedness* in the present. Here, much contemporary commentary on 1 Corinthians 7—Miroslav Volf being representative—misses the spirit of Paul's admonitions. See Volf, *Work in the Spirit: Toward a Theology of Work* (New York: Oxford University Press, 1991), 92–94, 103–7. Luther, however, did not miss it. In Luther's day, contentedness meant "stations" in life, which did *not* mean an utter lack of mobility or unjust support of the status quo (contra Volf, *Work in the Spirit*, 107–8). In fact, Luther and Melanchthon, the latter serving as the chief representative of the Reformation cause at the official level, encouraged others to pursue education, which meant mobility in sixteenth-century terms (as much, that is, as social structures of the time allowed).

11. Douglas J. Schuurman, *Vocation: Discerning Our Calling in Life* (Grand Rapids, MI: Eerdmans, 2004), 47, expresses it in this way: the general call of God to Christ will take specific shape in each Christian's life, just as a prism refracts light into an endless variety of colors.

12. Elton Trueblood, *Your Other Vocation* (New York: Harper, 1952), 65.

Vocational questions, it needs emphasizing, follow us through various stages of our lives—not just when we head off to college, not just when we graduate from college and enter the workforce, but in middle adulthood and later adulthood as well. In any case, the Christian wrestles with—and keeps in tension—two basic vocational questions: How is God calling me to serve him at this time, in this season of life? and What is my wider calling in life, for which I have been given particular gifts, abilities, capacities, and passions or burdens? Having a sense of the latter—an awareness of my wider calling in life—will give meaning and purpose to the particular season in which I presently find myself.

Permit me to illustrate. Two seasons of life, having seemingly nothing to do with each other, help anchor the awareness of personal calling in my own life not only to teach and write but, specifically, to address issues of justice. One season was when I lived in West Germany during the early 1980s, the result of having married a German citizen. My German father-in-law, as it happened, had spent all five years of the Second World War serving with the German army, the *Bundeswehr*, in Poland. Not only that, he had spent all five years of the war in Poland working as a railroad-car switcher—again, *in Poland*. Think of the death camps in that country, such as those in Auschwitz-Birkenau, Sobibor, Warsaw, or Treblinka. One does not need much imagination to wonder what Papa witnessed. Thus, marrying into German culture I am wed to more recent German history.

The second season of life that was formative and confirming of my calling to issues of justice was the early to mid-1990s, during which time I was doing criminal justice research in Washington, DC. There I saw again and again not only the necessity of theological conviction but also the need to be able to translate those convictions in compelling ways in the public arena. Our wider vocational calling, then, unites various seasons of our lives, even when we have difficulty making sense of them at the time.[13]

---

13. Before I was granted a "student seat" (*Studienplatz*) at the German university to study language (one of my main goals in living in West Germany during the 1980s), I was "forced" to work in a cemetery for the better part of a year, digging graves, since this was the only job I could find at the time when the unemployment rate in West Germany was at unprecedented levels. Needless

Perhaps the reader is thinking, "Daryl, all well and good, and very interesting, but what do we mean in practical terms by vocation?" "What does it mean for me to think vocationally?" Perhaps we can answer in the form of several qualifying definitions of the concept of vocation. Properly (and biblically) understood,

- Vocation entails the awareness that we do not choose our calling; rather, it "chooses" us. Just as none of us chooses our DNA, our families, or our children, in the same way we *receive* our vocation from God. In fact, it is more accurate to say that we *discover* rather than receive our vocation, and this discovery tends to be a gradual process.
- Vocation entails the meeting of genuine human need around us. While we cannot meet every need around us, we are equipped in such a way as to be able—through gifts and abilities, energy and influence—to meet some need in a strategic and practical sense.
- Vocation also entails our recognition of skills, talents, and abilities that have been given to each of us by God and of which we are stewards; moreover, it presumes an intentional and guided development of those skills, talents, and abilities.
- Vocation entails a willing desire to serve others, meet genuine need, and thereby serve the common good. What is the Great Commandment identified in the Old Testament and reiterated by Jesus in the New Testament? Love God and love your neighbor.[14] *That* is our calling.
- Vocation entails the recognition that in serving others and the common good we are expressing service and worship—true worship—to God.
- Vocation entails the recognition that we are placed in the world (even when we are not "of" it) and that this placement is in a particular sociocultural context of the world.
- Vocation entails the basic awareness that based on the image of God (i.e., his likeness), we are created for work, which is a form of worship.

---

to say, during this difficult season I struggled and did not have a strong "sense" of *vocatio*!

14. Lev. 19:18; Matt. 22:36–40; Mark 12:28–34; Luke 10:25–28.

- And finally, vocation entails the recognition of work's intrinsic worth, dignity, and value; therefore, work is its own reward in terms of a certain level of satisfaction. Work must not be our identity, but it does offer a measure of satisfaction, properly viewed.[15]

All these definitions or descriptions of vocation or calling have their foundation in theological truth. I refer specifically to the doctrines of creation, providence, redemption, and incarnation, all of which are interlocking and inform one other. A few comments on these doctrines are in order.

In creation we see God calling into existence what he had purposed before the foundations of the created order even appeared. And the centerpiece of creation is the human person, in which is found the *imago Dei*, the very likeness of God. Moreover, based on this likeness, humans are coregents of creation, cocreating, molding, shaping, and extending the created order.

Providence implies meaning and purpose, and it also implies redemption and restoration. It is a distortion to view "the hand of providence" as some rare intervention; rather, it is a moment-by-moment, hour-by-hour, day-by-day presence and guiding of human affairs.[16] Providence is ceaselessly, not occasionally, operative in the affairs of people and nations. This in itself renders daily life and the "mundane" meaningful and purposeful. It follows, then, that human affairs—and my individual life—work together toward a greater, broader design.[17] God's design, indeed, is both general and specific to each of us.

At the same time, it is important to clarify our understanding of divine providence. The doctrine of providence implies neither

---

15. Biblically and theologically, vocation is about serving others and glorifying God, not self-therapy or self-actualization. At the same time, we may expect that a measure of satisfaction comes through our service to God and others. Consider in this regard the discussion of Ecclesiastes 2:24–26; 3:12–13; 5:18–20; 8:15; and 9:7–10 in chapter 9.

16. The reality of God's providential care has been quite helpfully described by Harry Blamires, *The Will and the Way* (New York: Macmillan, 1957), 43–44.

17. In the words of Blamires, *The Will and the Way*, 69: "Vocation is the voice of Providence."

some form of fatalism nor a sort of determinism (to which we *have* to submit). Rather, it implies a purposefulness, which offers hope rather than resignation. Nor does providence cancel out the marvelous realm of free will and human moral agency. Judas's treachery, even when it was allowed to stand, did not defeat Jesus's work nor did it negate redemption; mysteriously, it was used by God toward his redemptive purpose.[18]

Relatedly, we may insist that redemption is part of God's very character, *not* an exception to it or some novel or wildly abstruse intervention that God needed to concoct.[19] And incarnation, which is part of the redemptive process, is part of God's character as well; it is his very nature, as the prologue to the Fourth Gospel makes abundantly clear: "In the beginning ... the Word was God.... And the Word became flesh and dwelt among us" (John 1:1, 14 RSV). God creates. God communicates. God restores. God sustains. And this creative redemptive program applies to "all things"—material and nonmaterial, visible and invisible, as Paul reminds us (Col. 1:15–20). All things belong to God in Christ through creation and redemption.[20]

Where does this lead us? The realities of providence, incarnation, and redemption, alas, lead us neither to pronounce judgment on the world nor curse it, nor to flee from it, nor to isolate ourselves within it, but rather to *enter* it—with all its sin and anguish—and by God's grace to help restore particular spheres of the created order. How? Through our lives and the God-given gifts of which we are stewards. When we offer ourselves in service to God and others, doors open so that redemptive light can shine into the created order. And when my self-offering joins that of millions of other believers, in the words of one theologian, there is "a wonderful, grand interconnectedness

---

18. See Matt. 26:24.

19. Blamires, *The Will and the Way*, 47.

20. John 1:1–3; Heb. 1:2. Douglas Schuurman, *Vocation*, 51, helpfully frames Christian confession as follows: "God created all things; sin infects all things; God redeems all things." For this reason, "Christians, like the Christ whose name they bear, share in God's redemptive and creative purposes in all things.... Therefore, Christian vocation includes all aspects of cultural and social life."

of the Holy Spirit" that realizes the biblical metaphors of salt, light, and leaven.[21]

Providence, redemption, incarnation, and vocation, then, go hand in hand; they are mutually dependent on one another. Together they furnish our theological baseline.

The benefits of thinking vocationally, it must be emphasized, are many; and they are both profound and quite practical. Thinking vocationally will prevent us from a sort of chaotic, out-of-control, day-to-day, meaningless lifestyle that can plague us when we have no sense of direction.[22] This mode of living, of course, takes its toll on us spiritually, mentally, and psychologically. For some of us, it can even lead to despair. Relatedly, thinking vocationally liberates us from what is often called the tyranny of the urgent. It also liberates us from the common but insidious sacred-versus-secular view of work and calling. And it keeps us from a false sense of duty and conformity to the world and its standards, while also freeing us from comparing ourselves with others and becoming people pleasers. Living in the reverential fear of God rather than in the fear of what others think is liberating, causing us to be at peace with ourselves and giving us a boldness and confidence.[23]

Theological Reflections on Work

It is not incidental that the primary doctrines of historic Christian faith describe God's work: he creates, he makes covenant, he redeems, he justifies, he sanctifies, and he promises consummation. From Genesis to Revelation, from creation to the new Jerusalem, "the biblical narratives overflow with work."[24] In the beginning of

---

21. Blamires, *The Will and the Way*, 62.

22. In this regard Calvin notes: "Therefore each individual has his own kind of living assigned to him by the Lord as a sort of sentry post so that he may not heedlessly wander about throughout life." John Calvin, *Institutes of the Christian Religion*, ed. John T. McNeill, trans. Ford Lewis Battles (Louisville: Westminster John Knox, 2006), 3.10.6).

23. No one has expressed the benefits of thinking vocationally more practically and usefully than Gordon T. Smith, *Courage and Calling: Embracing Your God-Given Potential*, rev. ed. (Downers Grove, IL: InterVarsity, 2011), 128–47.

24. Jensen, *Responsive Labor*, 22.

Genesis, moreover, work arises not because of the fall but because of the *imago Dei*.[25] Human work is patterned after the divine model: creative work is done for six days, followed by rest. Moreover, biblical commentators are quick to point out that in Jesus's parabolic teaching, work or work-related themes predominate, and in fact this is the case.[26] And even the apostle to the Gentiles does not abandon his trade after being called by God to take up the apostolic ministry. Even when his trade is not the focus of the New Testament, the apostle still makes tents. And we can assume that the disciples—*all* of them—continued in their professions. In the early church, there were no "clergy"; all were "laity." Fishermen still fished in the Sea of Galilee, even when they were made "fishers of men." In fact, our Lord himself, before a mere three-year messianic stint, spent the better part of thirty years apprenticing and working as a carpenter.

All this is simply to say that work is valuable because of creation, human nature, and the *imago Dei*. Few have argued for the value and dignity of work with greater rhetorical force than Dorothy Sayers, a contemporary of C. S. Lewis. In her 1947 essay "Why Work?" (subsequently included in the volume *Creed or Chaos?*[27]), she calls for "a thoroughgoing revolution in our whole attitude to work." For Sayers, work is not "a necessary drudgery to be undergone for the purpose of making money" but rather "a way of life in which the nature of man should find its proper exercise and delight and so fulfill itself to the glory of God." Work, then, according to Sayers, is best understood as "a creative activity undertaken for the love of the work itself" (assuming that the love of God is present).[28] Sayers believes that several underlying convictions and baseline assumptions need identifying; for her these include the following: (1) human beings image the very nature of God; (2) because of this there exists an almost sacramental

---

25. In the words of Cornelius Plantinga Jr., *Not the Way It's Supposed to Be: A Breviary of Sin* (Grand Rapids, MI: Eerdmans, 1995), 199, "creation is stronger than sin and grace is stronger still."

26. One finds over fifty occurrences in the Gospel accounts of Jesus resorting to parabolic discourse.

27. Dorothy L. Sayers, *Creed or Chaos?* (1949; repr., Manchester: Sophia Institute, 1974), 89–116.

28. Sayers, *Creed or Chaos?*, 89.

relationship between the human person and work; (3) in work the Christian should find spiritual, mental, and physical satisfaction; (4) work is a medium in which the human person offers himself or herself to God; and (5) the only truly "Christian" work is work that is well done.[29]

In fact, the very notion of rewards, clearly taught in the New Testament, presupposes the value of work when it is done with the proper motivation. On that final day, judgment will be according to our works, the apostle Paul insists (2 Cor. 5:10).[30] This means that our efforts here on earth in the present truly mean something; they mean enough, in fact, that their fruit will endure beyond this life. And even when the New Testament writers speak of a new heaven and a new earth, there will be some continuity with the present life. Our works and the created order will not simply be thrown on some cosmic ash heap; they will remain in some discernible form and fashion, even when that form is mysteriously *trans*formed.

The Christian church has not always had a healthy view of work. Historians are quick to point out imbalances and distortions in the church's view of the nature and value of work in virtually every era of the church's existence. One fairly constant theme in historical commentary is the distinction between the *vita contemplativa* and the *vita activa*. This distinction seems to have been very much alive among the ancients and the medievals. It is a distinction, however, that lacks a biblical basis, and for this reason the Lutheran breakthrough in the early sixteenth century was so important. The Protestant Reformation—particularly through Luther and Calvin—would address two primary distortions that have appeared at other times in human history but called for a particularly urgent response by the late-medieval period. The first was the notion of work as salvation—namely, that human activity and efforts can justify a person before a holy God. The second was the sacred-secular dichotomy, which existed because of the religious devaluation of earthly occupations, as personified in monastic orders and the priesthood. Luther's response was nothing short of prophetic: every Christian's "call" is to love the neighbor through his or her work and to serve in that

---

29. Sayers, *Creed or Chaos?*, 101, 108.
30. Cf. 1 Pet. 1:17; Rev. 20:12; Ps. 62:12; Prov. 24:12; and Eccl. 12:14.

particular "station," whatever it might be.[31] Work, then, for Luther, was a divine vocation. When people asked what they should do, the *last* thing Luther could recommend was to retreat into a monastery; rather, serve God and others *where you are*. Every believer is a priest, serving God and society through work.

Concluding Reflections

The subjects of our calling and of discerning our vocation typically lead at some point to a discussion of divine guidance. Few topics are more slippery, at least in Christian circles, than that of guidance. And because much confusion often attends Christian thinking about the subject, several comments here are perhaps appropriate. While it is true, as I have argued, that in calling us God speaks and communicates, this occurs typically through "whispers," circumstances, and the inaudible and not through a booming voice, trumpets, or lightning strikes—nor through laying out fleeces. Perhaps the best advice, then, in terms of learning discernment—which is a process—is that we develop a "listening heart," a quiet soul, an attentive inner posture. While this perhaps sounds terribly impractical and theoretical, it nevertheless needs emphasizing, in order that we avoid the common evangelical tendency to understand the will of God in four, five, or six formulaic steps. While this latter attempt might sell books, it fails to acknowledge the simple mystery of communing with God and developing a "listening heart."[32] "Be still, and know that I am God," admonishes the psalmist (Ps. 46:10 RSV). More importantly, developing a listening heart will free us from the fear or dread that we somehow will miss God, as if God's will is a train

---

31. For Luther "stations" correspond to social structures that are assigned by God; *vocatio*, then, is our response to those duties in our stations, as Luther saw it. See *Luther's Works*, ed. Jaroslav Pelikan, Helmut T. Lehmann, and Christopher Brown (Philadelphia: Fortress; St. Louis: Concordia, 1955–), 17:384.

32. On this see Suzanne G. Farnham et al., *Listening Hearts: Discerning Call in Community*, rev. ed. (New York: Morehouse, 2011).

that leaves the station at five minutes before eleven and if I am not on it, I am forever sunk.[33]

In addition to developing an inner quietness (which, let us be honest, is a *fight* in our cultural environment but which is *absolutely crucial* for our survival), we should do very natural things such as assess our own gifts and abilities and recognize how God has uniquely equipped us individually. This is one of the reasons being in community is so important; as part of Christ's body we are subject to the push-pull, give-and-take, and impulses of other parts of the body. In community we discover and sharpen those various gifts and capacities that God has given us.[34] Moreover, this personal assessment needs to be honest, and without comparing ourselves to others or succumbing to a sort of false humility. Basic personal motivations factor as well into fulfilling our vocational calling—for example, not being driven by money or prestige or cultural affirmation. Additionally, as already noted, we must genuinely desire to serve others, which is the real meaning of neighbor-love. Finally, we must keep in mind that calling and vocation are generally gradual in nature, a process of discovery, a pilgrimage, as it were. There is

---

33. Simply stated, God's will is foremost neither geographical nor circumstantial; rather, it is relational. The will of God is that we commune with God in the present.

34. In "The Ordered Life: Between Solitude and Community," chapter 12 of *Courage and Calling*, Gordon T. Smith describes two "anchors" that need to be working in symbiosis: being an integral part of community and finding solitude in our busy and complicated lives. We are members of the body of Christ and thus discover our calling not in isolation but in community with others. After all, in community there exists a healthy give-and-take in terms of needs, dialogue, wisdom, and discernment. Balancing this corporate need is the necessity of finding quiet for the soul in times of contemplation. Mentally, emotionally, and spiritually we cannot live without this component. And because the culture around us oppressively stamps this out, we must fight for it. This "space" doubtless will also need reinforcement through fasting—from food, pleasure, and technology. In solitude we find God; in solitude we are renewed; and in solitude we grasp a sense of our calling, part of which is simply being still and knowing that the Lord he is God (Ps. 46:10).

usually no straight line in that process; there are detours along the way with which we will need to reckon.[35]

Which brings me to the matter of the changing seasons in our lives. I opened with wisdom literature, and with wisdom literature I shall close. Not only does the book of Ecclesiastes contrast two opposing world- and life-views ("under-the-sun" secularism on the one hand over against a theistic outlook on the other), revealing their very different perspectives on human activity including work, the book also observes what is a painful discovery for most people—namely, there is a time and season for every purpose under heaven (Eccl. 3:1). In short, seasons of pain and sorrow, hardship and distress, dying and grief *will* visit us. To be ignorant of the wisdom perspective on life is to be blindsided by these intrusions, and for many, to fall into despair, even to the point of contemplating suicide. That we incur detours does not cancel out the fact of our individual vocational calling. It only underscores the fact that our calling is a journey, with twists and turns that require us, again and again, to receive the gift of God's grace, which *will be there* for the taking.

In the context of the emergence of the Confessing Church three generations ago, theologian Emil Brunner stated the truth of the importance of vocation. As an idea, Brunner noted, vocation "has been degraded, so disgracefully, into something quite trivial" and "has been denuded of its daring and liberating religious meaning" to such an extent that "we might even ask whether it would not be better to renounce it altogether." On the other hand, he insisted, "it is a conception which in its Scriptural sense is so full of force and so pregnant in meaning" that "to renounce this expression would mean losing a central part of the Christian message. We must not throw it away, but we must regain its original meaning."[36] Brunner made this declaration as storm clouds were gathering over Europe in the 1930s (the German original was published in 1932 under the

---

35. For a penetrating examination of the spiritual and psychological dimensions that belong to the process of discernment, see John P. Neafsey, "Psychological Dimensions of the Discernment of Vocation," in *Revisiting the Idea of Vocation: Theological Explorations*, ed. J. C. Haughey (Washington, DC: Catholic University of America Press, 2012), 163–89.

36. Emil Brunner, *The Divine Imperative* (Philadelphia: Westminster, 1947), 205–6.

title *Das Gebot und die Ordnungen*). One might conclude that, quite tragically, the church did not heed his call.

With Brunner, we too stand in a period of extraordinary upheaval. And with Brunner we might argue as well that to renounce the notion of vocation is to lose a central—if not *the* central—part of the Christian message. Time will tell whether the Christian church—at least in the West—will "regain its original meaning."

Do we wish all of life to be infused with meaning and purpose? May we all live with a settled sense of our personal vocational calling, which can anchor us regardless of the season.

Eight

Education as Vocation*

Although I have taught chiefly in the Christian university context for the last three decades, I first became more intimately acquainted with your fine institution about ten years ago through my oldest son. He had then just arrived here to work as the assistant coach of the men's soccer team, and shortly thereafter he met his future wife here. She is an accomplished graduate of this university. I can say that in the years since, my appreciation for John Brown University has increased.

Recently I was elated to participate here at your university in an economics and virtue symposium (yes, the two can and do coexist). Thus, it goes without saying that I am honored to return to address this esteemed institution on the occasion of your celebration of academic scholarship and excellence. There will always be a special place in my heart for JBU. Thank you for the invitation.

What does Jerusalem have to do with Athens? Or, as it is often asked, What does Athens have to do with Jerusalem? People usually get the order wrong, but it is the point behind the question that interests me. What *does* Jerusalem have to do with Athens? It was

---

*Chapel address delivered at John Brown University on April 19, 2018.

a rhetorical question posed by the second-century church father Tertullian, who worried that Christians might get sidetracked or misled by philosophers and educators of his day.

By "Athens," Tertullian was referring to intellectual culture and the life of the mind—namely, the study of language, philosophy, history, literature, the arts, and the sciences. And by "Jerusalem," he meant the life of faith and redemption through Christ. It is in his treatise *Prescriptions against Heretics*, written in AD 198, that Tertullian asks the Jerusalem–Athens question and cites philosophy, in particular, as the root of heresy and foolishness.[1] Since we have Christ, the end of all things, he reasons, why do we need intellectual culture? Why do we need to study and research? After all, on the last day you and I will not be judged according to how much pagan wisdom we have assimilated and how much we have studied.

Tertullian's rhetorical question regarding Athens and Jerusalem remains every bit as relevant eighteen centuries later as it was in his day. Consider C. S. Lewis, only three generations removed from us, in the mid-twentieth century. It is well known that Lewis experienced a sort of double conversion—a spiritual and intellectual conversion—in coming to Christian faith. In a most interesting autobiographical note found in his essay "Christianity and Culture," Lewis concedes that in becoming a Christian he swung from one extreme, pursuing intellectual and cultural activity, to the other, rejecting everything about culture and being tempted to withdraw. He writes:

> At an early age I came to believe that the life of culture (that is, of intellectual and aesthetic activity) was very good for its own sake. After my conversion, which occurred in my later twenties, I continued to hold this belief without consciously asking how it could be reconciled with my new belief that the end of human life was salvation in Christ and the glorifying of God. I was awakened from this confused state of mind by finding that the friends of culture seemed to me to be exaggerating. In my reaction against what seemed exaggerated I was driven to the other extreme, and began, in my own mind, to belittle

---

1. See volume 3 of *The Ante-Nicene Fathers*, ed. Alexander Roberts and James Donaldson (New York: Charles Scribner's Sons, 1903), available at http://www.newadvent.org/fathers/0311.htm.

the claims of culture. As soon as I did this I was faced with the question, "If it is a thing of so little value, how are you justified in spending so much of your life on it?"[2]

This is a fair question, is it not? If culture, the life of the mind, intellectual pursuit, scholarship, scientific research, and learning are of such little value (at least according to the Tertullians of our day), then how can we justify spending so much of our lives in it? I myself have spent almost a lifetime in it. Perhaps I have missed my calling? Perhaps I have made a grave error? Perhaps I have been fiddling while Rome is burning?

Tertullian's rhetorical question confronts us with a more basic question that every person must answer: Does education per se have value? If not, then why on earth would you shell out thousands of dollars a year to attend a university? Why do something so foolish?

But let us not give Tertullian too much credit in our day. My own experience parallels that of Lewis to a certain, though far lesser, extent. After my conversion as a young adult in the early 1970s at the tail end of the "Jesus Movement," I was surrounded by extremely zealous Christians who were consumed by only one thing: *What if Jesus comes back soon?* This sort of top-heavy eschatological focus, of course, was typical of the Jesus Movement. I recall those fascinating days of the 1970s when I worked with a Christian organization and did street theater and pantomime as a platform for evangelism. The zeal that characterized our community was notable. Team members were literally praying in their daily needs, including tubes of toothpaste; everyone was poor but content because we were zealous and serving the Lord. No one—and certainly not I—had any interest in education—until, that is, my own eyes began to open, both theologically and culturally, over time. It was during this season of doing street theater that I met my future wife, a European citizen, and we would spend the early years of marriage living in Europe. As I learned during those years of living abroad, there is nothing quite like living abroad for an extended period of time to teach you how

---

2. C. S. Lewis, "Christianity and Culture," in *Christian Reflections*, ed. Walter Hooper (London: Geoffrey Bles, 1967), 14.

important culture is, how important education is, and how important language is.

The Tertullians of any age, of course, remind us that we are in the world but not of it. They prefer to emphasize the latter half of that phrase—"not of it." At the same time, they tend to downplay or disregard the first half. But the truth is that after we are redeemed, we are then not immediately removed from the world; we are left here on earth and in various cultural contexts. Why? To mirror the glory and majesty and redemptive character of the Creator. Recently I read a book that I wish had come to me years ago when I was a young Christian. The title is *Heaven Is Not My Home*, and the subtitle is *Living in the Now of God's Creation*.[3] The author, Paul Marshall, serves as a senior fellow at the Hudson Institute, a think tank in Washington, DC. It is a book well worth the read, and its argument—as the title somewhat provocatively suggests—is that in some of our pious Christian circles, our theology has caused us to downplay our earthly citizenship, and with it the implications for faithful stewardship of the created order, in favor of a bloated eschatology that has encouraged in us the desire to be raptured away from earthly responsibility.

Alas, the Tertullian error of isolation or separatism fails to take seriously all of creation. It downplays or is resentful of human culture, and it fails to appreciate the width and breadth of redemption. This stands in strong contrast to the emphatic teaching of Paul in his letter to the Colossians: that Christ has redeemed "all things"—*all things* visible and invisible, material and immaterial (Col. 1:15–20). The teaching that Jesus Christ is both the Creator and Redeemer of all things serves to underscore the fact of the goodness and value of the created order.

But there is, of course, an equal and opposite error to that of isolation. It is the tendency toward capitulation. Like withdrawal, it too is an ever-present possibility in every generation. This mind-set fails to discern, to test, to probe, to question, and to affirm what is true in a world of mixed allegiances. While isolationists and separatists downplay or disregard the fact that creation is good, belonging to

---

3. Paul Marshall with Lela Gilbert, *Heaven Is Not My Home: Living in the Now of God's Creation* (Nashville: Word, 1998).

Christ, and hence is something to be cultivated, capitulationists are completely absorbed into the culture so that no discernible difference can be found in their lives. The temptation toward capitulation, of course, is all around us; it is the air we breathe, and it is a temptation of every generation. In the realm of education, one need only look at the experience of American colleges and universities to observe capitulation at work, as though it were almost inevitable. In a two-part essay titled "The Decline and Fall of the Christian College," which eventually became a book with the title *The Dying of the Light: The Disengagement of Colleges and Universities from Their Churches*,[4] author James Burtchaell has catalogued the remarkable number of colleges and universities that started out as church-affiliated and authentically Christian and then in time severed their commitment to the church and confessional Christian faith. Consider this very cursory (though telling) list:

- Originally founded as Presbyterian institutions: Princeton, Macalester, Hanover, University of Tulsa, Agnes Scott, Centre
- Founded as Baptist institutions: Vassar, Brown, Wake Forest, Spelman
- Founded as Quaker institutions: Haverford, Swarthmore, Whittier, Earlham, Guilford, Bryn Mawr
- Founded as Congregationalist institutions: Dartmouth, Yale, Williams, Smith, Fisk
- Founded as Lutheran institutions: Valparaiso, St. Olaf, Luther, Hartwick, Wittenberg
- Founded as Methodist institutions: Duke, Emory, Northwestern, University of Southern California, Syracuse, Vanderbilt
- Founded as Episcopalian institutions: University of the South (Sewanee), Hobart, Bard, William & Mary, Kenyon

The logical question is this: Where are the institutions that embody *both* faithfulness to Christ *and* academic excellence? Why does the

---

4. James T. Burtchaell, "The Decline and Fall of the Christian College," *First Things*, no. 12 (April 1991): 16–29; no. 13 (May 1991): 30–38; idem, *The Dying of the Light: The Disengagement of Colleges and Universities from Their Churches* (Grand Rapids, MI: Eerdmans, 1998).

empirical evidence seem to suggest that once we get serious about scholarship or having high standards, not wishing to be sectarian, the faith commitment almost always seems to lag or disappear? In the strongest terms, I wish to maintain that it does not have to be that way. It is not inevitable that to be forward-thinking or to be gifted means that we compromise. Now, it is true, we must acknowledge that sometimes where virtue and piety are found there is no talent or giftedness. And it is true on occasion that good, pious people are not attractive, while cunning, wicked, or unprincipled people are brilliant and appealing. But this is not God's design, based on creation and redemption; hence, that skewed model need not be our model.

Because of the image of God within us, we are created for excellence in all that we do. There is simply no excuse for wanting to have piety yet doing something that is second rate. The story is told—and it may well be apocryphal—that the late fourth-century bishop of the church Augustine was chastised on one occasion by a fellow Christian who asked him somewhat condescendingly, "Why do you go all the way across town and buy your sandals from that pagan cobbler who cares not one bit for your faith?" To which Augustine responded in essence, "Because he makes a better sandal." Shame on us if we do not do things well—if we do not create, build, study, and perform with excellence.

Standing alongside the foundational doctrines of creation and redemption is the doctrine of the incarnation. God took on human flesh. God became one of us. God entered into our experience. Let me ask of you this question: What do you think Jesus was doing for almost thirty years of his life before he formally began his brief, three-year "ministry"? He was apprenticing as a carpenter, learning from his father. Do you think the Son of God—the Incarnate One, the One who fashioned the universe—built bad furniture? Do you think that he did shoddy woodwork? The Prince of Glory is glorious, and not to have his standards mirrored in our work is a sham; it is simply deficient and unacceptable. I say this humbly, not judgmentally.

John Henry Newman, the author of one of the most important books ever written on the purpose of the university, *The Idea of a University*, wrote on the occasion of his first sermon at the University of Dublin: "I wish the intellect to range with the utmost freedom.... I wish ... the same individuals to be at once oracles of philosophy and shrines of devotion."[5] Consider the import of those words: "the same individuals" to be gifted, even brilliant, yet holy and humble. Newman understood the purpose of the university not just to be spiritual formation, important as that is, but the formation of intellectual culture. Developing intellectual culture, properly understood, does not undermine or denigrate Christian faith; rather, it is the sheer expression of bona fide faith. The university exists to help reunite and reconcile all things to God. God through Christ created all things, and God through Christ redeemed all things. We may, therefore, say that all things are doubly his, *especially* the realm of education. Therefore, we need not feel guilty when we love studying economics or spinning mathematical equations or doing scientific research or learning language or exploring human psychology and philosophy or performing dance and the fine arts. These are all part of creation, and *all things* have been redeemed, belonging to Christ.

The doctrines of creation, redemption, and incarnation, then, combine to transform everything in the human experience, especially education. Everything we do, when viewed through this lens, begins to take on a different shape, a glory and a wonder all its own. For me personally, that revelation came in the context of language study. When I went to live in West Germany in the 1980s, I was unable to speak a word of German. After living there for a period of years and studying German and linguistics at the German university level for two of those years, I came to enjoy learning for the first time in my life (before that I was never a great student, nor was I an avid reader). I also realized while living abroad that I have an aptitude for language, and during those years I came to recognize how important culture is and how necessary language study is in order to open doors within a culture for cumulative Christian witness. As we inhabit a specific sociocultural context to which God has called us, there is a sense in which communication is everything. Do Christians really understand the extent and ramifications of this reality? "In the beginning was the Word, and the Word was with God, and the Word was God.... And the Word became flesh" (John 1:1, 14 RSV). The Word was *incarnated.*

---

5. John Henry Newman, "Intellect, the Instrument of Religious Training," in *Sermons Preached on Various Occasions* (repr., London: Longmans, Green and Co., 1921), 13.

Are we not exceedingly glad that God, the master communicator, communicated his best to humanity? The eternal Word continues to incarnate himself to the world that he himself created—a task that has been committed to creation's redeemed.

Education, then, is part of our cultural, redemptive, and incarnational mandate. Because of the image of God within (that is, his likeness), we create, design, extend, shape, and develop all of creation. This is stewardship; we are stewards of all God's creation.

This brings us to the second part of my argument. Authentic integration is the fruit—the by-product—of a sturdy theology of creation, redemption, incarnation, and *one additional element*: I refer here to vocation. Quite simply, we in the church and in Christian liberal arts education must rediscover and reclaim the notion of vocation. Tragically, vocation is one of the most misunderstood—and neglected—areas of teaching in the Christian church. The word itself has been neutered and debased to mean "occupation," "job," "job training," or "employment." This neglect or distortion, it needs emphasizing, is not merely a case of extreme secularizing; it is also the result of misguided religious thinking that dominates our own Christian circles. Sadly, much evangelical teaching and preaching, if it has not fallen captive to the idolatry of church growth, focuses exclusively on the spiritual life or the vertical dimension of faith rather than its horizontal or social dimension, leaving us, I am sorry to say, bankrupt in the marketplace, where most of us spend much of our lives.[6]

Moreover, vocation (properly construed) is practically ignored at the seminary level, where Christian leaders and pastors are trained. And where the notion of vocation, on rare occasion, *is* treated, seminary education tends to inculcate and further the prevailing and mistaken sacred-versus-secular division. After all, those attending seminary typically are headed into the pastorate or church ministry. For this reason, not infrequently you will hear seminary students say, "I quit my job to go to seminary," or "I quit my job to go into

---

6. Lest I be misunderstood, I am not opposed to teaching that seeks to fortify the personal element of faith. What I lament is a focus of teaching that emphasizes what God is doing *in* me to the virtual exclusion of what he is doing—or wishes to do—*through* me.

Christian ministry." Notice the flawed assumption here: a "regular job" is less meaningful, it is less holy, and only "full-time Christian work"—whatever *that* is—is thought to be a higher calling. To which I say, balderdash! Much to the contrary, I must insist that a "secular" job is, in fact, a *holy vocation*. Brothers and sisters, the fact of the matter is that very few of us are called to the pastorate or church work or "full-time Christian ministry."[7] Most all of us are called to the marketplace. In our day, Christians who are lawyers, businesspeople, bankers, social workers, artists, and educators receive precious little help from the pulpit and pastoral leadership in terms of vocation.

In my four decades of being a Christian, I cannot recall hearing a single sermon or teaching on the marketplace and secular work as a high calling and holy vocation. Not a single one. Why? This is puzzling because vocation is a distinctively Christian concept that applies to *every* believer and which determines our fruitfulness and effectiveness in all of life. It encompasses the entirety of our lives—all our capacities, gifts, and proclivities—whether we are young or old. Each of you has a vocation, a calling, with gifts and abilities that correspond to that vocation. So we begin by clearing the table: there is no such thing as a higher or lower calling. There is no such thing as a sacred-versus-secular divide in life. Based on creation and redemption, everything is sacred (unless, of course, it is clearly shown through Scripture to be evil per se). Recall the first half of my address: all things were created by Jesus, and all things have been redeemed, reconciled to him, their creator and rightful owner.

Both Catholics and Protestants, it needs pointing out, have frequently created a false sacred-versus-secular dichotomy throughout the church's history. One of the most significant breakthroughs of the Protestant Reformation in the sixteenth century, particularly through the teaching of Luther and Calvin, was the insistence that all work, all occupations, and all activities are sacred and have value before God, as long as they are performed out of two govern-

---

7. I am not denying here the value of those who are called to the pastorate. I am simply arguing that the notion of "full-time Christian ministry" often has had the unfortunate effect of reinforcing the false dichotomy between the sacred and the secular. The workplace is every bit as high and holy a calling as vocational church work.

ing motivations: service to God and service to our neighbor. All work is sacred, whether one is a cabinet maker, a plumber, a farmer, a cobbler, a ruler, or a priest. It follows, then, that all Christians are priests (1 Pet. 2:4–9; Rev. 1:5–6). The concept of the priesthood of every believer, stressing the vocational calling of each person who confesses Christ, radically affected sixteenth-century life and society. In the same way, every successive generation needs to rediscover the Christian doctrine of vocation.

Here, then, is the first implication of the doctrine of vocation, a uniquely Christian idea: namely, a leveling or collapsing of any supposed sacred-versus-secular dichotomy and an elevating, sanctifying, and ennobling of every line of work under creation. That includes education and scholarship, whatever its specific focus and discipline. Let us remember that because all things have been redeemed, all things are fair game vocationally.

The second thing that the concept of vocation teaches is that every believer has been called and equipped with gifts for his or her particular calling. Paul writes to the Corinthians that each person has been assigned a place in life to which God has specifically called him or her. The Lutheran notion of having a station of life assigned—that is, a particular calling in terms of work and service—points to the doctrine of divine providence, which is to say that God leads and guides us continually, whereby we simply respond to his initiative in gratitude through our entire lives. To the Christians living in the imperial seat of Rome, Paul writes that we all have different gifts, according to the measure of grace given each of us (Rom. 12:3–8). And Peter tells us that we should steward the gifts that God has given us (1 Pet. 4:10).

Here we may pause for a moment and reflect. What is the question that virtually every university student dreads? Whether it comes from family or friends, it is likely the question, What are your plans after graduation? I shall never forget one such conversation I had with a former student of mine at Taylor University. This precious young woman whom I had in my theology class knocked on my office door *two weeks before graduation* and sheepishly asked if she might discuss a matter that had been vexing her. She absolutely dreaded heading back home in two weeks following her graduation. Why? Because she could not answer *the two big questions* that her parents would be asking her: What do you expect to be doing now after graduation? and Have you met anyone special?

Why the dread—a dread which is by no means found solely among students who are set to enter the job market, even when it understandably tends to plague this social group? I have personally found that not just students on the eve of graduation but older Christians as well, even retirement-age folks, struggle with the same concern—namely, identifying their vocational calling, a calling that includes work or occupation but that also transcends it. Permit me to gently probe, at this point, and ask, Do you know your calling, your vocation? What are your gifts and talents? Let it be clearly stated that there is a direct correlation between our gifts or talents and our calling. We do not need blinding-light revelations or the laying out of fleeces like Gideon in order to recognize what these gifts and talents are; rather, they show themselves quite naturally. This does not mean, of course, that there will not be seeming detours or seasons of our lives in which we struggle with a lack of clarity. It does mean, however, that we can be confident in God's leading and find satisfaction in our work—*all* work, regardless of where we are planted. Permit me once more to illustrate.

When I went to live in Germany in 1980, I did not know how long I would be living there; as it turned out, it was nearly four years. What I *did* know was that I needed to learn the language; as previously noted, I spoke not a sentence when I arrived. Before I found an opening in a language school, we needed income; that means I needed to find a job—*any* job. At the time, Germany was struggling with a 13 percent unemployment rate, which was catastrophic by their standards. So I went to the employment office in the city where we lived. There I was informed of three available job possibilities, two of them requiring training, which seemed out of the question at the time. The third did not and was temporary, a three-week gig working in—of all places—a cemetery. My long-term sense of calling, I can assure you, did *not* include digging graves and doing what was only glorified landscaping. And yet, not having any other alternatives but needing some sort of income, I took the job, thinking, "God, I cannot believe it, you lead me to Germany for who knows how long, and *this is what I get* in response!"

To make a long story short, a three-week temporary position became a permanent position (to my surprise), after which deliverance came and I was granted a "student seat" (*Studienplatz*) at the university to begin language study. That season of working in a cemetery was important, painful as it was, and God in his providence had a purpose behind it; I simply could not see it. I ended up spending several years studying language and linguistics at the university, so that in time I actually became quite proficient—proficient enough that some years later I translated a book (German to English) on proverbial wisdom in ancient Near Eastern culture written by a famous German Old Testament scholar.[8]

From digging graves I did go on to do language study and then returned to the United States for graduate studies, after which I did public policy research in Washington, DC, before entering the university classroom, where for several decades various threads in my calling have been united. I understand my own vocational calling, which includes my job but which extends beyond it, as a call to the academy and the church as a teacher and writer, and to bring Christian faith to bear on public life, including public policy.

Before I close, permit me to return to several previous and related questions: What is your vocational calling? What are your talents and abilities? What are your passions and burdens? As we assess our own inclinations and priorities, we can know that particular passions or burdens are from God when they *endure*—that is, when they do not lessen or fade over time. Our gifts, talents, and burdens have been given to us for two purposes: to serve God and to serve the needs of our neighbor. It is, therefore, dishonoring to the Creator to disregard or bury what has been given to us, as the parable of the talents teaches (Matt. 25:14–30). But I am convinced that most of us are looking for a calling, not a job.

In summary, (1) education is an important part of our cultural, redemptive, and incarnational mandate; and (2) education and our work are best understood in terms of vocation and calling. Therefore, within the Christian community we must rediscover and reclaim vocation, properly understood, if we are to thrive—whether in our

---

8. Claus Westermann, *Roots of Wisdom: The Oldest Proverbs of Israel and Other Peoples*, trans. J. Daryl Charles (Louisville: Westminster John Knox, 1995).

personal lives, in our work, or in the educational enterprise. The danger perhaps is not simply failing to appreciate intellectual life as much as it is failing to appreciate the *deep and inherently Christian significance* of intellectual life. We should be ever mindful that the university was conceived by the church; the university was born only because of the church. We must never forget that.

May we all, by God's grace, resist the temptation either to withdraw and separate ourselves from the culture or to capitulate and be wholly absorbed into the culture. May we be faithful stewards of all that God has created and redeemed. And may we all, in the words of John Henry Newman, be simultaneously "oracles of philosophy and shrines of devotion."

Virtually all of you are called to the marketplace, few of you are called to church work, and some of you are called to education in some way. In any event, may you thrive during this present season of your lives. May you know the hope of your calling, not just in a general sense of being called to Christian faith but also in a very particular sense in terms of knowing your individual vocational calling. And may you have listening, discerning hearts, so that you are in tune with—rather than being frustrated by—God's guidance. Finally, may you be anchored by the peace of Christ as you go through various seasons—seasons of change—as you move forward in the desire to fulfill your calling before God, in Christ, and by the Holy Spirit.

Nine

Wisdom and Work: Perspectives on Human Labor from Ecclesiastes*

Wisdom Literature and the Wisdom Perspective

Ecclesiastes represents one of the most—if not *the most*—intriguing and misunderstood books in the entire biblical canon. Few writings have generated more diverse interpretive approaches, and none has resulted in more diverse understandings than this remarkable piece of literature, even among professional scholars. This diversity at the technical level has not served the church, in terms of its teaching and preaching ministry, particularly well. Given the wisdom that is resident within this literary masterpiece, the neglect of its insights results in great loss.

Ecclesiastes is part of a literary genre called wisdom literature. Significantly, the wisdom perspective was common to wider ancient Near Eastern culture and not merely to Israel, even when Hebrew wisdom, canonized in the text of the Old Testament, has remained with us more than its ancient counterparts. The wisdom perspective concerns itself chiefly with how to live and thus is universal and

---

* This essay is adapted from a longer version that appeared in the *Journal of Markets & Morality* 22, no. 1 (Spring 2019), and is reproduced with permission.

enduring in its character, applicable to ancient as well as modern life. Particular features that are peculiar to the wisdom genre are worthy of note. Wisdom literature is inherently didactic in character and takes on a peculiar literary form. With a quest for understanding the human condition, it focuses chiefly on practical life experience and for this reason is marked by a particular language and vocabulary. In addition, because its concerns are primarily epistemological in nature, its format may be speculative or it can be declarative—for example, in the form of parables or wise sayings. Relatedly, its theological orientation is indirect and anchored in creation.

Wisdom is depicted in Scripture as having framed all of creation (Prov. 8:22–31; cf. Col. 1:17; 2:3; Heb. 1:2). Hence, its beginning is the fear of the Lord (Job 28:28; Prov. 1:7, 29; 2:5; 3:7; 9:10), who is sovereign over all of creation, and its value is supreme, surpassing that of gold or silver and all things deemed precious in the material world (Prov. 2:4; 3:14–15; 8:10). To be wise, then, is to be guided throughout life by this central aspect of common grace.[1] To have wisdom is to walk in harmony with the Creator.

Wisdom literature—and hence the wisdom perspective—is important for numerous reasons, as is suggested above. Three reasons in particular strike me as basic in our day. For one, we live in a foolish culture—a fact that applies to virtually all of modern Western societies—so that to make claims in the public sphere that call for virtuous behavior, moral formation, or moral discernment inevitably results in charges of being hate-filled, bigoted, and intolerant. To seek wisdom is decidedly out of step with the times. Second, most formal attempts in the twenty-first century to account for either virtue or vice tend to reduce (at least in Western culture) to biology, neuroscience, or related materialist constructions of the human person and the human brain. Third, and perhaps most importantly, standard Christian teaching and preaching, in almost wholesale fashion, ignores wisdom literature with its invaluable perspectives

---

1. In theological terms, common grace is distinct from particular grace. By the former, all creation is maintained and preserved through God's providential care; by the latter—i.e., what we call special revelation—we enter into communion with God through Christ by means of cleansing from sin and walking in newness of spiritual life.

and is often subservient to the cultural-ecclesial idols of church growth, seeker-friendliness, numerical assessments of success, and the like. We miss valuable insights into living, to our great peril, by ignoring wisdom literature—among these: the importance of virtue and moral formation, lessons from physical nature that bear upon human nature, the value of suffering, the reality of divine providence in light of life's mystery, and an anatomy of stewardship.

As already suggested, wisdom literature can take multiple forms—for example, parable, allegory, riddle, proverb, didactic poetry, or philosophical treatise, with the book of Ecclesiastes fitting into the latter category. And because of its genre, attempting to interpret Ecclesiastes is difficult, as evidenced by a perusal of most biblical commentaries and its general neglect in standard teaching and preaching. That works such as Job and Ecclesiastes are more speculative and less "practical" than, say, the book of Proverbs does not, however, detract from their essence as wisdom literature. Part of the wisdom perspective is to wrestle with the problem of suffering and life's mystery and to search for life's meaning. Although from a human vantage point divine wisdom is impenetrable, as it enters the human experience it nevertheless sheds partial light on the mystery of providence—light that will allow human beings to practice discernment, persist in the midst of suffering, put mystery in its proper perspective, and walk in harmony with their Creator. Ecclesiastes, then, may serve as a necessary antidote to shallow self-righteousness and unreflective belief.

Interpretive Strategy in Ecclesiastes

Whether in the past or the present, a large part of the problem in understanding Ecclesiastes is the character of the book. The major interpretive problem is to adequately understand and explain the book's apparent internal contradictions. The average layperson might be tempted to despair when realizing the extent to which Old Testament scholars themselves disagree over the book's interpretation and the degree to which they question the book's orthodoxy. The majority of commentators understand the message of Ecclesiastes to be fundamentally negative and despairing. For example, one commentator asserts: "In fact, it [Ecclesiastes] denies some of the things on which the other [biblical] writers lay the greatest stress—notably that God has revealed himself and his will to man."[2] And another laments: "Life is profitless...totally absurd. This oppressive message lies at the heart of the Bible's strangest book. Enjoy life if you can ... for old age will soon overtake you. And even as you enjoy, know that the world is meaningless. Virtue does not bring reward. The deity stands distant, abandoning humanity to chance and death."[3] And yet another commentator discounts the presence in Ecclesiastes of any "epistemological, ethical, or metaphysical" guidelines, being resigned to the book's message of life's "ultimate worthlessness."[4] In the end, by hereby rendering the book of Ecclesiastes so problematic, Old Testament scholarship tragically has rendered it virtually inaccessible to the contemporary reader.

Presented to the reader in Ecclesiastes is neither a sermon nor a narrative in the strictest sense, but rather a mixture of observations—and specifically, contrasting observations—about life's meaning and wisdom sayings, couched in an almost brooding skepticism, all of which together might seem at times to contradict and at other times to support earlier observations. Consistent with a standard technique found in wisdom literature, however, the wider strategy of the writer of Ecclesiastes[5] is to contrast and compare—that is, to juxtapose—and to repeat various insights. That is, the writer moves back and forth throughout the treatise seamlessly without telling

---

2. R. B. Y. Scott, *Proverbs and Ecclesiastes* (Garden City, NY: Doubleday, 1965), 191. Moreover, Scott writes: "In Ecclesiastes God is not only unknown to man through revelation; he is unknowable through reason, the only means by which the author believes knowledge is attainable." The book, in the end, constitutes "a philosophy of resignation," the writer's ethic "has no relationship to divine commandments," and "his views run counter to those of his religious fellow Jews" (191–92).

3. James L. Crenshaw, *Ecclesiastes* (Philadelphia: Westminster, 1987), 23.

4. J. W. Gericke, "Axiological Assumptions in Qohelet: A Historical-Philosophical Clarification," *Verbum et Ecclesia* 33, no. 1 (2012): 6.

5. I will simply assume "Qoheleth," which is a transliteration of the Hebrew word translated "Preacher" or "Teacher" (Eccl. 1:1, 2), to be the writer. However, this essay does not concern itself with questions of authorship, dating, canonicity, literary genre, or language—matters that are sufficiently addressed in standard critical commentaries.

the reader along the way, "Now, pay attention: this is a contrast" or "Now a shift." Not once, not twice, but continually this technique is employed, often to the consternation of the average reader, who is perhaps hoping for a clearer, straight-line approach to interpretation. A key in interpreting both the form and content of Ecclesiastes is to grasp the dialectical method underlying the entire work.[6] Contrast is the organizing principle.

Having observed dialectic in Ecclesiastes, we must sharpen this thesis a bit. Not only are two ways of thinking, two approaches to life, two views of ultimate reality being compared in the book, they are presented in sharpest relief. That is, they stand in diametric opposition. Let us call them antitheses, or, quite simply, contradictions. The despair that arises in Ecclesiastes emanates from the writer-teacher's oft-repeated lament that in spite of *everything*, he fails to find *anything* of meaning. If we allow the tensions and ambiguities in Ecclesiastes to stand, however, we may discover that there is interplay between two polarities of thought, between two contradictory perspectives. Contradiction does not cancel out coherence. Hence, what seem to amount to blatant contradictions in the human existence, alas, are reconcilable in the economy of God.[7] Consider the reflections gathered in 3:1–8—reflections that seem to bear out the reconciling of what are incongruities in human experience. There is a "time"[8] and "season"—and this "under heaven"—for "everything"; hence, seeming contradictions and absurdities, which encompass virtually everything in the human experience, have meaning and purpose *if* viewed according to a proper framework of reality. These opposites,

---

6. So Leland Ryken, "Ecclesiastes," in *A Complete Literary Guide to the Bible*, ed. Leland Ryken and Tremper Longman III (Grand Rapids, MI: Zondervan, 1993), 269.

7. If the writer were, in fact, a real pessimist to the bone, he would have struck a different note throughout the treatise. He would, it seems, have assumed an attitude of disgust, with death serving as *release* from this absurd and cruel world. But such represents neither his tone nor his rhetorical strategy.

8. The proper way in which to understand "time" here accords with "season"; thus, it should be rendered "occasion" or "appropriate time"; so Gerhard Von Rad, *Wisdom in Israel* (repr., Nashville: Abingdon, 1974), 138–43. The sense of these verses, then, has to do not with a mechanistic or deterministic predestination but rather with human discernment.

presented in the form of fourteen pairs of poetic verse, include the following: (1) birth and death, planting and uprooting; (2) killing and healing, destroying and building; (3) weeping and laughing, mourning and dancing; (4) removing stones and gathering stones, embracing and withdrawing; (5) searching and giving up, retaining and throwing away; (6) tearing down and sewing, being silent and speaking; and (7) loving and hating, war and peace.

While the verses of this didactic poem are some of the most well-known (or at least oft-cited) verses from the Bible, precisely how they inform the overall message of Ecclesiastes is less well known. In fact, because they appear to be blatant contradictions, they are routinely dismissed—when, that is, they are not misunderstood. Thoughtful meditation and reflection on what they suggest, from a wisdom perspective, and how they illuminate life's meaning and purpose are very much needed. While our natural reaction is to view many of the elements in these pairs as absurd, wretched, and scandalous, every one of them possesses meaning and purpose if interpreted by divine providence. (Whether human beings actually discern meaning and purpose therein is, of course, another matter.) Such a conclusion accords with the statement that follows: God "has made everything beautiful in its time" (3:11 NIV). Hence, an important lesson of this didactic material is *discernment* of (1) the particular season that impacts our lives and (2) what action or actions would be appropriate, given that particular season. The context here is quite clear: any measure of discernment presupposes the recognition of divine omnipotence and providence.

As we look at Ecclesiastes as a whole, assisting the reader in the interpretive process is the writer's repeated use of catchwords ("meaningless," "meaninglessness"[9]), catchphrases ("under the sun," "under heaven," "chasing after the wind," "what God has done," "the gift of God," "which God has given"), and recurring themes ("This, too, is meaningless"; "so that men will revere God"). Moreover, all aspects of human activity—that is, *everything* in human existence and human experience, whether accumulating knowledge, pursuing pleasures, seeking justice, toiling in one's work—are said to be "meaningless."

---

9. Translations of the Hebrew *hebel* (lit. "smoke," "vapor," or "breath") include "vanity," "futility," "absurdity," and "transience."

At the same time, periodic shifts occur in the writer's thinking. These shifts in perspective usually attend reference to God, or the Creator. Thus, at play in Ecclesiastes is a contrasting of two perspectives on life: one issues from what we might call "under-the-sun" secularism, while the other might be termed "under-heaven" theism. Two approaches to interpreting reality, two understandings as to what is meaningless or meaningful, two competing teleologies or ultimate ways of viewing human existence. Those things that appear meaningless when viewed "under the sun," alas, have meaning if they are viewed in the light of the Creator whose providential ways are impenetrable.

What is the purpose of the book of Ecclesiastes? In the words of one minority-view commentator, Ecclesiastes is a work of "apologetics"—that is, a work that defends divine providence by underscoring "the grimness of the alternative."[10] The world, in the end, is not so much a theater of the absurd as it is the arena of God's unfathomable glory.[11] If we let Ecclesiastes speak for itself and assume a literary unity (regardless of how difficult that unity may be to ascertain), three recurring and interconnecting elements comprise the writer's literary strategy: (1) a thorough, rational, and despairing examination of the meaninglessness of everything in the human existence; (2) God the Creator and his providential work behind life's mysteries; and (3) human beings' inability to discern God's doings.[12] In spite of the writer's depressing observations, which without further context are inclined to induce despair, he is not arguing that events in the cosmos are random and without purpose. There is a time and season for *everything*, he insists, even when this remains veiled in the human experience.

One conspicuous recurring shift in the book concerns the value of human toil and work. So, for example, 1:1–2:23 catalogs the meaning-

---

10. Michael A. Eaton, *Ecclesiastes: An Introduction and Commentary* (Leicester, UK: Inter-Varsity, 1983), 44.

11. So William P. Brown, *Wisdom's Wonder: Character, Creation, and Crisis in the Bible's Wisdom Literature* (Grand Rapids, MI: Eerdmans, 2014), 19–24, 159–80.

12. Von Rad, *Wisdom in Israel*, 227–37, is one of the few commentators both to acknowledge a literary unity in Ecclesiastes and recognize the interplay of these three themes.

lessness of varied expressions of human activity, including human labor. This lament, however, is followed by a shift in perspective in 2:24–3:15. Whereas human toil and work was "meaningless" in the lament ending in 2:23, it is presented in a vastly different light in 2:24–3:15, wherein the reader is told that the Creator "has made everything beautiful in its time" and "has also set eternity in the human heart" (3:11).[13] The consequence of this is that when a person eats and drinks and finds happiness in his work, this is a "gift of God" (3:13). This conclusion is strengthened by the following observation: "So I saw that there is nothing better for a man than to enjoy his work, because that is his lot" (3:22).

Similar shifts regarding human activity and work occur again later in Ecclesiastes. One of these is the following rather remarkable observation: "when God gives any man wealth and possessions, and enables him to enjoy them, to accept his lot and be happy in his work—this is a gift of God ... because God keeps him occupied with gladness of heart" (5:19–20). Notice the reasoning behind this statement: satisfaction in one's work is "a gift of God" (this is a repetition, and thus underscoring, of an earlier statement). And as if this were not enough, later on the writer reinforces this fact: "joy will accompany him [the God-fearer (v. 12)] in his work all the days of the life God has given him under the sun" (8:15)—this despite humans' inability to comprehend what God does.

What might we make of these statements and the context in which they are made? Again, we must keep the writer's intent—namely, juxtaposition—in view. One finds either statements scattered throughout Ecclesiastes that are blatantly self-contradictory in nature,[14] render-

---

13. The sense of the "eternity" that God has placed within the human heart may be understood in two fundamental, corresponding ways: first, as basic knowledge of the Creator, of self, and of moral accountability—namely, that which accords with the natural law, the law "written on the heart" (see Rom. 2:14–15)—and second, as a certain awareness of or yearning after meaning and purpose. Both aspects are anchored in our having been created in the image of God.

14. For example, on the one hand Ecclesiastes insists that wisdom is meaningless, like chasing the wind, and on the other hand extols wisdom in a number of places. Both of these viewpoints, at face value, cannot be correct—unless they are part of a literary strategy at work.

ing any rational attempt at interpretation meaningless, or two points of view that are in conflict with one another are being compared.[15] In his portrayal of work within a theistic framework, the writer is not seeking to idolize work—or *any* human activity, for that matter. Neither is he writing in the manner that popular self-help gurus of our day utilize—promising personal happiness, realization, and self-fulfillment. The universe is *theo*centric, not egocentric.

Wisdom and the Work of God in Ecclesiastes

Given the well-known interpretive problems briefly outlined above, as well as the fact that theology in wisdom literature is not explicit, it should not be all that surprising that little attention in the relevant literature has been devoted to the concept of God in Ecclesiastes. A fascinating and little-examined element in the book is the number of references to God that occur throughout the work. It is possible to identify as many as forty references to God—this in a book that has a total of 222 verses.[16] Surely the fact that there are so many divine references in this relatively brief treatise is significant. In the words of one commentator, "Clearly if you remove everything about God in this book, thinking to produce a text on secular wisdom, you utterly dismember it."[17] And indeed this appears to be the case. Moreover, in Ecclesiastes the writer always uses the term *Elohim*, which designates God in general and which is used in the Genesis creation narrative, and not *Yahweh*, the God who reveals himself

---

15. Hence, we must reject the conclusion of J. T. Walsh, "Despair as a Theological Virtue in the Spirituality of Ecclesiastes," *Biblical Theology Bulletin* 12, no. 2 (1982): 46, whose mistaken interpretation—an interpretation that is representative, to be sure—fails to discern juxtaposition at work and ignores the progressively building admonitions in the book toward enjoyment. According to Walsh, the writer's "world-weary cynicism" and "near agnosticism" mirror an "acceptance" of despair's "permanence."

16. So, for example, Daniel Lys, *L'Ecclésiaste: ou que vaut la vie? Traduction, introduction générale, commentaire de 1/1 à 4/3* (Paris: Letouzey et Ané, 1977), 78; and Roland E. Murphy, *The Tree of Life: An Exploration of Biblical Wisdom*, 3rd ed. (Grand Rapids, MI: Eerdmans, 2002), 57.

17. Jacques Ellul, *Reason for Being: A Meditation on Ecclesiastes*, trans. Joyce Main Hanks (Grand Rapids, MI: Eerdmans, 1990), 214.

to his people. But creation, if viewed ontologically, is not a neutral object, without meaning or reference. It is, rather, an object of supreme significance, both physically and morally: everything was "very good" (Gen. 1:31). That is, the God of all creation gives life, and that life is good, in the very likeness of the Creator himself. Given this depiction of God as Creator, it is thus very plausible that the writer uses *Elohim* to eliminate any sense of Hebrew particularity, not unlike the apostle Paul in his Athenian discourse (Acts 17:16–34), who begins with the "unknown God" to whom his listeners can best relate before offering fuller revelation of the God who has made himself known. The argument being set forth in Ecclesiastes, thus, is of a universal character: life's limitations, impenetrability, and seeming absurdities apply to all, leading to despair apart from the mystery of divine providence. And while Christians confess that this God is in fact knowable, Ecclesiastes constitutes a necessary reminder that God cannot be calculated, manipulated, localized, or humanly understood. "What God does"—a catchphrase in Ecclesiastes—is unknowable and impenetrable, and hence hidden. To say, however, that God is hidden is *not* to argue that God is utterly unknowable. Historic Christian belief affirms that it is possible to confess—and experience—that God is in part knowable, even when he seems hidden and when his works are inscrutable. While from a human vantage point this God strikes us as arbitrary,[18] his inscrutability and mystery have the effect of exploding any human pretensions, religious or secular in nature. Human beings simply cannot claim to be God's equal. Fallibility and depravity firmly establish humans' distance from their Maker.

What the writer *does* tell his readers about this Creator God is significant and worthy of consideration, aiding us in locating an interpretive strategy by which to understand the book. Ecclesiastes presents God in essentially three roles: as creator, as inscrutable and impenetrable sovereign, and as judge.[19] Consider some of what we

---

18. Ecclesiastes reminds us that God seems arbitrary when we have preconceived notions of what he is like or what he should do.

19. Derek Kidner, *A Time to Mourn, and a Time to Dance* (Nottingham, UK: Inter-Varsity, 1976), 15–17, is one of the few who understands Ecclesiastes to depict God in essentially three ways. I diverge in collapsing Kidner's second

know about God from the writer's argument and how these specific elements, in some form or fashion, express creation, inscrutability, and judging:

1:13—God gives a burden that is heavy to bear (cf. 3:10).

2:24–26—God grants satisfaction, enjoyment, wisdom, and happiness.

2:26—There exist some people who please God.

3:9—God assigns.

3:11—God has made everything beautiful in its time; he has placed a sense of the eternal in human hearts.

3:13—God gives gifts, one of which is satisfaction in human labor.

3:14–15—God makes everything; nothing can be added or subtracted from this reality.

3:15–17—God will judge all, the wicked and the righteous, and that judgment will be according to our deeds.

3:18—God tests human beings.

5:1–7—God is to be approached, worshiped, and served.

5:2—God is in the heavens whereas human beings live on earth—which is to say, he is incommensurate and "other."

5:7—God is to be revered.

5:18—God gives life.

5:19–20—God gives gifts such as wealth, satisfaction in work, and gladness of heart.

6:2—God gives wealth, possessions, and honor.

7:13–14—God orders things; what God has done is to be pondered.

7:18—God is to be feared.

7:29—God created the human person upright.

8:12–13—God is to be feared and revered.

---

and third divine features—sovereignty and inscrutability—into one (my second) while adding judgment as a third.

8:15—God gives life and joy in human labor.

8:16–17—What God has done is unsearchable.

9:1—The righteous and wise are in God's hands.

9:7—What we do in the moment is what pleases God.

9:9—God grants life.

11:5—God has made everything, which is to say, he guides things—even human evil—toward an ultimate purpose which he alone knows.

11:9—God will call human beings to account and judge.

12:1—God the Creator is to be remembered in our youth.

12:6–7—God is to be remembered before we grow old and near death.

12:13—God is to be feared and his commandments to be kept.

12:14—God will bring every deed—good and evil, hidden and open—into judgment.

Despite the presence of God's works in Ecclesiastes, many commentators take a negative view of the writer's theology. "Qoheleth's God is a hard ruler," writes one commentator, a ruler who "must be feared, not cherished.... This is an uncomfortable theology, and one need not accept it as valid—the other Biblical authors *wouldn't have*—but this is Qoheleth's teaching."[20] Another commentator similarly misses the mark by speaking of "Qoheleth's harsh criticisms of God" and asserting that the writer "blames" God.[21] The perceived harshness, from a human perspective, issues from the fact that God's ways and works are *impenetrable*. But this is as it should be; otherwise, we construct God in humanity's image. This sort of commentary fails to recognize that Ecclesiastes concerns itself, in a detached manner, with life's totality and not theology proper. Moreover, it misses or ignores the recurring admonition in the book concerning life's "enjoyment" and God's "gifts," which actually con-

---

20. Michael V. Fox, *A Time to Tear Down and a Time to Build Up* (Grand Rapids, MI: Eerdmans, 1999), 136–38 (emphasis added).

21. Peter Enns, *Ecclesiastes* (Grand Rapids, MI: Eerdmans, 2011), 116, 210.

stitute "theological statements of faith in a just and loving God."[22] In fact, we must insist, with one perceptive interpreter, that fear of God and joy coexist in Ecclesiastes.[23] And in the end we must insist, against most of the literature, that Ecclesiastes does not mirror a theological deficiency. In truth, its theology squares with that of the New Testament: "Consider therefore the *kindness and the severity* of God" (Rom. 11:22 RSV, emphasis added). Human response to the divine, according to Ecclesiastes, requires reverence, silence, acceptance, and awe—responses that, simply said, are properly due.

How, then, might the two themes of meaninglessness and joy in Ecclesiastes be reconciled? Thus far we have suggested that juxtaposition—and hence a back-and-forth contrasting technique pitting a despairing under-the-sun secularism and an acknowledging of the Creator whose ways are unfathomable—is the rhetorical strategy at work in Ecclesiastes. This shifting entails, among other things, a highlighting of celebration and human gratitude. In this light, considering several key passages throughout Ecclesiastes that serve as a counterpoint to the book's pessimism and nihilism is an illuminating next step. It is to these passages that we now turn.

Wisdom and Human Labor in Ecclesiastes: A Closer Look

Although meaninglessness is applied to all human activity "under the sun," it is not applied to human work *categorically*. It applies, rather, to anything that stands outside of or apart from a theocentric outlook on life. The alternative to an under-the-sun secularism is what might be called an under-heaven theism. And in the latter description, work is portrayed as an aspect of satisfaction and enjoyment that constitutes a gift from God.

The sheer frequency of the term "meaningless"/"vanity" (Heb., *hebel*)—appearing over thirty times—would lend the impression that the writer believed nothing in the temporal life could be called

---

22. Graham S. Ogden, *Qoheleth*, 2nd ed. (Sheffield, UK: Sheffield Phoenix, 2007), 26.

23. Eunny P. Lee, *Vitality of Enjoyment in Qohelet's Theological Rhetoric* (Berlin: De Gruyter, 2005).

good. But the Hebrew word *tôb* ("good") occurs even more frequently than *hebel* in the book—roughly fifty times.[24] The writer also employs the verb *sāmah* ("to enjoy") and the noun form *simḥāh* ("enjoyment," "joy") in the passages that are treated below (2:24–26; 3:12–13; 5:18–19; 7:14; 8:15; 9:7–10; 11:8–9). At the same time, he makes a clear distinction between authentic joy as a gift of God and the mindless frivolity of the fool. Together these indicators suggest a picture that departs radically from conventional thinking about Ecclesiastes: there *is indeed* meaning, purpose, and satisfaction in life, *if* life—from a metaphysical standpoint—is viewed properly.

Many commentators, as already suggested, are broadly unified in the assumption that the writer has a fatalistic, despairing view of life, and they either ignore or downplay the presence of a cluster of statements spread throughout Ecclesiastes that give a full-throated recognition of enjoyment and satisfaction in this temporal life. The presence of this material presents the interpreter with a serious obstacle if, that is, the message of Ecclesiastes is despair and the God depicted therein is harsh. Taken together, these positive statements—eight in number—blatantly contradict the meaninglessness thesis that is expressed throughout. Moreover, they are clearly more than mere "marginal notes" on the part of the writer; rather, by the manner in which they punctuate the entire treatise they constitute an important—and recurring—theme and therefore must be taken seriously as part of the writer's interpretive strategy.[25]

What is more, the next to last of these passages noted below (9:7–10) is the most forceful of the writer's admonitions toward enjoyment—emphatic advice to the young to make the most out of life while they can—and may properly be viewed as part of a bridge leading into the book's concluding section. Finding enjoyment is an important counterpoint and subtheme, even when it is not to be confused with pleasure-seeking (cf. 7:1–6). Significantly, in five of

---

24. R. N. Whybray, *The Good Life in the Old Testament* (London: T&T Clark, 2002), 186.

25. The fundamental assumption that enjoyment is a counter-thesis in Ecclesiastes undergirds R. N. Whybray's commentary *Ecclesiastes* (Sheffield, UK: Sheffield Academic, 1997) and his essay "Qoheleth, Preacher of Joy," *Journal for the Study of the Old Testament*, no. 23 (July 1982): 87–98.

these statements an explicit connection is made between work (Heb. '*āmāl*) and enjoyment—a state of affairs that does not exist in a secularist-materialist account of human life. Because of the trademark of repetition in wisdom literature, the reader may be assured that the recurring accent being placed on *contentment through human labor* is not a minor point. Moreover, eight times in Ecclesiastes the writer speaks of a human being's "lot" or "portion" (2:10, 21; 3:22; 4:9; 5:18; 9:6, 9; 11:2) that has been assigned by heaven; several of these appear in a positive context of one's delight or contentment through work.

The eight passages that speak of enjoyment may be understood as corresponding to eight intervals in the writer's argument. At each interval, joy and contentment are reaffirmed in contradistinction to the absurdities that characterize secular existence. The implication in each of these interval statements, moreover, is that temporal enjoyment should not be dissociated from the *source* of contentment since it is a gift of God. And far from being a distant God, as much commentary mistakenly asserts, "God keeps him [i.e., the human being] occupied with joy in his heart" (5:20 RSV).

First Interval Statement

2:24–26: There is nothing better for a man than that he should eat and drink and find enjoyment in his toil. This also, I saw, is from the hand of God; for apart from him who can eat or who can have enjoyment? For to the man who pleases him God gives wisdom and knowledge and joy; but to the sinner he gives the work of gathering and heaping, only to give to one who pleases God. This also is vanity and a striving after wind. (RSV)

These statements serve as a counterpoint to the futility, pain, and grief of toil and endless effort poured into labor done "under the sun" (2:17–23). They are in response to the failure of all attempts—philosophical (1:12–18), sensual (2:1–2), commercial (2:3–11), intellectual (2:12–17), and work-related (2:18–23)—to find meaning in human existence. They also answer the question concerning good posed earlier (2:1). Wisdom, knowledge, and joy—a joy that includes satisfaction in one's work—are gifts from "the hand of God" (2:24; also in 9:1) given to those who "please" him. Verse 24 contains the first of four "there is nothing better" rhetorical devices applied to work in the book.

Second Interval Statement

> **3:12–13:** I know that there is nothing better for them than to be happy and enjoy themselves as long as they live; also that it is God's gift to man that every one should eat and drink and take pleasure in all his toil. (RSV)

These statements serve as a counterpoint to human inability to fathom what God has done and will do from beginning to end (3:10–15). Eating and drinking and working symbolize the joy of being human. Verse 12 contains the second of four rhetorical devices applying to work in the book.

Third Interval Statement

> **3:22:** So I saw that there is nothing better than that a man should enjoy his work, for that is his lot; who can bring him to see what will be after him? (RSV)

This statement serves as a counterpoint to the finality of death and divine judgment (3:16–22). That judgment of both the wicked and the righteous encompasses "every matter" and "every work" done in this present life (3:17 RSV)—that is, it is a judgment according to works. Verse 22 contains the third of four "there is nothing better" rhetorical devices applied to work.

Fourth Interval Statement

> **5:18–20:** Behold, what I have seen to be good and to be fitting is to eat and drink and find enjoyment in all the toil with which one toils under the sun the few days of his life which God has given him, for this is his lot. Every man also to whom God has given wealth and possessions and power to enjoy them, and to accept his lot and find enjoyment in his toil—this is the gift of God. For he will not much remember the days of his life because God keeps him occupied with joy in his heart. (RSV)

These statements serve as a counterpoint to the pursuit of wealth and riches and their disappearance or loss (5:10–20). They underscore the genuine good, something that has been emphasized earlier (in 2:24; 3:12, 22); moreover, this is said to be a "gift of God," which is a reiteration of what was claimed earlier (3:13). These verses contain one of the densest concentrations of allusions to God in the book (along with 3:10–15). Furthermore, they make the explicit connection between one's relationship to God and joy in the heart.

Fifth Interval Statement

7:14: In the day of prosperity be joyful, and in the day of adversity consider; God has made the one as well as the other, so that man may not find out anything that will be after him. (RSV)

This statement serves as a counterpoint to potential disillusionment that arises from a lack of wisdom (7:1–8:1). It also harkens back to the earlier argument that humans cannot fathom what God does (3:1–22).

Sixth Interval Statement

8:15: And I commend enjoyment, for there is nothing better for man under the sun than to eat and drink and enjoy himself, for this will accompany him in his work all the days of the life God has given him under the sun.

This statement serves as a counterpoint to life's unfairness, life's seeming injustice, and the propensity for human wickedness (8:11–15). It also contains the fourth of four "there is nothing better" rhetorical devices applied to work.

Seventh Interval Statement

9:7–10: Go, eat your bread with enjoyment, and drink your wine with a merry heart; for God has already approved what you do. Let your garments be always white; let not oil be lacking on your head. Enjoy life with the wife whom you love, all the days of your vain life which he has given you under the sun, because that is your portion in life and in your toil at which you toil under the sun. Whatever your hand finds to do, do it with your might; for there is no work or thought or knowledge or wisdom in Sheol, to which you are going. (RSV)

These statements serve as a counterpoint to death as the universal destiny of all human beings (9:2–6). They also constitute a powerful witness to human moral agency and responsibility with their "seize the day" imperative, which find its expansion in the later admonitions to give and to sow seed (11:1–6).

Eighth Interval Statement

11:7–12:1: Light is sweet, and it is pleasant for the eyes to behold the sun. For if a man lives many years, let him rejoice in them all; but let him remember that the days of darkness will be many. All that comes is vanity. Rejoice, O young man, in your youth, and let your heart cheer you in the days of your youth; walk in the ways of your heart and the sight of your eyes. But know that for all these things God will bring you into judgment. Remove vexation from your mind, and put away pain from your body; for youth and the dawn of life are vanity. Remember also your Creator in the days of your youth. (RSV)

These statements serve as a counterpoint to the inevitability and finality of death in old age (11:8–12:7).

Enjoyment—by which the writer is signifying contentment or satisfaction and which is symbolized by eating, drinking (i.e., shared fellowship around the table), and working—is a divine gift as depicted in Ecclesiastes. Gifts are to be received. In fact, as noted above in several of the interval statements, the writer has used the rhetorical device "there is nothing better" four times throughout the treatise to emphasize the matter of life's enjoyment and the truth that it is a gift of God (2:24; 3:12, 22; 8:15).[26] God's gifts, moreover, are declared good in six of these intervals (3:12; 5:19; 7:14; 8:15; 9:7; 11:9).

---

26. See Graham S. Ogden, "Qoheleth's Use of the 'Nothing Is Better' Form," *Journal of Biblical Literature* 98, no. 3 (1979): 339–50; and idem, "Qoheleth's Summons to Enjoyment and Reflection," *Vetus Testamentum* 34, no. 1 (1984): 27–38.

Together, these markers underscore not the Creator's *harshness* but his *benevolence*.

In granting us satisfaction in our labor, God sanctifies, as it were, the ordinary. Moreover, the Judeo-Christian tradition knows no split or dichotomy between manual and mental labor, in contradistinction to the Greco-Roman tradition.[27] The reason for this difference is quite simply that we are created in God's likeness (Gen. 1:26–27). Furthermore, the enjoyment of our labor is not merely some momentary phenomenon—here one minute and then gone the next. Rather, it has a residual effect in the believer's life: "for this [i.e., satisfaction] will accompany him in his work all the days of the life God has given him" (8:15). Ecclesiastes depicts work in a way that is utterly relevant to our contemporary world and that always has been relevant to the world.

Concluding Thoughts on the "End of the Matter"

After all has been considered in Ecclesiastes, the writer's argument concludes (12:9–14). The "end of the matter" is that humankind is to revere God. If any wisdom is to be found among human beings, it will lead a person away from the absurdity of a secularist outlook and to the acknowledgment of the mystery of divine providence. In the end, the fear of God, which has been a recurring subtheme in Ecclesiastes (3:14; 5:7; 7:18; 8:12–13 [twice]; 12:13), is the final word (12:13–14).[28] As someone has rightly observed, in the message of Ecclesiastes we clearly have no *Chicken Soup for the Soul* approach to positive thinking or spirituality.[29] In addition, in his treatise the writer addresses everything that constitutes normative human activity, inclusive of human labor. The writer does not despise or devalue work; rather, he

---

27. On this see William P. Brown, "Whatever Your Hand Finds to Do: Qoheleth's Work Ethic," *Interpretation* 55, no. 3 (2001): 273.

28. Cf. Job 28:28; Ps. 111:10; Prov. 1:7; 9:10; 15:33. The fear of God as a theme is at home in the wisdom tradition, as indicated by the Old Testament book of Proverbs (e.g., Prov. 1:7; 9:10; 14:26, 27; 16:6; 19:23; 22:4; 23:17; 28:14).

29. Ryan P. O'Dowd, "Epistemology in Ecclesiastes: Remembering What It Means to Be Human," in *The Words of the Wise Are Like Goads: Engaging Qohelet in the 21st Century*, ed. Mark J. Boda, Tremper Longman III, and Cristian G. Rata (Winona Lake, IN: Eisenbrauns, 2013), 216.

recasts it.[30] Specifically within a theocentric context, work is portrayed not as meaningless toil but rather as satisfying and as a gift from God (2:24; 3:13; 5:18–20; 8:15; 9:10 [implied]). Work as both a sign of contentment and a divine gift is part of the writer's broader theme of enjoyment, as we have attempted to argue. Here we find neither the language of divine determinism nor a portrait of drudgery and toil; nor does Ecclesiastes mirror a harsh and distant God, as many would suppose. Its message, rather, represents a challenge to make the most of our gifts and abilities as well as our opportunities—a challenge that, unlike the rest of life, knows no (known) limits.

While most people are familiar with the emphasis in Ecclesiastes on the meaninglessness of life, little attention either in standard commentary or in the church's standard teaching and preaching is given to the book's emphasis on joy or satisfaction in work. The writer's observations, it should be remembered, agree with another wisdom saying: "In all labor there is profit" (Prov. 14:23a NASB)—a "profit" that is measured not foremost in economic terms but in *contentment*.

Perhaps Ecclesiastes is consigned to neglect—in the past and in our day—because it confronts us with what we fear the most. It is withering in its exposure of life's absurdity and nakedness when human existence has been bleached of an acknowledgment of God, whose ways are inscrutable. At bottom, in its own unique way Ecclesiastes is a guide—an invaluable one at that—to living faithfully in a world or culture that at best is agnostic and at worst is hostile to the One who is creator, sustainer, and judge of all things. Perhaps, then, it is high time that Western societies be exposed for what they are. From the wisdom perspective, a "fool" is not merely some imbecile; rather, he is one who resists the witness of truth as it is on display in creation, in human nature, and in human activity.

While a secularist-materialist perspective strips life and life's vocation of its inherently religious meaning, vocation properly understood infuses mundane secular life—the ordinary—with meaning and significance. Such renewed understanding of the ordinary occurred in significant ways five hundred years ago in Western history. One of the breakthroughs of early sixteenth-century Protestant reform was to recover a deeper understanding of the notion of vocation, fol-

---

30. Brown, "Whatever Your Hand Finds to Do," 279.

lowing over a millennium of the church's devaluing of human work aside from the calling to the priesthood and the monastery.

In Martin Luther's reaction to this devaluation, it is significant that the book of Ecclesiastes played no small role in helping shape his thinking on human labor and vocation. In *Notes on Ecclesiastes*, Luther offers the following reflection:

> No less noxious for a proper understanding of this book [Ecclesiastes] has been the influence of many of the saintly and illustrious theologians in the church, who thought that in this book Solomon was teaching what they call "the contempt for the world" [*contemptus mundi*].[31]

Here Luther cites as an example Jerome, who encourages fourth-century monastic life in the preface of his *Commentarius in Ecclesiasten*. For Luther, this meant that Christians should "forsake the household, the political order ... to flee to the desert, to isolate oneself from human society, to live in stillness and silence; for it was [deemed] impossible to serve God in the world."[32] Luther is at pains to counter the longstanding tradition of ascetic monasticism and isolation from the world. In his view, this was counter to a proper understanding—and acknowledgment—of creation's essential goodness (see Gen. 1:31). Monks, however, were *dis*engaged, which caused Luther to polemicize against the world-fleeing monastic tendency. In reading Ecclesiastes, Luther laments that "it is almost a bigger job to purify and defend the author" from mistaken ideas smuggled in by the church than it is to understand the book's meaning.[33] Two priorities, he concludes, are obscured: the author's purpose and the author's unique style. The author's aim, then, is clarified by Luther: "to put us at peace and to give us a quiet mind in the everyday affairs and business of this life, so that we live contentedly in the present."[34] In the end, Luther asserts, what Ecclesiastes condemns is not creation

---

31. Martin Luther, *Notes on Ecclesiastes*, in *Luther's Works* (hereafter *LW*), vol. 15, ed. Jaroslav Pelikan and Hilton C. Oswald (Philadelphia: Fortress; St. Louis: Concordia, 1972), 4.

32. Luther, *Notes on Ecclesiastes*, in *LW* 15:4.

33. Luther, *Notes on Ecclesiastes*, in *LW* 15:7.

34. Luther, *Notes on Ecclesiastes*, in *LW* 15:7.

or the created order but rather "depraved affection" and a lack of contentment.[35]

On occasion throughout its history, as in the sixteenth century, the Christian church has been permitted to gain renewed insight into its apologetic mission in the world. Part of that mission entails rediscovering the meaning and purpose of neglected domains of social life—for example, the arts or sciences, language and linguistics, or the study of history, philosophy, and culture. And not infrequently, those breakthroughs—as they did in the early sixteenth century—adjust our views of the marketplace as we grasp a deeper understanding of the concept of vocation.

Vocation properly understood has the effect of recalibrating our sense of duties and obligations within the larger ethical framework of God's providential care and purpose. Work, then, is perhaps the most significant element of the believer's vocational calling, even when it does not represent the totality of that calling. Thus, when Ecclesiastes commends work as a satisfying gift, yet the believer's day-to-day experience at work is *neither* satisfying *nor* viewed as a gracious gift, theological recalibration is in order.

Anything less than the experience of work as a satisfying gift is to fail to live in harmony with our Creator.

---

35. Luther, *Notes on Ecclesiastes*, in *LW* 15:8.

BIBLIOGRAPHY

Acton, John Emerich Edward Dalberg. *Selected Writings of Lord Acton.* Edited by J. Rufus Fears. 3 vols. Indianapolis: Liberty Fund, 1985–1988.

Anderson, Owen. *The Natural Moral Law: The Good after Modernity.* New York: Cambridge University Press, 2012.

Attarian, John. "In Dispraise of Tolerance, Sensitivity and Compassion." *Social Critic* 3, no. 2 (Spring 1998): 14–23.

Benedict XVI. Encyclical Letter on Integral Human Development, *Caritas in Veritate* (June 29, 2009). http://w2.vatican.va/content/benedict-xvi/en/encyclicals/documents/hf_ben-xvi_enc_20090629_caritas-in-veritate.html.

Benne, Robert. *Good and Bad Ways to Think about Religion and Politics.* Grand Rapids, MI: Eerdmans, 2010.

Blamires, Harry. *The Will and the Way.* New York: Macmillan, 1957.

Bratt, James D., ed. *Abraham Kuyper: A Centennial Reader.* Grand Rapids, MI: Eerdmans, 1998.

———. *Abraham Kuyper: Modern Calvinist, Christian Democrat.* Grand Rapids, MI: Eerdmans, 2013.

Bretschneider, C. G., H. E. Bindseil, et al., eds. *Corpus Reformatorum.* 101 vols. Halle: Schwetschke, 1834–1959.

Brown, William P. "Whatever Your Hand Finds to Do: Qoheleth's Work Ethic." *Interpretation* 55, no. 3 (2001): 271–84.

———. *Wisdom's Wonder: Character, Creation, and Crisis in the Bible's Wisdom Literature.* Grand Rapids, MI: Eerdmans, 2014.

Brunner, Emil. *The Divine Imperative*. Philadelphia: Westminster, 1947.

Brunner, Emil, and Karl Barth. *Natural Theology*. Translated by Peter Fraenkel. Reprint. Eugene, OR: Wipf & Stock, 2002.

Burtchaell, James T. "The Decline and Fall of the Christian College." *First Things*, no. 12 (April 1991): 16–29; no. 13 (May 1991): 30–38.

———. *The Dying of the Light: The Disengagement of Colleges and Universities from Their Churches*. Grand Rapids, MI: Eerdmans, 1998.

Calvin, John. *Institutes of the Christian Religion*. Edited by John T. McNeill. Translated by Ford Lewis Battles. 2 vols. Louisville: Westminster John Knox, 1960.

Cameron, Euan. *The European Reformation*. 2nd ed. Oxford: Oxford University Press, 2012.

Catholic Church. *Catechism of the Catholic Church*. Washington, DC: United States Catholic Conference, 1994.

Catholic Church and the Lutheran World Federation. *From Conflict to Communion: Lutheran-Catholic Common Commemoration of the Reformation in 2017*. http://www.vatican.va/roman_curia/pontifical_councils/chrstuni/lutheran-fed-docs/rc_pc_chrstuni_doc_2013_dal-conflitto-alla-comunione_en.html.

Chadwick, Owen. *The Reformation*. Middlesex, UK: Penguin, 1964.

Charles, J. Daryl. "Burying the Wrong Corpse." In *Natural Law and Evangelical Political Thought*, edited by Jesse Covington, Bryan McGraw, and Micah Watson, 3–34. Lanham, MD: Lexington, 2013.

———. *Natural Law and Religious Freedom: The Role of Moral First Things in Grounding and Protecting the First Freedom*. New York: Routledge, 2018.

———. *Retrieving the Natural Law: A Return to Moral First Things*. Grand Rapids, MI: Eerdmans, 2008.

———. "Toward Restoring a Good Marriage: Reflections on the Contemporary Divorce of Love and Justice and Its Cultural Implications." *Journal of Church and State* 55, no. 2 (2013): 367–83.

Covington, Jesse, Bryan McGraw, and Micah Watson, eds. *Natural Law and Evangelical Political Thought*. Lanham, MD: Lexington, 2013.

Crenshaw, James L. *Ecclesiastes*. Philadelphia: Westminster, 1987.

Crosby, John F. "Education and the Mind Redeemed." *First Things*, no. 18 (December 1991): 23–28.

Dilthey, Wilhelm. *Gesammelte Schriften*. 23 vols. Leipzig: Teubner; Göttingen: Vandenhoeck & Ruprecht, 1921–1974.

Dingel, Irene, Robert Kolb, Nicole Kuropka, and Timothy J. Wengert. *Philip Melanchthon: Theologian in Classroom, Confession, and Controversy.* Göttingen: Vandenhoeck & Ruprecht, 2012.

Dreher, Rod. *The Benedict Option: A Strategy for Christians in a Post-Christian Nation.* New York: Sentinel, 2017.

Eaton, Michael A. *Ecclesiastes: An Introduction and Commentary.* Leicester, UK: Inter-Varsity, 1983.

Ellul, Jacques. *Reason for Being: A Meditation on Ecclesiastes.* Translated by Joyce Main Hanks. Grand Rapids, MI: Eerdmans, 1990.

Elshtain, Jean Bethke. "Judge Not?" In *The Moral Life: An Introductory Reader in Ethics and Literature,* edited by Louis J. Pojman, 194–98. New York: Oxford University Press, 2004.

Enns, Peter. *Ecclesiastes.* Grand Rapids, MI: Eerdmans, 2011.

Farnham, Suzanne G., Joseph P. Gill, R. Taylor McLean, and Susan M. Ward. *Listening Hearts: Discerning Call in Community.* Rev. ed. New York: Morehouse, 2011.

Fenlon, Dermot. *Heresy and Obedience in Tridentine Italy: Cardinal Pole and the Counter Reformation.* Cambridge: Cambridge University Press, 1972.

Finnis, John. *Natural Law and Natural Rights.* Oxford: Clarendon, 1980.

Fox, Michael V. *A Time to Tear Down and a Time to Build Up.* Grand Rapids, MI: Eerdmans, 1999.

Frankl, Viktor E. *Man's Search for Meaning.* Boston: Beacon Press, 1959.

Gericke, J. W. "Axiological Assumptions in Qohelet: A Historical-Philosophical Clarification." *Verbum et Ecclesia* 33, no. 1 (2012): 1–6.

Gerson, Michael, and Peter Wehner. *City of Man: Religion and Politics in a New Era.* Chicago: Moody, 2010.

Goldstone, Richard. "War Crimes: When Amnesia Causes Cancer." *The Washington Post,* February 2, 1997, C4.

Grabill, Stephen J. *Rediscovering the Natural Law in Reformed Theological Ethics.* Grand Rapids, MI: Eerdmans, 2006.

Habermas, Jürgen, and Joseph Ratzinger (Pope Benedict XVI). *The Dialectics of Secularization: On Reason and Religion.* Edited by Florian Schuller. Translated by Brian McNeil. San Francisco: Ignatius, 2006.

Hamilton, Alexander et al. *The Federalist Papers.* New York: New American Library, 1961.

Harrison, Richard L., Jr. "Melanchthon's Role in the Reformation of the University of Tübingen." *Church History* 47, no. 3 (1978): 271–78.

Hildebrandt, Franz. *Melanchthon: Alien or Ally?* Cambridge: Cambridge University Press, 1946.

Howard, Thomas Albert, and Mark A. Noll. *Protestantism after 500 Years.* New York: Oxford University Press, 2016.

Hunter, James Davison. *The Death of Character: Moral Education in an Age of Good and Evil.* New York: Basic Books, 2000.

Jensen, David H. *Responsive Labor: A Theology of Work.* Louisville: Westminster John Knox, 2006.

John Paul II. Apostolic Letter on the Christian Meaning of Human Suffering, *Salvifici Doloris* (February 11, 1984). https://w2.vatican.va/content/john-paul-ii/en/apost_letters/1984/documents/hf_jp-ii_apl_11021984_salvifici-doloris.html.

———. Encyclical Letter on Certain Fundamental Questions of the Church's Moral Teaching, *Veritatis Splendor* (August 6, 1993). http://w2.vatican.va/content/john-paul-ii/en/encyclicals/documents/hf_jp-ii_enc_06081993_veritatis-splendor.html.

———. Encyclical Letter on the Relationship between Faith and Reason, *Fides et Ratio* (September 14, 1998). http://w2.vatican.va/content/john-paul-ii/en/encyclicals/documents/hf_jp-ii_enc_14091998_fides-et-ratio.html.

———. Encyclical Letter on the Value and Inviolability of Human Life, *Evangelium Vitae* (March 25, 1995). http://w2.vatican.va/content/john-paul-ii/en/encyclicals/documents/hf_jp-ii_enc_25031995_evangelium-vitae.html.

Joyce, Michael S. "On Self-Government." *Policy Review*, no. 90 (July/August 1998): 41–48.

Kennedy, Simon P. "Abraham Kuyper: Calvinist, Anti-Revolutionary Politician and Political Thinker." *Australian Journal of Politics and History* 6, no. 2 (June 2015): 169–83.

Kidner, Derek. *A Time to Mourn, and a Time to Dance.* Nottingham, UK: Inter-Varsity, 1976.

Kilner, John F. *Dignity and Destiny: Humanity in the Image of God.* Grand Rapids, MI: Eerdmans, 2015.

Kuyper, Abraham. *The Antithesis between Symbolism and Revelation.* Edinburgh: T&T Clark, 1899.

———. *Lectures on Calvinism.* Reprint. Grand Rapids, MI: Eerdmans, 1987.

———. *Ons Program.* 2nd ed. Amsterdam: J. H. Kruyt, 1880.

———. *Our Program: A Christian Political Manifesto.* Translated by Harry Van Dyke. Bellingham, WA: Lexham Press, 2015.

———. *Wisdom and Wonder: Common Grace in Science and Art*. Edited by Jordan J. Ballor and Stephen J. Grabill. Translated by Nelson D. Kloosterman. Grand Rapids, MI: Christian's Library Press, 2011.

Lee, Eunny P. *Vitality of Enjoyment in Qohelet's Theological Rhetoric*. Berlin: De Gruyter, 2005.

Lehmann, Karl, and Wolfhart Pannenberg, eds. *The Condemnations of the Reformation Era: Do They Still Divide?* Translated by Margaret Kohl. Minneapolis: Fortress, 1990.

Lehmann, Karl, Michael Root, William G. Rusch, and J. Francis Stafford, eds. *Justification by Faith: Do the Sixteenth-Century Condemnations Still Apply?* New York: Continuum, 1999.

Leithart, Peter J. "Pluralism's Pride." *Touchstone* 18, no. 7 (September 2005): 15–17.

Lewis, C. S. "Christianity and Culture." In *Christian Reflections*, edited by Walter Hooper, 12–36. London: Geoffrey Bles, 1967.

———. "The Humanitarian Theory of Punishment." In *God in the Dock: Essays on Theology and Ethics*, edited by Walter Hooper, 287–94. 1970. Reprint. Grand Rapids, MI: Eerdmans, 2002.

———. *Mere Christianity*. Rev. ed. New York: HarperCollins, 2001.

Lonergan, Bernard. *Insight: A Study of Human Understanding*. Edited by F. E. Crowe and R. M. Doran. Toronto: University of Toronto Press, 1992.

Luther, Martin. *D. Martin Luthers Werke. Kritische Gesammtausgabe*. 120 vols. Weimar: Herman Böhlaus Nachfolger, 1883–2009.

———. *Luther's Works*. Edited by Jaroslav Pelikan, Helmut T. Lehmann, and Christopher Brown. 75 vols. Philadelphia: Fortress; St. Louis: Concordia, 1955–.

Lutheran World Federation and the Catholic Church. Joint Declaration on the Doctrine of Justification. http://www.vatican.va/roman_curia/pontifical_councils/chrstuni/documents/rc_pc_chrstuni_doc_31101999_cath-luth-joint-declaration_en.html.

Lys, Daniel. *L'Ecclésiaste: ou que vaut la vie? Traduction, introduction générale, commentaire de 1/1 à 4/3*. Paris: Letouzey et Ané, 1977.

MacIntyre, Alasdair. *After Virtue: A Study in Moral Theology*. 3rd ed. Notre Dame, IN: University of Notre Dame Press, 2007.

Macklin, Ruth. "Dignity Is a Useless Concept." *British Medical Journal* 327 (2003): 1419–20.

Manschreck, Clyde. "The Bible in Melanchthon's Philosophy of Education." *Journal of Bible and Religion* 23, no. 3 (1955): 202–7.

———. *Melanchthon: The Quiet Reformer.* New York: Abingdon, 1958. Reprint. Eugene, OR: Wipf & Stock, 2008.

Marshall, Paul, with Lela Gilbert. *Heaven Is Not My Home: Living in the Now of God's Creation.* Nashville: Word, 1998.

May, William E. "The Sanctity of Human Life." In *In Search of a National Morality: A Manifesto for Evangelicals and Catholics*, edited by William Bentley Ball, 103–11. Grand Rapids, MI: Baker; San Francisco: Ignatius, 1992.

Mayer, Thomas F. *Cardinal Pole in European Context: A* via media *in the Reformation.* Aldershot, UK: Ashgate, 2000.

McGoldrick, James E. *Abraham Kuyper: God's Renaissance Man.* Auburn, MA: Evangelical Press, 2000.

McGrath, Alister E. *A Passion for Truth.* Downers Grove, IL: InterVarsity, 1996.

Melanchthon, Philip. *Commentary on Romans.* Translated by Fred Kramer. St. Louis: Concordia, 1992.

———. *Loci Communes.* Translated by J. A. O. Preus. St. Louis: Concordia, 1992.

———. *Melanchthon's Werke in Auswahl.* Edited by Robert Stupperich. 7 vols. Gütersloh: Gerd Mohn, 1951–1975.

Moynihan, Daniel Patrick. "Defining Deviancy Down." *American Scholar* 62, no. 1 (Winter 1993): 17–30.

Murphy, Roland E. *The Tree of Life: An Exploration of Biblical Wisdom.* 3rd ed. Grand Rapids, MI: Eerdmans, 2002.

Murray, John Courtney. *We Hold These Truths: Catholic Reflections on the American Proposition.* New York: Sheed and Ward, 1960.

Neafsey, John P. "Psychological Dimensions of the Discernment of Vocation." In *Revisiting the Idea of Vocation: Theological Explorations*, edited by J. C. Haughey, 163–89. Washington, DC: Catholic University of America Press, 2012.

Neuhaus, Richard John. *The Naked Public Square: Religion and Democracy in America.* 2nd ed. Grand Rapids, MI: Eerdmans, 1988.

———. *Time toward Home: The American Experiment as Revelation.* New York: Seabury, 1975.

Newbigin, Lesslie. *The Gospel in a Pluralist Society.* Grand Rapids, MI: Eerdmans, 1989.

———. *Truth to Tell: The Gospel and Public Truth.* Grand Rapids, MI: Eerdmans, 1991.

Newman, John Henry. "Intellect, the Instrument of Religious Training." In *Sermons Preached on Various Occasions*, 1–14. Reprint. London: Longmans, Green and Co., 1921.

Oberman, Heiko A. *The Two Reformations: The Journey from the Last Days to the New World*. Edited by Don Weinstein. New Haven, CT: Yale University Press, 2003.

O'Dowd, Ryan P. "Epistemology in Ecclesiastes: Remembering What It Means to Be Human." In *The Words of the Wise Are Like Goads: Engaging Qohelet in the 21st Century*, edited by Mark J. Boda, Tremper Longman III, and Cristian G. Rata, 195–217. Winona Lake, IN: Eisenbrauns, 2013.

Ogden, Graham S. *Qoheleth*. 2nd ed. Sheffield, UK: Sheffield Phoenix, 2007.

———. "Qoheleth's Summons to Enjoyment and Reflection." *Vetus Testamentum* 34, no. 1 (1984): 27–38.

———. "Qoheleth's Use of the 'Nothing Is Better' Form." *Journal of Biblical Literature* 98, no. 3 (1979): 339–50.

Orwell, George. Review of *Power: A New Social Analysis*, by Bertrand Russell. *Adelphi* (January 1939): 375.

Pelikan, Jaroslav. *The Riddle of Roman Catholicism: Its History, Its Beliefs, Its Future*. New York: Abingdon, 1959.

Pinker, Steven. "The Stupidity of Dignity." *The New Republic*. May 28, 2008. https://newrepublic.com/article/64674/the-stupidity-dignity.

Plantinga, Cornelius, Jr. *Not the Way It's Supposed to Be: A Breviary of Sin*. Grand Rapids, MI: Eerdmans, 1995.

Pole, Reginald. *Defense of the Unity of the Church*. Translated by Joseph G. Dwyer. Westminster: Newman, 1965.

President's Council on Bioethics. *Human Dignity and Bioethics: Essays Commissioned by the President's Council on Bioethics*. Washington, DC: The President's Council on Bioethics, 2008.

Ramsey, Paul. *Basic Christian Ethics*. New York: Scribner's, 1954.

Richard, James William. *Philip Melanchthon: The Protestant Preceptor of Germany 1497–1560*. New York: Putnam, 1898.

Rieff, Philip. *The Triumph of the Therapeutic: Uses of Faith after Freud*. New York: Harper & Row, 1966.

Rogness, Michael. *Philip Melanchthon: Reformer without Honor*. Minneapolis: Augsburg, 1969.

Ryken, Leland. "Ecclesiastes." In *A Complete Literary Guide to the Bible*, edited by Leland Ryken and Tremper Longman III, 268–80. Grand Rapids, MI: Zondervan, 1993.

Sayers, Dorothy. *Creed or Chaos?* Reprint. Manchester: Sophia Institute, 1974.

Scholes, Jeffrey. "Vocation." *Religion Compass* 4, no. 4 (2010): 211–20.

Schuurman, Douglas J. *Vocation: Discerning Our Calling in Life.* Grand Rapids, MI: Eerdmans, 2004.

Schwiebert, E. G. "The Background of the Times." In *The Reformation: Revival or Revolution?*, edited by W. Stanford Reid, 23–29. New York: Holt, Rinehart and Winston, 1968.

Scott, R. B. Y. *Proverbs and Ecclesiastes.* Garden City, NY: Doubleday, 1965.

Sigmund, Paul. "Subsidiarity, Solidarity, and Liberation: Alternative Approaches in Catholic Social Thought." In *Religion, Pluralism, and Public Life: Abraham Kuyper's Legacy for the Twenty-First Century*, edited by Luis E. Lugo, 205–20. Grand Rapids, MI: Eerdmans, 2000.

Skillen, James W., and Rockne M. McCarthy, eds. *Political Order and the Plural Structure of Society.* Atlanta: Scholars Press, 1991.

Skinner, B. F. *Walden Two.* New York: Macmillan, 1948.

Smith, Gertrude. "The Jurisdiction of the Areopagus." *Classical Philology* 22, no. 1 (1927): 61–79.

Smith, Gordon T. *Courage and Calling: Embracing Your God-Given Potential.* Rev. ed. Downers Grove, IL: InterVarsity, 2011.

Sowell, Thomas. *A Conflict of Visions: Ideological Origins of Political Struggles.* New York: Basic Books, 2002.

Stackhouse, Max. Foreword to *Religion, Pluralism, and Public Life: Abraham Kuyper's Legacy for the Twenty-First Century*, edited by Luis E. Lugo, xi–xviii. Grand Rapids, MI: Eerdmans, 2000.

Steinmetz, David C. "Reginald Pole (1500–1558): The Loss of Eden." In David C. Steinmetz, *Reformers in the Wings*, 53–65. Minneapolis: Fortress, 1971.

Strauss, Gerald. *Luther's House of Learning: Indoctrination of the Young in the German Reformation.* Baltimore, MD: Johns Hopkins University Press, 1978.

———. "The Social Function of Schools in the Lutheran Reformation in Germany." *History of Education Quarterly* 28, no. 2 (Summer 1988): 191–206.

Stupperich, Robert. *Der unbekannte Melanchthon: Wirken und Denken des Praeceptor Germaniae in neuer Sicht.* Stuttgart: Kohlhammer, 1961.

———. *Melanchthon.* Translated by Robert H. Fischer. Philadelphia: Westminster, 1965.

Tertullian. *Prescription against Heretics*. Translated by Peter Holmes. In *The Ante-Nicene Fathers*, edited by Alexander Roberts and James Donaldson, vol. 3, 243–67. New York: Charles Scribner's Sons, 1903.

Tocqueville, Alexis de. *Democracy in America*. Edited and translated by Harvey Mansfield and Delba Winthrop. Chicago and London: University of Chicago Press, 2000.

Troeltsch, Ernst. *Vernunft und Offenbarung bei Johann Gerhard und Melanchthon*. Göttingen: Huth, 1891.

Trueblood, Elton. *Your Other Vocation*. New York: Harper, 1952.

VanDrunen, David. *Divine Covenants and Moral Order: A Biblical Theology of Natural Law*. Grand Rapids, MI: Eerdmans, 2014.

———. *Natural Law and the Two Kingdoms: A Study in the Development of Reformed Social Thought*. Grand Rapids, MI: Eerdmans, 2010.

Van Til, Kent A. "Subsidiarity and Sphere Sovereignty: A Match Made in …?" *Theological Studies* 69, no. 3 (2008): 610–36.

Veith, Gene Edward. "Vocation: The Theology of the Christian Life." *Journal of Markets & Morality* 14, no. 1 (Spring 2011): 119–31.

Vlekke, Bernard H. M. *Evolution of the Dutch Nation*. New York: Roy, 1945.

Volf, Miroslav. *Work in the Spirit: Toward a Theology of Work*. New York: Oxford University Press, 1991.

Von Rad, Gerhard. *Wisdom in Israel*. Reprint. Nashville: Abingdon, 1974.

Vries, John Hendrik de. "Biographical Note: Abraham Kuyper 1837–1920." In Abraham Kuyper, *Lectures on Calvinism*, i–vii. Reprint. Grand Rapids, MI: Eerdmans, 1987.

Walsh, J. T. "Despair as a Theological Virtue in the Spirituality of Ecclesiastes." *Biblical Theology Bulletin* 12, no. 2 (1982): 46–49.

Westermann, Claus. *Roots of Wisdom: The Oldest Proverbs of Israel and Other Peoples*. Translated by J. Daryl Charles. Louisville: Westminster John Knox, 1995.

Whybray, R. N. *Ecclesiastes*. Sheffield, UK: Sheffield Academic, 1997.

———. *The Good Life in the Old Testament*. London: T&T Clark, 2002.

———. "Qoheleth, Preacher of Joy." *Journal for the Study of the Old Testament*, no. 23 (July 1982): 87–98.

Witte, John, Jr. *Law and Protestantism: The Legal Teachings of the Lutheran Reformation*. Cambridge: Cambridge University Press, 2002.

Witte, John E., Jr., and Thomas C. Arthur. "The Three Uses of the Law: A Protestant Source of the Purposes of Criminal Punishment?" *Journal of Law and Religion* 10, no. 2 (1993/4): 433–65.

Woldring, Henk E. S. "Multiform Responsibility and the Revitalization of Civil Society." In *Religion, Pluralism, and Public Life: Abraham Kuyper's Legacy for the Twenty-First Century*, edited by Luis E. Lugo, 175–88. Grand Rapids, MI: Eerdmans, 2000.

Wolters, Albert M. *Creation Regained: Biblical Basics for a Reformational Worldview*. 2nd ed. Grand Rapids, MI: Eerdmans, 2005.

Subject and Author Index

Abraham Kuyper Prize, xn6, 104
accountability, 15, 37, 114, 166
   conscience, 90, 97
   image of God and, 15, 108–9, 111
   moral, 122–23
activism, social action, 10, 14
Acton Institute, xiv–xv, 108
African wisdom, 116–17
agnosticism, agnostics, 3, 23, 163n15, 174
America, United States of, 80, 108, 145
   democracy, 2–3, 49–50, 109–10
   founders, natural law, 38–39, 86, 110
   military, 53–54, 58
   post-consensus culture, 2–4, 5–6
Anabaptists, 11, 18, 61–62, 77–78, 98, 100
anarchy, 85, 109
ancient Near Eastern wisdom, 116, 121, 152, 155
animals, 30–31, 39
antinomianism, 77–78
Aquinas, Thomas, 43, 48, 93, 95, 99
   justice, 44–45, 54n2, 55
Aristotle, 29–30, 32, 44, 45, 55, 73, 76

atheism, 23, 34, 91, 94–95
Athens, vii–viii, xi, 21–22, 23–25, 164
Augsburg Confession, 64, 70
Augustine of Hippo, Augustinian, 48, 62, 65, 146
   dual citizenship vii–viii, 26, 42
   justice, 46, 49–50, 55
authority, 43–44, 54, 62, 74, 91

Barnes, Craig, 104
Barth, Karl, 36–37, 67, 69n15, 100
Benedict Option, xn7, 2
Benedict XVI, Pope, Joseph Ratzinger, 12–14, 65, 84–85, 103
bridge building, xi, 11, 15–16, 21–24, 41, 81, 84–85
Brunner, Emil, 36–37, 138–39
Burtchaell, James, 145

Calvinism, 92–93, 95, 97, 104
Calvin, John, 48, 65, 69, 78, 95–96, 98
   human depravity, 20n38, 36, 99–100
   natural law, 99–100
   vocation, work, 133n22, 135, 149–50

Camus, Albert, 3–4
capitulation to culture, viii, xv, 11, 98, 144
  church, 42, 103–4, 105
  education, 145–46, 153
Catechism of the Catholic Church, 43–44, 101–3
charity, love, 13, 84
  justice and, 49, 55–59, 84
  neighbor-love, 41, 43, 48–49, 55, 56–58, 135–36, 137
  truth and, 12–16
Christians, 44–45, 63, 78–79
  cultural mandate, 11, 18–19, 24, 26, 50–51, 108–9, 110–16, 119, 148
  dual citizenship, vii–viii, 26, 41–44, 74–75, 144
  suffering, 40–41
  witness, 12–17, 126–27, 144, 147, 152, 176
  worldview, 27–29, 73–74, 82
church, the, 45, 62, 63, 64
  bridge building, 47, 85
  capitulation to culture, 42, 103–4, 105
  common good, 25–26, 50–51
  cultural stewardship, 50–51
  education, universities, 145–46, 148, 153
  idolatries of, 126, 148, 156–57
  public faith, witness, ix–x, xii, 14, 17, 26, 98–99, 103–4, 176
  sacred-versus-secular dichotomy, xiii–xiv, 19, 93, 125–26, 133–35, 148–50, 174–75
  unity, 76, 81, 87, 105
  vocation, calling, 124–26, 127, 134–35, 138–39, 174, 176
  work, view of, 135–36, 149–50, 174–75
Cicero, 44, 73
common good, 6, 7, 8–10, 38, 83, 86, 119
  advancing, 11, 18, 26, 42–44, 90, 130, 152
  church and, 25–26, 50–51
  law, 38, 46–49, 55
  state and, 43–44
common grace, viii, xiii, 50–51, 89–91, 96–99, 101, 103, 116, 156
communication, 13, 24, 81–82, 112–13, 147–48
  of God, 15, 67, 112–13, 124, 132, 136, 147–48
communism, 43, 50
Confessing Church, 138
conscience, 20, 22, 23, 34, 80n50, 109
  accountability, 90, 97
  natural law and, 36–37, 100
  social, 14, 98
Council of Trent, 62
Covey, Stephen, 125
creation, ixn5, xiii, 20, 25–26, 50–51, 68, 144–45, 164
  doctrine of, xv, 17–20, 96, 98–99, 110, 111–12, 131–33
  by Jesus Christ, 25–26, 51, 111–12, 132, 144
Creator, xv, 144, 161–62, 164, 164–66, 19
  human dignity, 32–33
  incarnation, 15–16, 112, 125
  knowledge, revelation of, 20, 24, 79, 122, 167
  moral order, 46–47, 75, 122
  ordinances, divine, 74, 90–92, 95, 96–97, 165
  relationship with, 152, 156–57, 166, 173, 176
  sovereignty, 17–18, 50–51, 96, 111, 164–66
  See also God
criminal deviance, 4–5, 9
criminal justice, 14–15, 48, 55, 80, 129
cultural mandate, Christian, 11, 18–19, 24, 26, 50–51, 108–9, 110–16, 119, 148

culture, 21–22, 51
  faith and, vii–x, xiv, 83, 89–90, 98, 141–47
  foolish, 121, 142, 156, 168, 173, 174
  intellectual, 142–43, 146–47
  post-consensus, 2–4, 5–6, 47, 66, 86
  stewardship, 11, 18–19, 24, 26, 50–51, 108–9, 113

Darwin, Charles, 4, 91, 98
death, 12, 33, 109, 158–59, 170, 172
democracy, 9, 109–10
  American, 2–3, 49–50, 109–10
  liberal, xiv, 109–10
depravity, human, 20n38, 35–36, 38, 68, 74, 99–100, 164
dignity, human, 15, 41, 43–44, 51, 134
  image of God, 32–35, 57
  justice, 45, 56
  personhood, 29–33
discernment, xv, 6, 11, 58, 128, 160
doctrine, dogma, 16–17
Dooyeweerd, Herman, 100
dual citizenship, vii–viii, 26, 41–44, 74–75, 144

Ecclesiastes, book of, 117–18, 121–22, 138
  antitheses, contradictions, 159–60
  enjoyment, 167–73
  God in, 163–67, 171, 173
  meaninglessness, 160–62, 167–68
  Qoheleth, 158n5, 166
  understanding, interpreting, 155, 157–63, 175–76
  work, 161–63, 167–74
Eck, Johannes, 72n30
economics, 108–11
  process, outcomes and, 116–19
  stewardship, 111–16
ecumenical relations, 65–66, 81, 86–87, 103
  Catholics and Protestants, xi–xii, xiii, 68, 69, 86–87, 94–96, 97–98, 102–3, 105
  Evangelicals and Catholics Together, 103
  Lutherans and Catholics, 64–66, 102–3
education, 80, 82, 96, 142–44, 146–47, 150, 152–53
  capitulation to culture, 145–46, 153
  liberal arts, 71–72, 77, 82n55, 112, 132, 148
  seminaries, divinity schools, viii–ix, xiii, 127, 148–49
  universities, 71–74, 82, 141, 143, 145–47, 148, 150–51, 153
England, 80
enjoyment, 161–62, 165–66, 167–73
equality, 45, 115
Erasmus, 62
escapism, isolation, vii, xiv, 10–11, 93, 98, 153, 175
  monasticism, 2, 19n36, 93, 98, 136, 175
  withdrawal, 17–19, 26, 42, 78, 83, 104, 108, 110, 142–44
eschatology, vii, xiv–xv, 17, 104, 108, 111, 143
  new heavens and earth, 19, 111, 135
eternity, 47, 162, 165
ethics, 29, 47, 53, 55–56
  integrity, 54–55, 58–59
  protection, 48–49
  relativism, 109–10
  See also moral; moral law
Eucharist, 75
European Union, 63
Eusebius, xin8
evangelicals, viii–ix, 17, 83, 136, 148
evil, 3–6, 8, 50, 86–87
  of society, 38–39, 48
  suffering, 40–41
evolution, Darwinian, 4, 91

faith, 69, 92–93, 114–15
  culture and, vii–x, xiv, 83, 89–90, 98, 141–47
  personal, private, ix–x, 10, 92, 104, 148
  public witness, ix–x, xii, 14, 17, 26, 98–99, 103–4, 148, 176
  reason and, xi, 75, 83, 84–85
faithfulness, xi, xv, 145–46, 174
  in stewardship, 11, 26, 113, 115
fear of the Lord, 133, 156, 162, 165–67, 173
Fifth Lateran Council, 62
foolish culture, 121, 142, 156, 168, 173, 174
France, French Revolution, 38, 93
Frankl, Viktor, 122–13
Frederick the Wise, Prince, 71, 72, 85n61
freedom, 4, 14, 34, 43–44, 64, 75, 78, 85, 109–10, 120
free society, 55
  virtue and, xiv, 107–11, 119–20
free will, 3, 40, 75, 132

gender issues, xn6, 104–5
general revelation, 20, 22, 24, 25, 75, 90, 116
Germany, 65, 69n15, 78, 86, 103, 129, 147, 151–52
  education, 73–74, 82
gifts, 71, 137
  common good, advancing, 11, 18, 26, 90, 130, 152
  of God, xv, 122, 127n9, 138, 160, 162, 165–66, 167–73, 174–76
  stewarding, 108, 110–16, 120, 132, 152
  vocation and, 149–51
Gnosticism, ix, 18
God, 22
  calling of, 124–25, 136–37, 165
  communication, 15, 67, 112–13, 124, 132, 136, 147–48
  in Ecclesiastes, 163–67, 171, 173
  fear of, 133, 156, 162, 165–67, 173

  gifts of, xv, 122, 127n9, 138, 160, 162, 165–66, 167–73, 174–76
  judge, 164–66
  moral law, 91–92, 96–97
  will, 91, 136–37
  work, 19, 133–34
  See also Creator; image of God, creation in
Golden Rule, 56, 49, 56, 75
Goldstone, Richard, 58–59
grace, 68–69, 75, 101, 138
  common, viii, xiii, 50–51, 89–91, 96–99, 101, 103, 116, 156
  special, xiii, 67
gratitude, 125, 150, 167
Great Commandment, 43, 57, 130
  neighbor-love, 41, 43, 48–49, 55, 56–58, 135–36, 137
Grotius, Hugo, 48, 85–86

Habermas, Jürgen, 84–85
Hauerwas, Stanley, 67, 83n57, 100
Heaven is Not My Home, 144
Holocaust, the, 1, 34, 86, 122–23, 129
human depravity, 20n38, 35–36, 38, 68, 74, 99–100, 164
humanitarian intervention, 48–49, 53–55, 56
human nature, 29–31, 46–47, 78, 101, 119
  body-soul composite, 32–33, 46–48
  common, 20, 25, 29–30, 32–34, 47, 79
  constrained, unconstrained, 37–39
  perfectibility, 38, 95
human rights, universal, 1, 20, 31, 34, 43–44, 45, 50, 85, 86
Hunter, James Davison, 2n3
Hus, Jan, 62

idols, idolatry, 126, 127n8, 148, 156–57, 162–63
image of God, creation in, xi, 19, 32–33, 45, 101, 148
  accountability, 15, 108–9, 111

dignity, 32–35, 57
moral impulse, 20, 34–35, 46–47, 108
natural law, 25, 79–80, 83
sin and, 35–37, 41, 66
work and, xiii, 130–31, 133–35, 146, 173
impulse, moral, 20, 34–35, 46–47, 108
incarnation, xv, 24, 33, 110, 119–20, 131–33, 146–48, 152
Creator, 15–16, 112, 125
doctrine of, 111–13, 132–33, 146, 147–48
incarnational humanism, 19–20
individualism, 43
injustice, 5, 15, 48, 50, 70, 171
reactions to, 23–24, 55
integrity, 54–55, 58–59
intolerance, 3, 7, 9–10, 15, 66, 110, 156
isolation. See escapism, isolation

James, epistle of, 76, 84
Jerome, 175
Jerusalem, vii–viii, 51, 133, 141–42
Jesus Christ, ix–x, 12, 56, 95, 119, 125, 130, 144
calling to, 127–28, 137n34, 150, 153
creation, 25–26, 51, 111–12, 132, 144
judging, 5, 6
law and, xii, 43, 78, 91–92
Logos, Word, 15, 24, 33, 112–13, 147–48
parables, 26, 41, 57–58, 113–15, 134, 152
redemption, 18–19, 74, 111–12, 132, 142, 144–45, 147–48, 149
suffering, 119–20
wisdom, 113–15, 117
work, 68, 146
Jesus Movement, 143
Job, 40, 157
John Brown University, 141

John Paul II, Pope, 12, 34, 50, 102–3, 126n7
faith and reason, xi, 83
liberal democracy, xiv, 109–10
Luther, Martin, 64
suffering, 40–41
Joint Declaration on the Doctrine of Justification, 64, 102
judgment, 5, 6, 111, 164–66
final, viii, 135, 142, 170
judgment, moral reasoning, 36–37, 46–47, 100
judgments, moral, 3–6, 8–10, 108
judgmentalism, 3, 5–6
justice, 37, 44–46, 49–50, 55
charity and, 49, 55–59, 84
criminal, 14–15, 48, 55, 80, 129
dignity and, 45, 56
just war, 48–49, 54, 58
moral law and, 97, 99–100
society and, 44–45, 49–50, 49–50
punishment, 4, 15, 56–57, 59n5
as virtue, 44, 55–56
justification, 62–63, 64, 69, 74, 76, 102
Joint Declaration on the Doctrine of Justification, 64, 102
just war, 48–49, 54, 58

Keller, Timothy, xn6, 104–5
Kuyper, Abraham, 89–93
common-cause cooperation, 93–96, 98–99, 103
common grace, 89–90, 96–98, 101, 103
culture, 103–5
moral order, 90–92
natural law, 99–100, 101
public square, 104–5
Roman Catholics and, 92–93, 101–3, 105

language study, 21, 142, 143–44, 147, 151–52
law, xii, 3, 18, 45–46, 77–78, 84–85
Christians and, 78–79

common good, 38, 46–49, 55
  divine, 46–47, 79
  human, civil, 45, 46, 79–80, 99, 101
  international, 85–86
  Jesus Christ and, xii, 43, 78, 91–92
  Old Testament, 78, 91–92
  See also moral law; natural law
Leo XIII, Pope, 94
Lewis, C. S., 16, 38
  culture and, 142–43
  law of nature, 22–24
  moral self-responsibility, 4, 15, 56n3
liberal arts, 71–72, 77, 82n55, 112, 132, 148
liberalism, 38, 98, 104
life-views. *See* worldviews
Locke, John, 7, 48
Logos, Word, 15, 24, 33, 112–13, 147–48
love. *See* charity, love
Lutherans, 68n13, 145
  Book of Concord (1580), 70
  Catholics and, 64–66, 102–3
  Joint Declaration on the Doctrine of Justification, 64, 102
  Melanchthon, Philip and, 70, 81
  vocation, 19n36, 135
Luther, Martin, 28, 48, 76, 93, 99
  Catholics and, 64–65
  Ecclesiastes, 175–76
  justification, 62–63
  law, 80n51
  Melanchthon, Philip and, 69–70, 71–73, 74–77, 78, 81, 83
  natural law, reason, 75–76
  reason, 75–76, 83
  reformation, 61–62
  stations, vocational, 19n36, 127–28, 135–36, 149–50

MacIntyre, Alasdair, 2n3
Mafia, the, 49–50
marketplace, xiii, 11, 47, 59, 126–27, 148–49, 153, 176
Marshall, Paul, 144
materialism, 3, 34, 91, 98, 156
meaning, 131, 157, 159–60, 168, 174–75
  Man's Search for Meaning, 122–23
  vocation and, 123–24, 129, 169
meaninglessness, 121–22, 133, 160–62, 167–73
Melanchthon, Philip, 69–74
  law, 77–78
  Loci Communes, 70, 73, 76n42, 79–80
  Luther, Martin and, 69–70, 71–73, 74–77, 78, 81, 83
  Lutheran Reformation, 65–66, 70–71, 77–78, 81
  moral persuasion, 81–82
  moral philosophy, 77–78
  natural law, 74–75, 79–80, 83, 85, 86–87
  as teacher, 70, 71, 72–74, 81–83
  theological foundations, 80–81
  Thomas Aquinas and, 74, 75
  worldview, 82–83
monasticism, 2, 19n36, 93, 98, 136, 175
moral, 9, 34
  formation, 156–57
  impulse, 20, 34–35, 46–47, 108
  order, 46–47, 75, 122
  persuasion, 15–16, 21–24, 66, 79–80, 81–82, 119
  reasoning, xiv, 36–37, 46–47, 66, 100, 172
  self-responsibility, 4, 15, 56n3, 12–13, 15
  truths, xii–xiii, 109–10
morality, 3, 55, 95
  legislating, 8–10
  natural law, 23–24, 34, 45, 55, 75, 97–98, 101, 103, 122
moral law, 1, 22–24, 34, 45–46, 58, 66, 80, 83
  God ordained, 91–92, 96–97
  Golden Rule, 49, 56

justice and, 97, 99–100
Ten Commandments, 34, 35, 75, 78, 79, 95, 101
Moynihan, Daniel Patrick, 5
Murray, John Courtney, 66

Native Americans, 85
natural law, xi–xii, 67, 86, 90–92
   bridge building, xi, 11, 15–16, 21–24, 41, 81, 84–85
   conscience and, 36–37, 100
   ecumenical dialogue, 86–87
   human nature, 20, 25, 29–30, 32–34, 47, 79
   human rights, universal, 1, 20
   image of God, 25, 79–80, 83
   morality, universal, 23–24, 34, 45, 55, 75, 97–98, 101, 103, 122
   moral reasoning, judgment, 36–37, 46–47, 100
   Protestants, x–xii, 25, 67–69, 99–100
   public policy, 48–49
   Reformers, xii, 25, 69, 85, 99
   retribution, 40, 115
   Roman Catholics, xii, 25, 99, 100, 101–3
   sin and, 67–68, 99
   sociocultural upheaval and, 1, 49–50, 66–67, 85–86
   tyranny, 49–50, 86
   works righteousness, 68–69, 77–78
nature, observing, 117–18, 157
Nazis, 50, 122–23
neighbor-love, 41, 43, 48–49, 55, 56–58, 135–36, 137
Netherlands, 86–87, 96–97
   Anti-Revolutionary Party, 96
Neuhaus, Richard, 9
Newman, John Henry, 146–47, 153
nihilism, 3, 167

ordinances, divine, 90–92, 95, 96–97, 165
Orthodox Church, xn7, xiv, 126
Orwell, George, 86

pantheism, 3, 94–95
parables, 57–58, 113–15, 134
   good Samaritan, 41, 57–58, 113
   talents, 26, 113–15, 152
Paul, apostle, ixn5, 25, 28, 72, 112, 135, 150
   Athens, xi, 21–22, 23, 24–25, 164
   natural law, 20, 36–37, 47, 75, 76n42, 79, 97, 99–100, 122
   redemption, 18–19, 76, 132, 144
   vocation, 43, 127–28n10, 150
peace, 44, 50, 133, 153, 175
Pelikan, Jaroslav, 63, 102
personhood, 29–33, 39, 43, 51
persuasion, 15–16, 24–26
   bridge building, xi, 11, 21–25, 41, 81
   moral, 15–16, 21–24, 66, 79–80, 81–82, 119
Plato, 44, 56
pluralism, xn6, 7–9, 10, 15, 99
   structured, 97, 104–5
Poland, 50, 86, 129
Pole, Cardinal Reginald, 62
post-Christian era, 1–2
post-consensus culture, 2–4, 5–6, 47, 66, 86
poverty, the social problem, 94–96
Presbyterians, 145
   Presbyterian Church in America, xn6
   Presbyterian Church (USA), xn6, 104
   Princeton Theological Seminary, xn6, 104–5, 145
   Kuyper, Abraham, 90, 92–94, 97, 98, 104–5
Protestants, xii, 67–68, 126
   Catholics and, xi–xii, xiii, 68, 69, 86–87, 94–96, 97–98, 102–3, 105
   common-cause cooperation, 93–96, 98–99, 103
   evangelical, viii–ix, 17, 83, 136, 148
   mainline, ix, 11, 104

natural law, x–xii, 25, 67–69, 99–100
orthodox, xii, 67–68, 99
Reformed, xiii, 43, 89–90, 94–95, 96–97, 100, 127
revisionist, 67, 68, 99
providence, divine, viii, xiii, 69, 110, 111–12, 119, 122, 161–62
redemption and, 131–33
vocation and, 128, 131–33, 150, 176
wisdom and, 157, 160
public policy, 25, 28, 41, 152
humanitarian intervention, 48–49, 53–55, 56
public square, xiv, 55
Christians in, 8–11, 12–16, 17–20, 24–26, 41–44, 51, 104–5
sphere, vii, xii–xiii
punishment, 4, 15, 56–57, 59n5
Puritans, 127

Qoheleth, 158n5, 166

Ramsey, Paul, 48–49
Ratzinger, Joseph, Pope Benedict XVI, 12–14, 65, 84–85, 103
reality, 19, 22, 67, 119
Christian, 8, 17, 50–51, 96, 107, 111, 147, 165
fallenness, sin and, 35–37, 38–39, 78
interpreting, 27–29, 161
moral, xiii, 7–8, 20, 35, 66, 75
ultimate, 28–29, 159
reason, 34, 67–68, 75–76, 79
faith and, xi, 75, 83, 84–85
reasoning, moral, xiv, 36–37, 46–47, 66, 100, 172
redemption, 26, 40–41, 110, 131–33
doctrine of, xv, 17, 18–20, 96, 98–99
by Jesus Christ, 18–19, 74, 111–12, 132, 142, 144–45, 147–48, 149
of all things, 10, 50–51, 144–45

Reformation, Protestant, 41–63, 94, 127
Catholics and, 61–62
reformations, 61–63
work, view of, 135–36, 149–50, 174–75
Reformed Protestants, xiii, 43, 89–90, 94–95, 96–97, 100, 127
Reformers, Magisterial, xii, 25, 62, 69, 85, 99
relativism, 7, 13, 55, 109–10
retribution, 40, 115
Reuchlin, Johann, 71
rewards, 18, 114, 131, 135, 158
rights, human, 1, 20, 31, 34, 43–44, 45, 50, 85, 86
Roman Catholic Church, 64, 92–93, 111, 126
cafeteria Catholics, x, 11
Catechism of the Catholic Church, 43–44, 101–3
common-cause cooperation, 93–96
Evangelicals and Catholics Together, 103
Kuyper, Abraham and, 92–93, 101–3, 105
Lutherans and, 64–66, 102–3
natural law, xii, 25, 99, 100, 101–3
Protestants and, xi–xii, xiii, 68, 69, 86–87, 94–96, 97–98, 102–3, 105
Reformation, 60–61
Second Vatican Council, 64
subsidiarity, 43, 102
Rwanda, 53, 54, 58–59

sacred-versus-secular dichotomy, xiii–xiv, 19, 93, 125–26, 133–35, 148–50, 174–75
Samaritan, good, 41, 57–58, 113
satisfaction in work, 122, 131, 135, 151–52, 162–63, 165, 168, 173–74
Sayers, Dorothy, 16–17, 134–35

science, 4, 18, 38, 51, 71, 82, 156
  common grace, 90–91
  study of, 51, 71, 82, 142, 176
secularism, xiii, 9, 63, 84–86, 98, 126, 148, 173
  materialist, 169, 173–74
  under-the-sun, 122, 138, 161, 167–73, 174–75
self-responsibility, moral, 4, 15, 56n3, 12–13, 15
seminaries, divinity schools, viii–ix, xiii, 127, 148–49
service, 19, 21, 64, 114, 127, 132
  stewardship as, 114, 130
  work, vocation as, 129–30, 135–36, 137, 150
sexuality, xn6, 104–5
Sinai law, 91–92
sin, fallenness, 18, 37–38, 78, 95
  image of God, 35–37, 41, 66
  natural law and, 67–68, 99
  reality of, 35–37, 38–39, 78
Singer, Peter, 39
Skinner, B. F., 4
Smith, Gordon T., 137n34
socialism, 38, 50, 94
  communism, 43, 50
social theory, 37–39
society, societies
  evil of, 38–39, 48
  free, xiv, 42–43, 55, 107–11, 119–20
  justice and, 44–45, 49–50, 49–50
  values, 42–43
  vision, 37–39
sociocultural upheaval, natural law and, 1, 49–50, 66–67, 85–86
South Africa, 58–59
sovereignty, 17–18, 50–51, 96, 111, 164–66
  sphere, vii, xii–xiii, 42–43, 74–75, 89, 97–98, 102, 104–5
Sowell, Thomas, 37
Spain, 85
special grace, revelation, xiii, 67

sphere sovereignty, 42–43, 74–75, 89, 97–98, 102
  public, vii, xii–xiii, 104–5
Stackhouse, Max, 103–4
state, the, 43–44, 45–46
Staupitz, Johann von, 62
stewardship, viii, xiii, 119, 132, 148
  of culture, 11, 18–19, 24, 26, 50–51, 108–9, 113
  economics, 111–16
  faithfulness, 11, 26, 113, 115
  of resources, gifts, 108, 110–16, 120, 132, 152
  service, 114, 130
subsidiarity, 43, 102
suffering, 39–41, 118–20
  meaning of, 123–24, 157
suicide, ix, 27–28, 123, 138

talents, parable of the, 26, 113–15, 152
Taylor University, 150–51
Ten Commandments, 34, 35, 47, 75, 79, 95, 101, 78
Tertullian, vii–viii, 51, 142–44
theistic view, theism, 34, 95, 122, 138
  Ecclesiastes, under-heaven, 161, 163, 167–73
theology, 79, 80–81
  vocation, work, 127–33, 133–36
Thielicke, Helmut, 67, 100
Thomas Aquinas, 43, 48, 93, 95, 99
  justice, 44–45, 54n2, 55
Tocqueville, Alexis de, 2–3, 49, 109
tolerance, xn6, 3, 6–8, 9–10, 86
  intolerance, 3, 7, 9–10, 15, 66, 110, 156
  judging, 5–6
totalitarianism, xiv, 3, 5, 24, 33n7, 42n29, 43, 85–86
  democracy and, 109–10
  Mafia, the, 49–50
truth, 8, 25, 34, 37, 66
  charity, love and, 12–16
  culture and, 21–22
  moral, xii–xiii, 109–10

195

tyranny, 2–3, 3–4, 109, 133
  natural law and, 49–50, 86

universities, 71–74, 82, 141, 143, 145–47, 148, 150–51, 153

virtue, 7, 40, 80, 116, 119–20, 156–57
  charity, neighbor-love, 55–56
  economics, 108–11
  free society and, xiv, 107–11, 119–20
  justice, 44, 55–56
Vitoria, Francisco de, 85
vocation, calling, vii, xiii–xiv, 138–39, 148–50
  calling of God, 124–25, 136–37, 165
  Christian doctrine of, 11, 19, 124–26
  church on, 124–26, 127, 134–35, 138–39, 174, 176
  contentment, 127–28n10, 169, 172, 174, 175–76
  discerning, identifying, 136–38, 150–52
  gifts and, 149–51
  meaning and, 123–24, 129, 169
  providence and, 128, 131–33, 150, 176
  seasons, stages, 128–29, 137–38
  service, 129–30, 135–36, 137, 150
  stations, Lutheran, 19n36, 127–28, 135–36, 149–50
  theology of, 127–33, 133–36
  thinking vocationally, 130–31
  work and, 125–26
  See also work, labor, job
Volf, Miroslav, 128n10

Walsh, J. T., 163n15
Washington, DC, 55, 129, 144, 152
will of God, 91, 136–37

wisdom, 47, 54, 58, 171
  acquiring, 117–18, 119
  African, 116–17
  ancient Near Eastern, 116, 121, 152, 155
  cross-cultural, universal truth, 116–17, 155–56, 164
  of Jesus Christ, 113–15, 117
  providence and, 157, 160
  suffering and, 118–19
  tradition, 113–15, 116
wisdom literature, 113, 116–18, 121–22, 138, 155–57, 158–59, 163, 169
withdrawal, 17–19, 26, 42, 78, 83, 104, 108, 110, 142–44
Wittenberg, University of, 71–72, 76n39, 76n41, 82, 85
Word, 15, 24, 33, 112–13, 147–48
worldviews, 27–29, 82, 138
  Christian, 27–29, 73–74, 82–83
  materialism, 3, 34, 91, 98, 156
  presuppositions, 28–29, 43–44
  theism, 34, 95, 122, 138, 161, 163, 167–73
  See also secularism
Wolters, Albert, 99
work, labor, job, 76, 128, 161–63, 167–4
  church view of, 135–36, 149–50, 174–75
  enjoyment of, 161–62, 165–66, 167–73
  excellence, 145–46
  of God, 19, 133–34
  as idol, 127n8, 162–63
  image of God and, xiii, 130–31, 133–35, 146, 173
  of Jesus Christ, 68, 146
  marketplace, xiii, 11, 47, 59, 126–27, 148–49, 153, 176
  rewards, 18, 114, 131, 135, 158

satisfaction in, 122, 131, 135, 151–52, 162–63, 165, 168, 173–74
as service, 129–30, 135–36, 137, 150
theology of, 127–33, 133–36
works righteousness, 68–69, 77–78, 111, 135

World War II, 1, 20, 34, 129, 138–39
   Nazis, 50, 122–23
   Poland, 86, 129
Wycliffe, John, 62

Yoder, John Howard, 67, 83n57, 100
Yugoslavia, former, 53, 58–59

Scripture Index

OLD TESTAMENT

Genesis
1...18
1:26–27......................................173
1:31....................................164, 175
9...34
9:5..35

Exodus
20:13..35

Leviticus
19:18....................................130n14

2 Kings
2...72

Job
4:8..115n5
28:28............................156, 173n28

Psalms
1...116
24:1..26
34...114
37...114
46:10.............................136, 137n34
49...114
62:12...135
73...114
111:10...................................173n28

Proverbs
1:7.................................156, 173n28
1:29...156
2:4...156
2:5...156
3:7...156
3:14–15......................................156
8:10...156
8:22–31......................................156
9:10.................................156, 173n28
11:18.......................................115n5
14:23a.......................................174
14:26.....................................173n28
14:27.....................................173n28
15:33.....................................173n28
16:6.......................................173n28
19:23.....................................173n28
20:29...117

22:4	173n28
22:8	115n5
23:17	173n28
24:12	135
28:14	173n28
30	118
30:24–28	117

Ecclesiastes

1:1	158n5
1:1–2:23	161–62
1:2	158n5
1:12–18	169
1:13	165
2:1	169
2:1–2	169
2:3–11	169
2:10	169
2:12–17	169
2:17–23	169
2:18–23	169
2:21	169
2:23	162
2:24	169, 171, 172, 174
2:24–26	131n15, 165, 168, 169–70
2:24–3:15	162
2:26	165
3:1	138
3:1–8	159
3:1–14	118
3:1–22	171
3:9	165
3:10	165
3:10–15	170, 171
3:11	47, 122, 160, 162, 165
3:12	170, 171, 172
3:12–13	131n15, 168, 170
3:13	122, 162, 165, 171, 174
3:14	122n1, 173
3:14–15	165
3:15–17	165
3:16–22	170
3:17	170
3:18	165
3:22	122, 162, 169, 170, 171, 172
4:9	169
5:1–7	165
5:2	165
5:7	122n1, 165, 173
5:10–20	171
5:12	162
5:18	165, 169
5:18–19	168
5:18–20	122, 131n15, 170–71, 174
5:19	172
5:19–20	162, 165
5:20	169
6:2	165
7:1–6	168
7:1–8:1	171
7:13–14	165
7:14	168, 171, 172
7:18	122n1, 165, 173
7:29	165
8:11–15	171
8:12	122n1, 165
8:12–13	173
8:15	122, 131n15, 162, 166, 168, 171, 172, 173, 174
8:16–17	166
9:1	166, 169
9:2–6	172
9:6	169
9:7	166, 172
9:7–10	131n15, 168, 171–72
9:9	166, 169
9:10	115n6, 174
11:1–6	172
11:2	169
11:5	166
11:7–12:1	172–73
11:8–9	168
11:8–12:7	172
11:9	166, 172
12:1	166
12:6–7	166
12:9–14	173
12:13	122n1, 166, 173
12:13–14	173
12:14	135n30, 166

SCRIPTURE INDEX

NEW TESTAMENT

Matthew
5:16	125
5:17	78
7:1	5
22:36–40	130n14
24:47	115n5
25	113
25:14–30	26, 113, 152
26:24	132n18

Mark
12:28–34	130n14

Luke
10:25–37	41, 57
10:25–28	130n14

John
1	25
1:1	24, 132, 147
1:1–3	112, 132n20
1:1–5	15
1:3	15
1:14	15, 24, 112, 132, 147
4:1–42	57
8:32	14
17	81

Acts
15:10	77
15:13–21	77
17	xi
17:16–34	xin8, 21, 164
17:22–34	22
17:34	xin8

Romans
1	79
1:20	20, 37
2:14–15	23, 34, 162n13
2:15	25, 47, 75, 99, 122
11:22	167
12	127
12:3–8	150
13:4	42, 46n37
13:6	42

1 Corinthians
7	127–28n10
7:1	127n10
7:17	127n10
7:20	127n10
7:24	127n10
9:11	115n5
9:19–22	21
9:19–23	xin8
12–14	127n9

2 Corinthians
5:10	135
9:6	115n5

Galatians
6:7	115n5

Ephesians
1:10	112
4	127n9
4:15	13

Philippians
2:8	120n8

Colossians
1	18, 112
1:15–20	132, 144
1:17	156
2:3	156

Hebrews
1:2	18, 25, 132n20, 156
1:2–3	111–12
4:15–16	120n8

James
2:19	76n42
2:24	76n42

SCRIPTURE INDEX

1 Peter
1:17 .... 135n30
2:4–9 150
4:10 150

Revelation
1:5–6 150
20:12 .... 135n30

www.ingramcontent.com/pod-product-compliance
Lightning Source LLC
Chambersburg PA
CBHW071341080526
44587CB00017B/2923